THE BULL OF MINOS

THE BULL OF MINOS

The discoveries of Schliemann and Evans

Leonard Cottrell

With a new introduction by Peter Levi

Bell & Hyman Limited

This edition published in 1984 by
BELL & HYMAN LIMITED
Denmark House
37–39 Queen Elizabeth Street
London SE1 2QB

First published by Evans Brothers Ltd in 1953
Revised edition 1955
Reprinted 1957
Reprinted 1962
Reprinted with revisions 1971

British Library Cataloguing in Publication Data
Cottrell, Leonard
    The bull of minos.——New illustrated ed.
    1. Knossos (Ancient city)
    I. Title
    939'.18   DF221.C8

ISBN 0 7135 2432 4

Designed by Harold Bartram
Typeset by Tradespools Ltd, Frome, Somerset
Colour reproduction by Positive Colour Ltd, Essex
Printed and bound in Spain by Printer industria gráfica s.a. Barcelona
D.L.B. 21098-1984

CONTENTS

Furthermore, after he (Theseus) was arrived in Creta, he slew there the Minotaur (as the most part of ancient authors do write) by the means and help of Ariadne; who being fallen in fancy with him, did give him a clue of thread, by the help whereof she taught him, how he might easily wind out of the turnings and cranks of the Labyrinth.

[*Plutarch* (North's translation).]

To the memory of Harry Fawcett, valued friend

Facsimile of faience Snake-
Goddess

INTRODUCTION

Leonard Cottrell had travelled all over the world and his experience of life and knowledge of history were unusually wide. All the same, *The Bull of Minos* reads not like a learned text, but more like the record of a love affair. It has a passionate freshness and it still conveys the same enthusiasm and liveliness with which he wrote it between 1951 and 1953. It is a minor classic and still, I believe, the best book of its kind.

He wrote it at the right time and at the first possible moment for such a book. The turmoil of controversy between scholars had begun to die down and the bones of the truth about Crete and Mycenae had become apparent. Even by 1951, soon after the German occupation and the disastrous civil wars that followed, travelling in Greece was easier than it had been in the thirties. The archaeological services and the museums were better organized, the sites and temples were not yet swathed in barbed wire, and there were few tourists. Ten years later, the Greece Cottrell knew, with its sense of immediate contact with the past and even with mythology, was already beginning to die as the modern world advanced.

The Bull of Minos belongs to the moment when it was written, and as a popular introduction to Greek bronze age archaeology it is unlikely ever to be bettered. Cottrell approached the problems with sharpness, intelligence and innocence as most people would like to do. But archaeology is always moving on and changing our perspectives. Even the greatest archaeologist does not simply draw back a blanket and reveal a world. That is as true of the Pyramids and of the Royal Tombs of the Macedonian Kings as it is of Troy and Mycenae and Knossos. It is almost true to say that the more spectacular the revelation is, the more problematic it is. It does not make much human or historic sense until it is fitted into context, and that involves a long process in which arguments crumble, ideas have to be abandoned and one problem leads into another. There is even an archaeology of archaeology itself. Old neglected finds have to be rediscovered and old findings studied again from a new point of view. Cotrrell put Schliemann and Evans into their proper setting. We must now do the same for *The Bull of Minos*.

In later editions of *The Bull of Minos*, Cottrell was forced by the continual advances of knowledge to add two appendices to his book, and Professor Wace wrote a scholarly introduction with still more material. In this edition, published after Cottrell's death in 1974, we have discarded one of the appendices, retaining only the one in which he discussed Linear B which will still be of interest to readers. In this introduction I will try to put the whole book into context and to explain what has been discovered since Cottrell's time.

The greatest increase in our knowledge of early Greece since 1951 has been the massive multiplication in the sheer quantity of evidence. Before Schliemann began digging, almost the only testimony to life in ancient, pre-classical Greece had been the Homeric poems written in the eighth or possibly the ninth century BC and describing a period, historical, legendary, or a little of each, from a much more distant past. Of these distant ages, (that is the Greek bronze age of high civilizations down to about 1100 BC), almost the only physical evidences that existed before Schliemann's excavations were the site of Troy (which was famous and quite often visited), the entrance pillars to Agamemnon's tomb in Mycenae, which were already decorating Lord Sligo's garden door in Ireland, and the foundations of Homeric geography laid down by W.M. Leake, the great identifier of ruins. Cottrell's picture of the breakthroughs made by Schliemann is therefore only slightly dramatized. Schliemann was interested only in great poetry and high civilization. The Greek dark ages (from about the 11th to the 8th centuries BC) were still almost completely unexplored by archaeologists, even when *The Bull of Minos* was written. Things had not been found from this period because no one was looking for them or interested in them. That gap has now been largely filled in by the work of Desborough, Snodgrass and many others.

The early history of Greece as we now know it is as follows. The Cretan palace civilization, with its wonderful courtly art and its luxuries, was taken over in its last phase (about 1400 BC) by the Mycenaeans, who had entered Greece as an immigrant people and learned their art and their technology under Cretan influence. We know something about the fall of the Mycenaeans, but not enough. Archaeology shows the collapse and ruin of the great fortified towns, but it also shows a survival (with declining technical skills and economic resources) of what appear to be the same people. Whether the disaster that overwhelmed the Mycenaeans was a great tribal raid, or migration from the north that advanced and withdrew like the sea, or a revolutionary rising of some kind, remains uncertain.

Alan Wace, who wrote the original introduction to *The Bull of Minos* was a precise scholar of scrupulous exactness. He insisted, with great integrity and considerable intellectual power, that Knossos in its last phase of glory was a Mycenaean colony, although this was a view which infuriated Sir Arthur Evans who believed that Knossos was a purely Cretan achievement. In his introduction to the last edition Wace offered the following review of how the archaeology of Greece appeared in 1952: 'In recent years the Greek mainland has again become the centre of interest with renewed excavations at Tiryns and Mycenae and with the discovery of the House of Cadmus at Thebes and of the Palace of Nestor at Pylos', and at Mycenae a new circle of royal graves a generation earlier than Schliemann's. Crete also has yielded riches that would have amazed Evans: the Palace of Chania, the ancient Kydonia, (the whereabouts of which was first pinpointed by the painter John Craxton), the palace at Mallia further studied by the French, at Phaistos further studied by the Italians, the brilliant palace at Kato Zakro excavated by the Greek archaeologist Platon, and the interesting small rural palace excavated by Gerald Cadogan, let alone the buried palace on the island of Santorini. All these have built up a picture of Crete more splendid and less centralized than Evans supposed, even though Knossos is still its supreme centre.

It is interesting to isolate one moment of archaeology and see how our view of it has widened with the benefit of more discoveries than had been made when Cottrell wrote. On considering a sketch of a standing man that was found on a tablet in the oil-merchant's house at Mycenae, Cottrell was led to speculate excitedly, that it might be 'an artist's draft for a wall fresco, as at Knossos ... We know that the Mycenaeans were in the habit of adorning their plastered walls with frescoes of men and women, chariots and hunting scenes.' In the light of more recent discoveries, such as those at Santorini, we can add significantly to what Cottrell wrote. We have learned, for instance, that the artists of the great palaces painted walls of flying fish, Cretan mountains in spring with lilies and extraordinary thistles, a forest full of blue monkeys, a harbour crowded with ships, boy fishermen, and what seem to be two little boys boxing. Our sense of Mycenaean art and life is very much fuller than was possible in 1951. The ritual and heraldic scenes on the golden thumb-rings from Mycenaean graves may very well be taken from some great series of sacred paintings that has perished. Figures in Mycenaean sacred art seem to occur in more than one medium. Perhaps the word sacred is wrong. To judge from the Santorini frescoes, and the Cretan bull game, the Minoan world was one where everything was both secular and sacred.

One would be mistaken to think that theirs was a happier world than ours. John Chadwick points, in his additional commentary to the 1973 *Documents*, (the standard work on Linear B), to undeniable evidence of human sacrifice: skeletons in a kneeling position in the mouth of a tomb. Homer confirms the nasty custom. So does the presence of a woman found buried beside her husband at Lefkandi. We have a detailed, eye witness account of such a ceremony by an Arab traveller in southern Russia in the tenth century AD. Historians have sometimes favoured other ways of measuring a human society. The eighteenth-century French *Encylopédie* pardonably remarks that the *Iliad* is a great and heroic poem in spite of the awfulness of its cooking, while French generals are unheroic in spite of their admirable cuisine. The list of spices in use at Knossos is not unimpressive, and no doubt the vegetables were fresh.

The most important new excavation of a prehistoric Greek site that has taken place since Cottrell wrote *The Bull of Minos* is that at Santorini. Santorini is the ancient Thera, an island not so very far from Crete. Its harbour is a volcanic crater where a new island appeared as recently as the eighteenth century, and it has long been known that it blew up with a most enormous bang, and buried a palace as Vesuvius buried Pompeii. When the Greek colonels were in power, they laid great importance on national culture and archaeology, and appointed

Professor Marinatos as Director General of the archaeological services, and its resources were concentrated on his excavation.

Marinatos was a pre-war archaeologist, a little larger than life. His record was distinguished, but in some ways he was a buffoon, and close to being a charlatan. By putting him in a powerful position, the colonels let Marinatos loose on Santorini. There in the end he died, when a wall of his own excavation crumbled under his heavy feet. From that palace by far the most attractive and best preserved of all Cretan frescoes have been recovered. Their delicacy, intimacy and beauty express better even than the flying fish of Phylakopi a quality of springtime that the best Cretan palace art has.

But Marinatos wanted Santorini to be all-important and, not content with the thrilling treasures of art discovered there, he chose to stretch the evidence to support wilder and more dramatic claims of his own. He wanted his volcanic explosion to be found to have destroyed the entire Cretan palace civilization (which it did not). Theories about it grew ever more exaggerated. Santorini was Atlantis. Whole cities had been drowned by a giant tidal wave. An American scholar even observed that the Santorini explosion explained the opening of the waters for Moses, and the cloud by day and the fire by night that led Israel through the desert. In fact the canticle of Moses, with dates suitably adjusted, was the only eye witness account of the Santorini volcano in action. For Marinatos even the fresco of apes and some old monkey bones represented a special, native Greek form of monkey. Those were heady days.

There are serious questions left over from this disgraceful episode which are still unanswered. The effect of the Santorini explosion is unknown, but it must have been spectacular, and some evidence suggests that it impoverished Cretan agriculture for years by seriously harming the soil. But no respectable scholar still defends the neat volcanic package deal that Marinatos marketed. I would greatly have enjoyed a full-scale assessment of Marinatos by Leonard Cottrell. It was Marinatos, with Blegen before the war, who discovered the site now called Pylos, where Nestor's bath, mentioned in Homer, is proudly exhibited. As a young man he wrote with verve on the phallic cult of stalactites in a Cretan cave. He spoke the most pompous Greek I ever heard.

Another important addition to knowledge that Cottrell would have wanted to incorporate in this book is the discovery of pottery goddesses, two feet high or more, at Hagia Eirene on Kea, and in excellent condition at Mycenae where they include a snake goddess. Those at Mycenae were found by Lord William Taylour. Most of them are spooky and rather sinister objects. At Hagia Eirene the broken off head of one of these ladies was placed in a circle of stones in the ninth century or so in the rubble of a palace room, evidently for the purposes of worship. At a lower level of the same room lay the body of the same statue and some other pieces of statuary. Might that indicate that the same goddess had continued to be worshipped in the same place in successive ages? Later, the goddess seems to have suffered a sex change, the god who was later worshipped on that spot was Dionysus (unless the goddess was a nymph, and Dionysus merely her companion).

Mervyn Popham's excavations at Lefkandi in Euboea throughout the seventies would certainly have attracted Leonard Cottrell, and furnish a good example of how progress is made. It was never a great city, but was an undisturbed place, and attracted not a megalomaniac (however touched by genius), but a scholar. Indeed it has been a nursery of scholars over the ten years and more of its excavation. At Lefkandi, Popham was able to recover every successive stage from the earliest simple settlement through the whole Mycenaean age to the time when Mycenaean soldiers stormed the town and took it over for themselves. To judge from their pottery, these soldiers were probably refugees from Athens. They did not last at Lefkandi for ever. In the tenth century BC Lefkandi had trading connections with Cyprus and the Levant, and at that time a man and his wife were buried there who gave rise to many new questions and debates about Greek religion.

The excavation itself is a saga of frustrations and last minute success that Leonard Cottrell would have described better than I can. What was revealed was a building with wooden columns and a curved wall like an apse, in which the couple had been first burned and then buried. A short time after their burial, a corner of the building had collapsed in a landslide or an earthquake (revealing Mycenaean remains). The building was then almost completely dismantled and the entire palace covered over with a mound of earth. Clearly some anger of the gods and some mysterious power of the dead were being controlled.

The unique burial and reburial strikes chords with the cult of the great, heroic dead which Homer records. The man buried at Lefkandi seems to have had connections with Cyprus and to have been more probably a merchant than a king, but this distinction could easily have been blurred. The *Odyssey* shows how the voyages of heroes could overlap with the colonizing of warriors, the activity of pirates and probably also the journeys of a merchant. The attitude of the later Greeks to the ancient dead is a fundamental problem in the study of Homer, and the relation of Homer to life. In the late eighth century BC we know from archaeological evidence that Mycenaean tombs were re-opened for the worship of the dead, and we also know that these dead men were often identified with the heroes of mythology, particularly with those Homer had named. It is therefore extremely interesting to have the very early case of Lefkandi. The attitude this reburial seems to express is not quite the same as the Homeric worship of the dead, but certainly shares with that cult some underlying assumptions about the dead having continuing potency. I believe the Lefkandi corpses were being hidden and not propitiated at their second burial; it is possible that the great mound of earth was meant to keep the dead from walking.

Leonard Cottrell wisely avoided any full discussion of what he called the Homeric Problem (the question of whether the *Iliad* was the work of one man, or whether it evolved through several generations of poets). In his day that was a savage battlefield. The realists, who believed in the unity of Homer as an act of mighty artistry, fought their adversaries who felt the poems had developed by work of mouth and feats of memory over generations, with gleeful mockery. I recollect a public discussion of Homer between two Oxford dons in 1954 that was like a Punch and Judy fight with wet fish. Today the subject has quietened down. Almost everyone understands something about how traditional poetry could be orally transmitted, existing only in varying performances, and it is easy to see how Homer was formed by such a tradition. But most Homeric scholars, at least in Britain, now agree that the *Iliad* as we have it is substantially one man's work. It can be understood only as a poem, a single great work.

The question of whether the *Iliad* contains stray bits of information that descended from the Mycenaeans is another issue. To Schliemann this belief was a guiding inspiration. Modern archaeologists believe they have outgrown Homer and that their subject now exists in its own right. Classical scholars take Homer seriously as a great poet, but not as an accurate historian. But most of them seem to think there are a few vestiges of Mycenaean historical truth in Homer, and everyone agrees there could be some.

Today most archaeologists set little store by the Homeric poems as evidence for the material culture of Mycenaean Greece. The strange subject called 'Homeric Archaeology' which attempts to relate Homer to physical monuments, and which is used, at least at Oxford, as an excuse to introduce young classical scholars to archaeology and to open their minds to the tradition of Schliemann and Evans, now has to deal with more and more dark age material. The dark age is the period when the *Iliad* and the *Odyssey* actually germinated, though it still cannot be understood without reference to the earlier period of the Cretan and Mycenaean achievements.

The attempt to show the continuity of ancient place names which seemed in 1956 a thrilling enterprise, has now been all but abandoned. Most of the Mycenaean names died out or became too unimportant to be recorded. The process of forgetting may have taken five hundred or a thousand years. Chadwick points out that the most detailed account we have of place names which the Pylos tablets might be expected to reflect, dates only from the reign of Augustus. The Greeks showed great interest in Homer's geography, at least from the fifth century BC onwards, and whatever was known about place names under Augustus, some of which has reached us, was drawn from centuries of learned controversy. So later Greek ignorance of real Mycenaean place names is a strong argument for their early disappearance from all epic poetry and even from mythology. In the fifth century BC the Greeks knew where Homer's Sandy Pylos was, and they opened a Mycenaean grave on the island of Sphakteria in the Pylos lagoon and worshipped the bones there. In the age of Hadrian they pointed out Nestor's bath and showed a fresco of the old gentleman on the wall. But excavation at Ano Englianos has revealed that the true Mycenaean Pylos was several miles away and inland; it was not all sandy, and Homer knew nothing about it.

Leonard Cottrell spoke of Mycenae in the time of Homer as an insignificant ruin. However we know that Agamemnon truly was worshipped there in the late eighth century BC and that the tombs of the Mycenaean dead were re-opened at that period for the purposes of worship all over Greece. One is therefore tempted to believe there was a basis in reality for Homer's poetry or at least for the religious cults he described. We even have what seem to be figurines commemorating the discovery of a re-opened Mycenaean tomb. Two shepherds and a dog are depicted peering down into the dome from above. The door of the tomb stands open to reveal a godlike hero or a Mycenaean ghost. We also know that (as Cottrell tells us in a footnote), not three but nine levels of Troy have been traced. Cottrell's footnote was based on Blegen's excavations at Troy, and some of the pottery Blegen discovered has now been shown to be fifty or a hundred years later than he thought. It is possible that Troy itself was inhabited close to Homer's time, just as Mycenae certainly was.

Archaeology is an activity that explores the continuity of the history it unearths. Tracing the links between one culture and another, one period and another, lies at the core of archaeological science. And the relationship between the cultures Schliemann and Evans unearthed at Troy, Mycenae and Knossos was a question of key interest to Leonard Cottrell in *The Bull of Minos*, as it is to anyone who starts to be fascinated by ancient Greek history.

Alan Wace believed that the range of artefacts made during the dark ages showed 'natural developments'. He believed in the Dorian invasion when a new people invaded Greece and destroyed the Mycenaeans (although today historians question it), and that it brought 'not a cultural but only a political change', being an invasion mounted by Greeks against Greeks. The deciphering of Linear B, which demonstrated that the Mycenaeans spoke, and were, Greeks, appeared to him as a triumphant confirmation of a cultural continuity that embraced the growing number of ancient cities where tablets were separately discovered. There is no doubt that the essential point he made about the derivation of 'protogeometric' and later Greek designs on pottery from late Mycenaean patterns, with no break in continuity, is true and has been confirmed by thirty years of later study. But arguments about the continuity and discontinuity of dark age traditions in Greece still take place. The truth is a matter of detail, and it will never be fully understood except by specialized study. In certain areas, the evidence is lacking and it can easily be made to produce paradoxes. In the introduction to the old edition of *The Bull of Minos*, Wace gave a bland assurance of natural evolution and 'a fairly broad period of transition'. In the Foreword to the *Documents*, he made the same case, but with stronger wording. Over the last thirty years the general direction of his argument has been so productive that by now the accumulation of detail has made it seem unnecessary. It has almost become a received truth. It is a task of archaeology to replace probable conjectures and general ideas with abundant detail.

The Bull of Minos is a quest, a discovery of the past and an account of those who discovered it. What it shows above all is the extraordinary result of individual genius. The two giants of prehistoric archaeology in Greece were Schliemann in the nineteenth century and Sir Arthur Evans in the early part of this. They were very much men of their own time, great individualists of astonishing powers, and it is important that they were both rich. Schliemann was born poor but he made a fortune, and used the techniques of big American engineering projects in the excavation first of Troy then of Mycenae and other important sites. His inspiration was Homer's *Iliad*. It is worth noticing that the prestige of classical Greek art and architecture, rediscovered in Europe only in the late eighteenth and nineteenth centuries, made the excavation of pre-history appear at the time comparatively worthless. By his obsession with Homer, Schliemann took a leap backwards in time, and the stunning prestige of his discoveries made the time between the Mycenaeans and the classical Greeks look dark indeed.

Arthur Evans inherited wealth. He was widely travelled and experienced, well educated, and the son of a famous archaeologist. He had no training in excavation, but he learned from experience, and he was able to put his results before the world 'in such a form that all could understand the importance of his discoveries and appreciate their full implications.' The attraction of such a career and such a mighty contribution to knowledge is irresistible. He became convinced on respectable scholarly evidence, which as a young man he was the first to notice, that the Cretans, under the legendary King Minos, were able to write. He bought the site of Knossos and built his house there – the Villa Ariadne. He found inscribed tablets within a fortnight of beginning to excavate. When Cottrell wrote *The Bull of Minos*, these tablets had not been interpreted although there had been numerous scholarly conjectures about them, and a few inspired guesses.

Evans in his mysterious Kingdom of Minos created an empire of his own, and in the later part of his life relations between those archaeologists who thought Mycenae all-important and those who worshipped Evans and Knossos were not easy. Professor Wace was a very great Mycenaean archaeologist, but his public career was badly affected by the hostility of Evans. I doubt whether Leonard Cottrell knew about the details of that quarrel. Its solution, which he gets right by following the steps of Pendelbury, is of fundamental importance.

There is no longer any room for doubt that there was a Mycenaean period at Knossos, although Evans was passionate about his Cretan civilization, and resisted the true conclusion. I have heard it said that he died not in that serene grandeur in which Cottrell prefers to see him, but of a heart attack on being told, quite falsely as it turned out, that the Germans had destroyed the Knossos archaeological collections.

Evans has come under severe attack. The storm burst when the language of the Linear B script had been deciphered and scholars had begun, in the early sixties, to discuss the differences between one set of tablets and another. Linear B tablets had been found at Pylos, Thebes and Mycenae, as well as at Knossos, and it appeared that the Mycenaean Greek language as deciphered showed no development in something like 200 years – a conclusion that seemed unacceptable. It was therefore tempting to try to alter the date, either of the fall of Pylos (one of the last Mycenaean fortresses and kingdoms to hold out) or of the Knossos tablets, which were the earliest examples. The possibility of doing the latter depended on the daybooks, the day by day journal of excavations kept by Duncan Mackenzie for Evans at Knossos. When examined they were said to contradict Evans's published results, which he was then accused of having cooked. There followed a furious and prolonged quarrel between Professor Palmer, a philologist, and Professor Boardman, an experienced archaeologist. The longer the battle raged, the more often the philologist had to change his ground, and the more triumphantly the details of the work of Sir Arthur Evans stood the strain that was put on them. It is certain, as it could never have been without this heated controversy, that Evans excavated Knossos with scientific care.

In other ways he was less scrupulous. I know from an eye witness of one occasion when Evans was leaving Crete and intending to smuggle out an ancient ring that he had found and proposed to keep. When he saw customs men come on board, since he was under suspicion, he calmly flung his ring into the harbour, where it must still be. That was not such a horrid crime in his generation as it would be thought today. Without collecting and its passion, archaeology would never have begun, just as without the naive reading of Homer as a true record, neither Troy nor Mycenae would have been dug. But anyone who acquires antiquities secretly is vulnerable to fakers and false provenances. Some of the objects, though very few, that passed through Evans's hands have come under suspicion. The pretty ivory snake lady in the Boston Museum seems to be by the same hand as the boy bull leaper now in the Ashmolean, which once belonged to Evans. She has been suspected, though the statues from Mycenae rather confirm her respectability; probably nothing is wrong with her except the golden tips of her breasts. The boy was described in a letter by Bosanquet without the golden kilt he now wears. These suspicions are not very serious and might easily be explained away. But romance is a drug, and the romance of antiquities does sometimes lead to exaggeration. Leonard Cottrell was romantic, but completely honest and protected always by a dryness. He was also an extremely sharp and thorough journalist. It is by these qualities, even more than the communication of his own excitement, that his book has lasted so well.

Recent excavations have shown that Knossos was larger than Evans knew. The Palace of Knossos was about the size of a big Oxford or Cambridge college, though of course more crowded. The problem of how large the population was is a difficult one, and all the opinions of the scholars are perforce provisional, and open to reassessment following further study or excavation.

At present we have discovered graves, but no dwelling place (before Mycenae was built), for the early Mycenaeans, and a splendid palace, but no graves, for the rulers of Knossos. This has led to the suggestion that the first Mycenaeans lived in a city of tents, as the Arabs did before they built Cairo. That is just possible. But is also led, about ten years ago, to another suggestion that belongs to the lunatic fringes of

archaeology. This was the idea that Knossos itself might be nothing but a funeral monument – a great city of the dead. The ingenious perversity of this idea has a certain appeal, although it is hard to see why the dead would want the first flushing lavatory in the recorded history of mankind. It is not to be taken seriously, alas.

For Leonard Cottrell the extent of the use of writing remained a puzzle. It is certainly odd that we have no written literature in verse or prose that has survived, but only archives. It was clear enough that the Mycenaeans could read, as Cottrell rightly argued from the tablets found in private houses and the careful inscriptions on some vases and jars. Why, he wondered, did they never inscribe the names of dead kings on their gravestones. Were some things too sacred to be written down? Were there painted inscriptions? Or did it never occur to them that the names of those dead whose graves were a landmark could be forgotten? It is quite likely they assumed, as Homer does, that a grave which is a landmark or a seamark, would be remembered; even in classical times Greek families knew their ancestry by heart for three hundred years back. And yet the graves certainly were forgotten. In later times a claim to ancestry could substantiate a claim to land, if one could point to an important tomb. But the earliest inscriptions on offerings at heroic tombs, like the one at Menidi, are only 'to the hero'. The names were applied later. We should think of this belated naming of the tombs as a sudden cult of ancestors that was inspired by the wish to lay claim to territory, and that therefore had a social and an economic explanation.

Frank Stubbing suggested that a powerful oral tradition, even in Homeric hexameters, might go back to the Mycenaeans. I am sure Stubbings is right to believe that the Mycenaeans might have had oral traditions. No poetry has ever been discovered among their archives, so since they certainly had poetry of some kind, it must either have been written on something non-durable like palm leaves, or it was purely oral. If they did have an oral tradition, the link was broken and none survived. There is unfortunately no way of ascertaining whether their poetry was epic, still less whether it was written in hexameters.

The most satisfying result of the decipherment of Linear B has been the detail it supplies about the life of Knossos and of Pylos in its last days. Pylos held out after Mycenae had fallen, so something of the urgent drama of the end of an age can be read from the palace archives. The tribute of the villages was still coming in, and ivory was still being inlaid into wood. There were ivory lions' heads, and the Queen's jug, perhaps an heirloom, was in the shape of a bull's head decorated with seashells. But extra rations were being sent to coastal strongholds, the army had been strengthened and was scattered in garrisons. We do not read of many ships, and the coast cannot have been effectively guarded. The leases and loans of tenant farmers were a ramshackle hopeless system. Records were kept of offerings to numerous gods. The gods correspond almost, though not quite, to the names of the Greek gods Homer knew. The pottery of Pylos, of which there was a huge quantity, was an inferior version of the pottery of Mycenae – a provincial version. I used to believe, and have written

Opposite The Lion Gate, Mycenae

elsewhere, that the palace fresco of Mycenaean warriors fighting barbarians showed colonial war, but I now understand it was only a copy of a North African painting, just as the crowded ship scene at Santorini has been said to derive from Egypt. All the same, these pictures must have had strong local resonance, and there is no doubt that the last generation of Pylos lived a threatened life and foresaw its own downfall.

The deciphering of the Linear B tablets, and the revelation that they were written in a form of Greek, was made in 1953 and fully published in 1955 by Michael Ventris and John Chadwick. The story is a thrilling and romantic one, retold by Cottrell at the end of *The Bull of Minos*. The inscribed tablets, writen on clay, sometimes in the shape of palm leaves, and baked hard in the fires that destroyed the palaces, contain palace archives – mainly administrative lists that record the collecting of taxes, the value of offerings to the gods, the distribution of seedcorn or of rations. Some scholars were at first sceptical of the Ventris and Chadwick interpretation, but few have remained so and every later discovery has confirmed their findings.

Linear script A now seems to be a close, slightly older relative of B. But the code breaking methods used to decipher B relied on having a large number of samples of the script, and we still have too few samples of A to make sense of it. Between the time of Ventris' death in a motor accident in 1955, and the second (1973) edition of *Documents*, knowledge advanced further. It now appears that the syllabic script used until much later in Cyprus is a first cousin of Linear B, and that they both derive from Linear A. When we get enough material to decipher Linear A it is going to have important consequences for the early history of Cyprus as well as Crete. It is already clear from the date of a fragmentary tablet from Enkomi in Cyprus (about 1500 BC) that Cyprus got the script from the Cretans and not the mainland Greeks. In some directions the Kingdom of Minos continues to expand.

Nineteenth century archaeology makes fascinating reading, as Cottrell saw. It contains plenty of bold action described by men who were excellent writers. (Lawrence of Arabia was an archaeologist before 1914. In fact he was recruited into the secret service, as well as the profession of archaeology, by Hogarth, who features in this book.) Not only is it thrilling to know something of the real past that Homer could only imagine, and to be constantly expanding what we know about the early Greeks. Archaeology itself has changed, so that now we like reading about the more active, less intellectual pleasures it once offered. It has now become a science; it is no longer in the hands only of rich men, and there is less place nowadays for those individual strokes of genius which Cottrell so brilliantly records. Schliemann and Evans and Hogarth are as interesting as their own excavations. How swiftly the world alters.

Peter Levi
1984

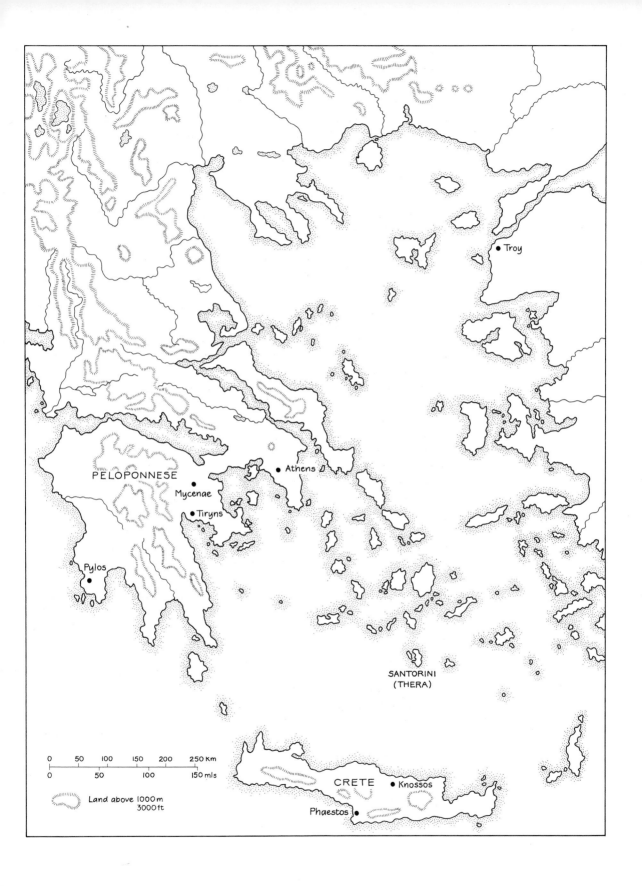

Troy

PELOPONNESE

Athens

Mycenae

Tiryns

Pylos

SANTORINI
(THERA)

0   50   100   150   200   250 Km
0   50   100   150 mls

Land above 1000 m
3000 ft

CRETE   Knossos

Phaestos

PREFACE

When I wrote the first edition of this book I had no idea that it would go on selling year after year and be published in some ten languages. But the appeal of the Mycenaean Greeks and the Cretan Minoans, who lived between three and four thousand years ago and created on the European continent rich civilizations comparable with Egypt in her prime, is apparently perennial.

I believe, also, that much of its appeal must lie in the characters who figure so largely in it, the great archaeologists Heinrich Schliemann and Sir Arthur Evans, the first of whom discovered the Mycenaean civilization of Greece, and the second of whom excavated and partially reconstructed the superb Minoan palace at Knossos in Crete, the legendary home of King Minos.

These men were the main heroes of the story, but many other distinguished scholars have continued to contribute to it, including the late Professor A. B. Wace to whom my gratitude is due for kindly reading my manuscript, and for his valuable suggestions. There is also another outstanding character, the brilliant young architect the late Michael Ventris who, over a period of seventeen years, in fact from the age of seventeen, succeeded in doing what scores of scholars had tried and failed to do. He deciphered the mysterious Minoan writing-system which Evans had called 'Linear B' to distinguish it from a similar but different writing system, 'Linear A' which remains undeciphered. 'Linear B' turned out to be a primitive form of Greek as spoken by the Mycenaeans (Homer's 'bronze-clad Achaeans'), a Greek-speaking people who entered Greece a thousand years before the Greeks of classical times. More of this is dealt with in my later book, *The Lion Gate*, which is a sequel to *The Bull of Minos*. Ventris, alas, was killed in a car crash at the age of thirty-four.

It remains for me to express my gratitude to the authors whose works form the principal basis of this book.

Any author attempting to write a book on the rise of the Minoan civilization must inevitably draw deeply from Sir Arthur Evans's great work *The Palace of Minos*. My chief debt of gratitude is, therefore to Sir Arthur's literary executors, to the Clarendon Press, and to Messrs. Macmillan, for allowing me not only to quote from the book, but also to reproduce some of the unique illustrations of Minoan culture in which it is so rich.

I am also grateful to the BBC who made it possible for me to visit Greece and Crete in connection with my radio documentary programmes on Heinrich Schliemann and Sir Arthur Evans.

I gained special pleasure and benefit from Emil Ludwig's life of Schliemann, from Schliemann's own works, especially *Ilios* with its fascinating autobiographical details, and the works of Schuchhardt, Dörpfeld, and Karo.

For the personal background to Sir Arthur Evans's life the most complete and authoritative source is *Time and Chance* written by his half-sister, Dr. Joan Evans, and published towards the latter end of the Second World War. I also remember with gratitude the late Sir John Myres, who in his eighties was kind enough to welcome me to his Oxford home, and gave me a first-hand impression of his lifelong friend such as I could never obtain from the printed word alone.

Next to *The Palace of Minos*, John Pendlebury's *Archaeology of Crete* remains one of the most complete and readable surveys of the prehistoric civilization. I was first brought into contact with Pendlebury's work by H. W. Fairman, Professor of Egyptology at the University of Liverpool, who had dug with Pendlebury on the site of Akhnaten's city of Tell-el-Amarna, in Egypt. After visiting Tell-el-Amarna myself in 1947, it became my ambition to visit Knossos, where Pendlebury was Curator for a number of years. When I realized that ambition and studied the Palace of Minos with Pendlebury's *Guide* in my hand, it was with some sadness, for the young scholar, who loved the Cretan people, had been one of the leaders of the Cretan Resistance and had died in the struggle. Had he lived, he might have become a worthy successor to Evans, who liked and respected him.

Special thanks are also due to the staff of the British School at Athens, who helped to arrange my visit to Knossos, and to the London Staff of the School, especially its able Secretary, Miss Edith Clay. I am also particularly grateful for the professional guidance of Dr Frank Stubbings, University Lecturer in Classics at Cambridge.

With two exceptions, all the quotations from *The Iliad* and *The Odyssey* are from the recent translation by Mr. E. V. Rieu, published in the Penguin series.

Finally, I remember with affection the late Mr and Mrs Piet de Jong. Piet de Jong was the last British Curator of the Palace of Knossos before it was handed over, with the Villa Ariadne, to the Greek authorities in 1952. He had been appointed by Sir Arthur Evans as his architect in 1922; but the hard, self-denying work which de Jong and his wife carried out to efface the results of war-time neglect of the Palace and its estate was not the least of his achievements. Had Sir Arthur himself lived he would have been the first to congratulate his former architect; may I, therefore, as a disinterested outside observer, record the fact that when the Palace of Minos was finally handed over to Greece, its sound condition, and that of the Villa Ariadne and its accompanying estate, was largely due to this modest Yorkshireman and his wife who had to cope with post-war difficulties which Sir Arthur was happily spared.

LEONARD COTTRELL 1971

PROLOGUE

I left Athens at mid-day in the *Automatrice*, a reasonably fast Diesel train which for four hours trundled along beside the sun-glittering Gulf of Salamis, through pale green valleys hemmed in by low, treeless hills of grey limestone, past dust-grey villages set among the dark spear-like cypresses. The light was white and intense, the magical light of Hellas which shadows impartially the fluting of a Doric column or the hard lines of a peasant's face. We passed Megara, near which the hero Theseus kicked the giant Sciron into the sea (where he turned into a tortoise), and then after miles of gnarled olive-trees, slowed and stopped at New Corinth.

I had over an hour to wait at the squalid railway station, which seemed as if designed to destroy all romantic preconceptions of Greece. On the dirty, paper-littered platform sat sad-eyed women in drab, shapeless clothes, and a few listless men, cloth-capped and collarless. Among them was a sullen youth with a strained, handsome face, who looked older than his years. He had lost a leg in the Civil War and hobbled painfully on crutches. A few meagre-looking fowl pecked between the tracks, and a small ragged boy moved along the platform with a trayful of 'souflakia'—fragments of meat on wooden skewers; but he had few customers.

So this was Greece. It served me right for my selfish preoccupation with the past. What else had I any right to expect in Greece in 1951? Invaded in turn by Italians and Germans, then, when other countries had gained peace, subjected to a bitter Civil War, Greece was now impoverished and exhausted. Was this a time for half-baked romantics to come poking about among her ruins? So I reproached myself, wishing either that I could have visited the country in happier times, or that I had the temperament of a contemporary reporter who could apply himself fearlessly and frankly to her present-day problems.

Another train took me southward again, crawling slowly round the skirts of the 2,000-foot mountain on which stands the Acrocorinthus. Dramatically it rose from the darkening plain, a dome of limestone capped by the ruins of the Temple of Athena, and the citadel from which the ancient Corinthians commanded the Isthmus. By the time its black silhouette had passed out of view the sun had set, and only an occasional cluster of lights revealed a village among the folded hills. My fellow-passengers were mostly peasants, the women usually in black, with head-scarves, and laden baskets resting on their broad laps. They chatted, but the sun-tanned men usually sat silent. Occasionally a pipe would be removed from beneath a curled moustache; a brief remark would accompany a flash of strong white teeth; then the pipe would be replaced, the arms folded, and dark eyes beneath round black turbans would resume their detached but un-hostile contemplation of the stranger.

As I watched them my spirits rose a little. In fact, so fascinating were those grave, contemplative faces that I almost forgot to get out at my destination. Glancing up when the train had been halted for nearly a minute I happened to see a station name-board in the yellow light of an oil lamp. It was *Mycenae*. Even as I snatched my bag from the rack and scrambled out of the carriage the absurdity of the situation struck me. To see the name of Agamemnon's proud citadel, Homer's 'Mycenae, rich in gold', the scene of Aeschylus's epic tragedy, stuck on a station platform, was too bizarre. And yet there it was. And there was I, the sole occupant of the platform, watching the red rear-light of the little train as it slowly receded into the night.

A full moon was rising, and the groves of olive-trees rustled gently in the night wind, which brought with it the faint scent of thyme. I looked around for the car which my friends in Athens had told me *might* be waiting to take me to the village inn at Charvati, two miles away. It was not there. So, hitching my bag on my shoulder I set off along the straight, olive-bordered lane towards the hills which showed clearly in the moonlight. As I walked I felt happier. Without knowing why, I began to believe that Mycenae would not disappoint me.

A few lights gleamed through the trees ahead. Some way off a dog barked and another answered. The hills were quite close now, and I could see the scattered houses of the village clustered on the lower slopes. The houses lay on the left of the road. On the right the plain of Argos stretched open to the sea, which, although I could not see it, I knew was only a few miles away. The inn, I had been told, was by the roadside, set back behind a break in the trees. Could this be it, this small, dark, flat-fronted building without a light showing? Yes, there was the sign, hung from a tree by the roadside. I shone my torch and read 'La Belle Hélène de Menelaus'.

If it had adorned a large, neon-lit hotel with a car park and a gold-braided porter, the inn-sign would have seemed smart-aleck and vulgar; but not as it was, hung in front of this unpretending house in an unpretending village. I knocked, waited, knocked again; but the house seemed deserted. There was no sound within, and not a light showed. The dog barked again, a long way off. The oleanders stirred in the slight breeze, and again came that faint, fresh smell of thyme. I felt curiously elated and expectant, not at all cast down by this apparent indifference to my arrival. My Athenian hosts had warned me that although they had sent a telegram to the proprietor of the inn there was no certainty that it would arrive.

Then came a light step crossing the hall; the door opened, and there emerged, first a slim white arm holding aloft an oil lamp, then the owner of the arm. She was about twenty-three, fair-skinned, with a wide, firm mouth, strong, rounded chin, and deep, dark eyes under a smooth brow. She stood for a moment on the top step, looking down at me. Her dress was that of a peasant, a simple cream-coloured frock

Above The citadel of Mycenae

Right View looking outwards
from the citadel at Mycenae

24

with a scarlet jacket carelessly thrown over it, but her face was like one of the sculptured maidens of the porch of the Erechtheum on the Athenian Acropolis. It was too absurdly romantic—the plain of Argos—Helen of Troy had been called 'Argive Helen'—the name on the inn-sign, the Homeric setting.

There were two men, and an older woman who seemed to be the mother of the girl who had admitted me. Evidently the telegram had not come and my arrival had taken them unawares, but now, recovering from their surprise, they bustled about the house, up and down the stairs, in and out of dining-room and kitchen, eager to make me comfortable. The older of the two men, tall, lean and dark, with stubble on his long chin, appeared to be in charge. As he shouted orders, lamps were brought into the stone-flagged dining-room, the girl spread a cloth and laid the table, while her mother hurried upstairs to prepare my bed. The other man, who seemed to be brother of the first, then entered carrying a three-legged shallow brazier filled with glowing coals. This he placed beneath the table so that I might warm my feet. As the brazier-carrier was hurrying out again his brother caught him by the arm and pointing to him, said to me:

'Orestes!' And then, indicating himself, he added, 'Agamemnon!'

We all bowed and smiled. I did not dare inquire the name of the girl. It would have been too disappointing if she had not been named Helen

The Lion Gate

or Andromache. Now she entered again, bearing my meal—a superb omelette, a fine cheese, and a bottle of pale golden wine—the familiar resin-flavoured *retzina* which is drunk all over Greece.

Dinner over, I wandered around the room, examining the photographs on the walls; pictures of the citadel of Mycenae, with its Lion Gate, its cyclopean walls and the huge beehive-shaped 'tholos' tombs which I had studied so often in weighty volumes at home. To think that these glories lay only a mile away in the dark hills, awaiting exploration tomorrow, filled me with excitement. On a table lay a copy of Professor Wace's newly published book on Mycenae, with his written greetings to my cheerful hosts. Wace, they had told me in Athens, had stayed here during the previous year while superintending his latest 'dig' at Mycenae.

While turning Wace's pages I found Agamemnon, my host, standing at my elbow with the inn's Visitors' Book. He held it under the light, pointing with a brown finger at an entry on a page dated 1942. It was a foreign signature, difficult to read at first. Then, with a start, I recognized it—Hermann Goering. My host flicked the pages and pointed to another signature—Heinrich Himmler. Somewhat shaken, I took the book from his hand, sat down and carefully read through the names entered during the early years of the war. I also found Goebbels, together with many scores of officers and men of *Panzer-divizionen*, from generals to privates.

What had attracted the Nazi chiefs and so many German soldiers to this spot? They had come to pay tribute to the memory of Heinrich Schliemann. Eighty years ago that great German archaeologist had come here after his triumphs at Troy, and dug from beneath the citadel treasures which proved that Homer's 'golden Mycenae' had been aptly named. Schliemann had died more than fifty years ago, yet his influence was still felt. Was it not a habit of Schliemann to give his workmen Homeric names, and often to stand godfather to their children? No doubt the Agamemnon who stood watching me now, with the book in his hands, had been so sponsored.

For a time I lay awake, reading Wace's book by candlelight, and listening to the faint sound of the night wind, and the occasional croak of a frog. When I snuffed the candle, I was too excited to sleep. Again and again my thoughts kept returning to the parson's son from Mecklenburg who believed in the literal truth of Homer; the self-made merchant turned archaeologist whose instinct proved more accurate than the learning of scholars; that exasperating, bewildering yet likeable mixture of shrewdness and naïvety—Doctor Heinrich Schliemann. From Schliemann my thoughts turned to Homer, the poet whom he idolized and by whom he was led to make those discoveries which set up such a fluttering in the academic dovecotes.

But before we can understand what Schliemann did to the historians, it is necessary to know something of the academic world into which the eccentric German erupted. To that world, and its view of Homer, I devote my first chapter.

1 HOMER AND THE HISTORIANS

I am going to assume that not all readers of this book will be specialists in Greek epic poetry or the prehistoric civilizations of the Aegean. Many, perhaps, will be in that vague but happy state of half-knowledge which I enjoyed before I was drawn down into the vortices of Homeric research. This is, they may know their Homer, either in the original or in one of those excellent modern translations (such as that made by Mr E. V. Rieu and published in the Penguin series), they may have a working knowledge of Greek classical history and may recall that at some time in the last century someone dug up 'Homer's Troy' and 'Homer's Mycenae' and thus proved to everyone's delight that the *Iliad* and the *Odyssey* were 'true'. If only the facts were as simple as that! But, alas, they aren't.

On the other hand, even readers who have not yet read the great epic poet of Greece will be familiar with the stories, be they history or legend, which Homer wove into his poems. They will have heard how the Trojan Prince, Paris, stole the lovely Helen from her husband Menelaüs of Sparta, of how Menelaüs and his brother Agamemnon 'King of Men' led the Achaean host to Troy and laid siege to it for ten years. The wrath of Achilles; the slaying of the Trojan hero, Hector; the stratagem of the Wooden Horse, planned by the cunning Odysseus, which led to the sack of Priam's city; the long return home of the much-enduring Odysseus, the Wanderer; all these are part of Europe's rich heritage of legend. In England alone poets from Chaucer to Louis MacNeice have drawn upon the Homeric themes and characters, as no doubt will writers yet unborn. For Homer, father of European literature, has entered to some extent into the thought and speech of every one of us, even those who have never consciously read a line by him.

Less than a hundred years ago the only knowledge—if it could be called such—of the early history of Greece was that obtainable from Greek mythology, and especially from the great epic poems of Homer, the *Iliad* and the *Odyssey*. Practically everything before about 800 BC was regarded as legend. The historian George Grote, whose monumental *History of Greece* was published in 1846, could write in his Preface:

... I began the real history of Greece with the first recorded Olympiad, or 776 BC ... For the truth is, that historical records, properly so called, do not begin until after this date; nor will any man, who candidly considers the extreme paucity of attested facts for two centuries after 776 BC be astonished to learn that the state of Greece in 900, 1000, 1100, 1200, 1300, 1400 BC, etc.—or any earlier century which it may please chronologists to include in their computed genealogies—cannot be described to him with anything like decent evidence . . .

. . . The times which I thus set apart from the region of history are discernible only through a different atmosphere—that of epic poetry and legend. To confound together these disparate matters, is, in my judgement, essentially unphilosophical. . . .

Thus sternly wrote Mr Grote, and justly, too, in the light of what was known at that time. For though the classical Greek (600–300 BC) regarded much of their epics as literal history, there was nothing in them which a modern historian would be justified in regarding as evidence. True, the epics sometimes described individuals who *could* have been credible historical figures, whose actions often took place in a precise geographical setting; yet they were so intermixed with obvious myths and supernatural happenings as to make it almost impossible to recognize where legend ended and reality began. For instance, Odysseus, the Wanderer, during the earlier part of his journey home from Troy, follows a route which can be traced, island by island, on a modern map, and which proves Homer's knowledge of Aegean topography. But after a while the Wanderer wanders off the map into fairyland, to the island of Circe, to the home of the hideous Lestrygonians and the land of the Cyclopes, even to Hades itself, where only our imaginations can follow him.

Of course the *Odyssey*—the 'first novel of Europe'—being an obvious romance, might be expected to contain many elements of fairy tale. But even the sterner *Iliad*, which tells of the siege of Troy, and which the Greeks of classical times regarded as authentic history, has its mythical ingredients. The gods take sides in the war, appear to the heroes, and fight in both armies—though usually disguised as human warriors. Some of the heroes are god-descended. Achilles is the son of Thetis, the sea-nymph, Helen is the daughter of Zeus himself. Xanthus, one of Achilles' horses, has the power of human speech and warns his master of his impending death. But admittedly these are subordinate elements in the story, which in the main is grimly and brilliantly realistic, and could only have been written by one who was personally familiar with the Trojan plain.

Who was this great poet, whose works were thought by the classical Greeks to embody their early history? The historian Herodotus, who lived between *c.* 484–425 BC believed that Homer had lived about four hundred years before his own time, that is, in about the ninth century BC, though later authorities placed his date far back in the twelfth century (present-day opinion on the whole favours Herodotus' date). No real histories of his life existed, though many legends grew up around his name. Several places competed for the honour of being his birthplace—Smyrna, Argos, Athens, Salamis, and Khios, but the last has the strongest claim. Tradition is insistent that he was an 'Ionian' Greek, that is that he belonged to those Greeks who were driven out of the mainland by the invading Dorians (*circa* 1000 BC) and founded the Ionian colonies on the west coast of Asia Minor.

One fact is certain: that Homer, whether he created his epics in the eight, ninth, or tenth centuries before Christ, was making use of much more ancient material—a store of myths, legends and folk-tales which had come down to him from a remote past. We also know that much of this epic material which Homer used survived, side by side with the Homeric poems, into classical times. This can be proved by the fact that several legends and stories which Homer only glanced at were used by later poets and dramatists as fully developed epics or plays. Historians call this material, on which both Homer and later Greek poets drew, the *Epic Cycle*.

Although I would not dare attempt to summarize the whole of the *Iliad* and the *Odyssey*, I think it might help those who have not read these epics to describe briefly those episodes which have a bearing on Schliemann's discoveries.

The *Iliad*, which is generally supposed to be the earlier poem, deals with an episode in the Trojan War—the Wrath of Achilles—and its tragic consequences. Its opening is tremendous:

The Wrath of Achilles is my theme, that fatal wrath which, in fulfilment of the will of Zeus, brought the Achaeans so much suffering and sent the gallant souls of so many noblemen to Hades, leaving their bodies as carrion for the dogs and passing birds. Let us begin, goddess of song, with the angry parting that took place between Agamemnon King of Men, and the great Achilles son of Peleus....

Notice that Homer calls his Greeks 'the Achaeans'. This is the name he most often uses to describe them, though occasionally he calls them Danaans. Often they are described by the name of the district or island from which they come, e.g. the Locrians, from Locris, the Arcadians 'from the lands where Mount Cyllene lifts its peak' and so on.

When the *Iliad* opens the Achaeans are encamped beside their ships on the edge of the Trojan plain. Before them lies King Priam's city of Troy, or Ilium, which they have unsuccessfully besieged for nine years. (Troy can easily be identified on a modern map of Turkey. It lies on the coast of Asia Minor, near the entrance to the Dardanelles.)

Agamemnon, 'King of Men', is the leader of the Achaean host. He is comparable to a feudal overlord of the Middle Ages, exercising a loose suzerainty over his subordinate chiefs (though they also are called Kings), but not having complete authority. In fact his authority is challenged in the very first book of the *Iliad*, when Achilles, King of the Myrmidons, and the greatest warrior in the Achaean host, heaps abuse on him for threatening to take from Achilles his slave-girl, Briseis, part of his legitimate spoils of war.

'You shameless schemer,' he cried, 'always aiming at a profitable deal! How can you expect any of the men to give you loyal service when you send them on a raid or into battle? It was no quarrel with the Trojan spearmen that brought *me* here to fight. They have never done *me* any harm. They have never lifted cow or horse of mine, nor ravaged any crop that the deep soil of Phthia grows to feed her men; for the roaring seas and many a dark range of mountains lie between us. The truth is that we joined the expedition to please you; yes, you unconscionable cur, to get satisfaction from the Trojans for Menelaüs and yourself—a fact which you utterly ignore.'

Menelaüs, King of Sparta, was Agamemnon's brother, and the ostensible cause of the war was the outrage offered to Menelaüs by Paris (sometimes called Alexander) son of King Priam of Troy. Entertained in Menelaüs's home at Sparta, Paris had seized the opportunity of his host's temporary absence to steal the affection of his wife, the lovely Helen, daughter of Zeus, and to take her with him to Troy. The legendary cause of this, though Homer only glances lightly at it, was Aphrodite, who, having been chosen by Paris as the most beautiful of the goddesses, promised him as a reward the loveliest woman in the world—Helen of Sparta. Agamemnon, determined to avenge the insult to his brother and his family, called upon the Achaeans from many parts of Greece, and from the islands, to sail under his leadership to Troy and win Helen back.

The Second Book of the *Iliad* contains the famous Catalogue of Ships, describing in considerable detail, where the Achaean contingents came from; a long, and, to our minds, rather tedious list, though to Homer's hearers it was of great importance. But there is an interesting point concerning this catalogue, one which puzzled an earlier generation of scholars. Most of the towns and citadels which Homer describes as of great wealth and power were in his own day, and in classical times, mere ruins, if they existed at all. For example,

The citizens of Argos and Tiryns of the Great Walls; the men of Hermione and Asine, towns that embrace a deep gulf of the sea; and those from Troezen, from Eionae, and from vine-clad Epidaurus, with the Achaean youth of Aegina and Mases, were led by Diomedes of the loud war-cry....

And most important of all

The troops that came from the great stronghold of Mycenae, from wealthy Corinth and the good town of Cleonae....

These, and others, the poet tell us

... in their hundred ships, King Agamemnon son of Atreus led. His following was by far the finest and most numerous. He was a proud man as he took his stand with his people, armed in gleaming bronze, the greatest captain of all, in virtue of his rank and as commander of by far the largest force.

Yet, in the ninth century, when Homer wrote, Mycenae was of little importance, and in later classical times, when every Greek schoolboy knew and recited Homer, it was a ruin. So was 'Minyan Orchomenos', and 'Tiryns of the Great Walls', and many another city which, according to the legends, was once rich and great.

This fact puzzled some scholars, because there were, in support of the legend that Agamemnon had lived at Mycenae, great walls which a later generation thought had been built by giants—the Cyclopes; similarly at Tiryns there were these Cyclopean walls. Nevertheless most scholars inclined to the belief that the Homeric stories were folk-myths and nothing more.

To return to the *Iliad*; the quarrel between Agamemnon and Achilles ends in bitter rancour. Agamemnon, determined to assert his authority, takes Achilles' slave-girl to replace the girl Chryseis, whom he has been forced to return to her father Chryses. This aged man was a priest of Apollo, who had let loose a plague on the Greeks, because Agamemnon had stolen Chryses' daughter. Achilles, whilst refraining from a direct attack on Agamemnon, retires with his Myrmidons to their tents and refuses to take any further part in the battle.

'That day is coming,' he tells Agamemnon, 'when the Achaeans one and all will miss

The abduction of Helen by Paris, illustrated centuries after Homer on an attic skyphos of about 480 BC

me sorely, and you in your despair will be powerless to help them as they fall in their hundreds to Hector, killer of men.'

In the third book the armies advance to meet each other, but Hector, principal warrior on the Trojan side, steps forward and proposes that his brother Paris should meet Menelaüs in single combat, whoever wins being entitled to Helen. A truce is declared and the two armies sit down opposite each other to watch the duel. Paris is defeated, but his guardian goddess Aphrodite saves him in the nick of time and spirits him back to the city, much to the disgust of both sides, since Paris is as unpopular with his own countrymen as he is with the Greeks.

But the gods are adamant and, tempted by the goddess Athene, Pandarus, one of the Trojan allies, shoots an arrow at Menelaüs, wounding him and so breaking the truce. This time fighting breaks out in earnest. The gods themselves join in the battle, and the valiant Diomedes, an Achaean hero, even succeeds in felling the war-god Ares, besides wounding Aphrodite when she tries to rescue her son Aeneas. Hector and Paris return to the battlefield and again Hector issues a challenge to any Greek to meet him in single combat. The great Telamonian Aias accepts the challenge, but the fight is indecisive, though tough, and ends with the combatants chivalrously exchanging gifts. meanwhile Achilles continues to sulk in his tent.

It is worth bearing in mind the *methods* of fighting described in the *Iliad* because they have a considerable bearing on the archaeological discoveries to be described later. In the period of classical Greece, e.g. in such battles as Marathon (490 BC) and Thermopylae (480 BC), the typical Greek soldier was the *hoplite*, clad, as Professor Gilbert Murray says,

31

in sold metal from head to foot; helmet, breastplate, and backplate, small round shield, and greaves, all of metal.

(Rise of the Greek Epic.)

Now it is true that the *Iliad* is full of references to the round shield 'plated in bronze', to 'the clash of men in bronze breastplates', and 'the flashing of bronze, men slaying and men slain'. The Greeks of classical times, hearing such descriptions, would imagine the typical heavy armour of the *hoplitae*, such as you can often see represented on classical vase-paintings or groups of classical statuary. Not only that, but, as Murray points out, some, though not all, of the tactics described, suggest the close-formation, tightly disciplined manoeuvres of the fifth-century warriors.

The Trojans came on, like lines of waves on the sea, line behind line, flashing in bronze, together with their commanders.

But there are other descriptions of methods of fighting which bear no resemblance to those of classical times, or even to those of Homer's own period, so far as these can be ascertained. For example, when the Greek hero, Telamonian Aias, goes to meet Hector in the above-mentioned duel, he carries a shield

like a tower, made of bronze and seven layers of leather. Tychius, the master-currier, who lived at Hyle, made this glittering shield for him with the hides of seven big bulls, which he overlaid with an eighth layer of bronze. Holding this shield before his breast, Telmonian Aias went right up to Hector before halting to defy him.

Evidently this shield 'like a tower' covered the entire body, and was quite unlike any type of shield depicted in classical times, or even in the ninth century, when Homer lived. Where did the poet get his description? Scholars were puzzled. Nor was this the only reference to a leather body shield. In Book Four there is a passage describing Hector walking back from the battlefield to the town.

As he walked, the dark leather rim of his bossed shield tapped him above and below, on the ankles and on the back of the neck.

Obviously this would have been impossible if the hero had been carrying an ordinary round shield with an arm-band. Evidently he was wearing a large body shield slung over his shoulders by means of a leather baldric.

And to take one final example there is a scene in Book Fifteen when Hector and his followers have forced the Achaeans right back to their ships, and are threatening to storm the wall which the besiegers have built to protect themselves. Here Hector slays many Greeks, among them one Periphetes, a Mycenaean.

He had just turned to fly when he tripped against the rim of his shield which he carried to keep missiles off and which came down to his feet. Thrown off his balance, he fell backwards, and as he reached the ground his helmet rang loudly on his temples, at once attracting Hector's notice. . . .

which was too bad for Periphetes. If he had been carrying a small round shield of the classical type or even of the ninth-century pattern, such an accident could not have happened. Where, asked the scholars, did Homer get the idea of these big cumbersome leather shields? And

why were they mixed up with much more frequent references to shields of the more familiar type?

There were other anachronisms too. For instance, in Homer's time and afterwards, weapons, whether swords or spears, were almost invariably of iron. In the *Iliad* and the *Odyssey*, with one or two insignificant exceptions, weapons are of bronze. Iron is known, but is used almost entirely for tools. Again, the Homeric heroes use chariots, which do not seem to have been widely used in Homer's day and had passed out of fashion in classical times.

To complete our very rapid review of the story, Agamemnon, worried by the Trojan success, sends an embassy to Achilles. It consists of the wily Odysseus, King of Ithaca and hero of the *Odyssey*, the aged Nestor, King of Pylos and 'elder statesman' among the Achaeans, and the redoubtable Telamonian Aias, he of the great shield. They convey Agamemnon's promise to return Briseis, together with an enormous gift, as compensation for the insult Achilles had been offered, but the hero returns a contemptuous answer. It is not until the Trojans threaten the ships that Achilles takes notice. Even then he only permits his beloved friend and squire, Patroclus, to borrow his armour and go out to the assistance of the hard-pressed Greeks. But Hector kills Patroclus and strips him of his armour.

Only then does Achilles realize the tragic result of his own intransigence. In bitter rage, and re-equipped with dazzling new armour made by the god Hephaestus himself, he returns to the fight with his Myrmidons. The Trojans are hurled back, Achilles meets Hector in single combat, slays him beneath the walls of Troy and then drags the body in the dust behind his chariot. Every morning he drives the chariot, with its burden, round the pyre on which lies the corpse of Patroclus. He honours his dead friend with a great funeral, after which games are held. The heroes contend with each other in running, boxing, duelling with the spear, chariot-racing, archery, wrestling and javelin-throwing.

The greatest moment of the *Iliad* is undoubtedly the end, when the aged King Priam comes at night to the Achaean camp to ransom the body of his dead son. It is one of the most moving passages in the literature of the world, and I make no apology for quoting from it again, in Mr Rieu's effective translation. Kneeling before Achilles, the slayer of his son, Priam says:

Achilles, fear the gods, and be merciful to me, remembering your own father, though I am even more entitled to compassion, since I have brought myself to do a thing that no one else on earth has done—I have raised to my lips the hand of the man who killed my son.

Priam had set Achilles thinking of his own father and brought him to the edge of tears. Taking the old man's hand, he gently put him from him; and overcome by their memories they both broke down. Priam, crouching at Achilles' feet, wept bitterly for man-slaying Hector, and Achilles wept for his father, and then again for Patroclus. The house was filled with sounds of their lamentation. . . .

The other great epic, the *Odyssey*, describes the long-delayed arduous return of the 'much-enduring' Odysseus to his home after the sack of Troy. In the *Odyssey* we also learn what happened to some of the other Achaean heroes who figure in the *Iliad*. We meet Menelaüs, back again at his palace in Sparta, with the repentant Helen beside him. No longer the *femme fatale*, she is now the perfect housewife:

... Helen with her ladies came down from her lofty perfumed room, looking like Artemis with her golden distaff. Adreste drew up for her a comfortable chair; Alcippe brought a rug of the softest wool; while Phylo carried her silver work-basket, a gift from Alcandre, wife of Polybus, who lived in Egyptian Thebes, where houses are furnished in the most sumptuous fashion. This man had given Melenaüs two silver baths, a pair of three-legged cauldrons, and ten talents in gold; while in addition his wife gave Helen beautiful gifts for herself, including a golden spindle and a basket that ran on castors and was made of silver finished with a rim of gold. ...*

It is in the *Odyssey* that we learn what happened to Agamemnon, King of Men, on his return to Mycenae. Old Nestor, speaking to Telemachus, son of Odysseus, describes the treachery of Aegisthos, Agamemnon's cousin, who seduced Clytemnestra, the King's wife, while he was away at Troy.

While we that were beleaguering Troy toiled at heroic tasks, he spent his leisured days, right in the heart of Argos where the horses graze, besieging Agamemnon's wife with his seductive talk. At first Queen Clytemnestra turned a deaf ear to his dishonourable schemes. She was a sensible woman, and beside, she had a man with her, a minstrel by profession, to whom Agamemnon when he left for Troy had given strict orders to watch over his queen. But when the fatal day appointed for her conquest came, Aegisthus took this minstrel to a desert isle, left him there as carrion for the birds of prey, and carried Clytemnestra off to his own house, fond lover, willing dame. ...

In another part of the *Odyssey*, Menelaüs completes the tale of his brother's doom.

Agamemnon set foot on the soil of his father with a happy heart, and as he touched it, kissed his native earth. The warm tears rolled down his cheeks, he was so glad to see his land again. But his arrival was observed by a spy in a watch tower, whom Aegisthos had had the cunning to post there. ... Aegisthos set his brains to work and laid a clever trap. He selected twenty of his best soldiers from the town, left them in ambush, and after ordering a banquet to be prepared in another part of the building set out in a horse-chariot to bring home the King, with his heart full of ugly thoughts. Agamemnon, never guessing that he was going to his doom, came up with him from the coast, and Aegisthos feasted and killed him as a man might fell an ox in its manger. Not a single one of the King's following was left, nor of Aegisthos' company either. They were killed in the palace to a man.

The classical poet Aeschylus, whose superb tragedy *Agamemnon* is based on the same theme, makes the guilty Queen even less sympathetic. According to his version, Clytemnestra was herself the slayer of the King, Aegisthos merely her accomplice. Such was the tragedy enacted at Mycenae.

Before ending this chapter I must apologize to all lovers of Homer for making such a scanty offering from the great man's table, though I hope it may at least tempt others to enjoy the full Homeric feast. Nor shall I attempt at this stage to discuss the so-called 'Homeric Problem'—whether the poems are the conscious and deliberate creation of one man, or represent the work of generations of poets

---

* Of this passage a sceptical archaeologist friend writes: 'I know people often say that Helen in the *Odyssey* is reformed and domesticated but she seems to need an awful lot of handmaidens to bring in her knitting.'

working within a common tradition. All I wish to emphasize now is the extraordinary realism of Homer, and the problem which this set the scholars of the last century. Although the epics, especially the *Odyssey*, contain much that is magical and supernatural, yet their descriptions of everyday life, of houses (from palaces to a swineherd's hut), of farming and seamanship, of warfare, of the domestic occupations of women, of clothes and jewellery and works of art, are so intensely *real* that even the most sceptical professors of the early nineteenth century found it hard to understand how the poet could have imagined them all.

Homer's geography, too, shows a detailed knowledge, not only of mainland Greece, but of the Aegean islands, of capes, harbours and sea-routes, of Syria and Asia Minor. In describing the Trojan plain, he makes the reader *see* its physical features, the winding river Scamander and its companion, the Simois, the two springs near the city, one warm, one cold; the fig-tree near the Scaean Gate, and, dominating it all, towering Mount Ida*, where Zeus sat, watching the battle.

Yet the fact remained that when George Grote published his *History of Greece* in 1846, there was apart from these topographic details, not a scrap of material evidence—not one fragment of a building, piece of pottery, jewellery, or armour to prove that the world which Homer described had ever existed outside his imagination. And the academic world nodded their heads approvingly when they read Grote's grave summing-up of the Trojan War.

Though literally believed, reverentially cherished, and numbered among the gigantic phenomena of the past, by the Grecian public, it is in the eyes of modern enquiry essentially a legend and nothing more. If we are asked whether it be not a legend embodying portions of historical matter, and raised upon a basis of truth . . . if we are asked whether there was not really some such historical Trojan war as this, our answer must be, that as the possibility of it cannot be denied, so neither can the reality of it be affirmed. We possess nothing but the ancient epic itself without any independent evidence. . . .

But in the year Grote's book appeared there was a young man working in a shipping office in Amsterdam, who was destined to make the great scholar's words irrevocably out of date.

---

* Not to be confused with the other Mount Ida in Crete.

35

2 SCHLIEMANN THE ROMANTIC

A seven-year-old boy, in the dress of 1829, sits at a table in a heavily-furnished room. A large book lies before him, in which he is completely absorbed. It is a Christmas gift from the boy's father, the Protestant parson of a little town in Mecklenburg, North Germany. The work—Jerrer's *Universal History*—is almost as heavy as the child, but that does not worry him as he pores over an engraving which shows the walls of burning Troy. Through the Scaean Gate comes Aeneas, bearing on his back his aged father Anchises. The boy turns to *his* father, half-dozing by the fire, and says:

'Father, did you tell me that Troy had completely gone?'

'I did.'

'And that there's nothing of it left at all?'

'Nothing at all.'

'But Jerrer must have *seen* Troy, or how could he have drawn it here?'

'Heinrich, that is simply a fanciful picture.'

The boy looks more closely at the drawing. Still he is not satisfied.

'Father, did Troy have great walls like these in the picture?'

'Probably.'

'Then' (triumphantly), 'they can't *all* have gone. Some must still be there, hidden under the ground. I'd love to dig them up. Father, some day shall I go and dig them up?'

The elder Schliemann, a disillusioned man, nods wearily.

'I shouldn't be surprised. And now be quiet. I want to sleep.'

Anyone who is inclined to regard that incident as too fanciful need only turn to page three of Schliemann's *Ilios* where they will find it described by the great man himself. There is no need to doubt its essential truth, for it has the unmistakable Schliemann characteristics which reveal themselves throughout his life; a romantic preoccupation with the past, inflexible determination, and complete literal minded-ness. He seems to have inherited the first trait from his father.

Though my father was neither a scholar nor an archaeologist he had a passion for ancient history. He often told me with warm enthusiasms of the tragic fate of Herculaneum and Pompeii, and seemed to consider him the luckiest of men who had the means and the time to visit the excavations that were going on there.

But Schliemann the elder was also a drunkard, a sceptic and a lecher, who took only a sporadic interest in his six children, and although he taught Heinrich Latin, the boy had to leave school at the age of fourteen and become an apprentice in a grocer's shop in the small town of Furstenburg.

I was engaged (he wrote) from five in the morning until eleven at night, and had not a moment's leisure for study. Moreover I rapidly forgot the little that I had learnt in childhood; but I did not lose the love of learning; indeed I never lost it, and, as long as I live, I shall never forget the evening when a drunken miller came into the shop. . . .

The miller, whose name was Niederhoffer, was a failed Protestant clergyman who had taken to drink, which, however,

had not made him forget his Homer; for on the evening that he entered the shop he recited to us about a hundred lines of the poet, observing the rhythmic cadence of the verses. Although I did not understand a syllable, the melodious sound of the words made a deep impression on me. . . . From that moment I never ceased to pray to God that by His grace I might yet have the happiness of learning Greek.

Troy and Homer became an obsession with him.

What weighs upon our heart, be it joy or sorrow (he writes in his portentous way) always find utterance from our lips, especially in childhood; and so it happened that I talked of nothing else to my play-fellows, but of Troy and of the mysterious and wonderful things in which our village abounded. I was continually laughed at by everyone except two young girls, Louise and Minna Meincke, the daughters of a farmer in Zahren, a village only a mile distance from Ankershagen (Schliemann's home).

With one of these girls, Minna, he carried on a curious childhood romance which seems to have consisted mainly of visits to all the antiquities in the neighbourhood, such as the medieval castle of Ankershagen where a robber knight named Henning von Holstein was said to have buried treasure.

Minna showed me the greatest sympathy and entered into all my vast plans for the future. . . . It was agreed between us that as soon as we were grown up we would marry, and then at once set to work to explore all the mysteries of Ankershagen; excavating . . . the vast treasures hidden by Henning, then Henning's sepulchre, and lastly Troy; nay we could imagine nothing pleasanter than to spend all our lives in digging for relics of the past.

Fantastic childhood ambitions are common enough, even among ordinary men who forget them as they grow older. But to Heinrich Schliemann they remained real and permanent. At fourteen, when he left Ankershagen to work in the grocer's shop, he met Minna again after an absence of five years, and the extraordinary couple (both only fourteen) burst into floods of tears and fell into each other's arms.

I was now sure that Minna still loved me, and this stimulated my ambition (he wrote). Nay from that moment I felt within me a boundless energy, and was sure that with unremitting zeal I could raise myself in the world and show that I was worthy of her. I only implored God to grant that she might not marry before I had attained an independent position.

This would have been sheer rhodomontade in most men. Schliemann meant every word of it. And though he lost his childhood Minna, he spent more than half his life looking for a substitute; nor could be begin his great archaeological work until he had found one, thirty years later.

In the meantime he lived a life of fantastic adventure such as only a romantic novelist could have invented. His father's never-ending amours and his outbreaks of drunken violence made life at home impossible. Heinrich broke away and got a job in Hamburg as a grocer's assistant at £9 0s 0d per annum, but his weak frame was unequal to the work. One day, trying to shift a heavy cask he injured his chest and spat blood. He tried another job but his weak lungs forced him to give it up. Still determined not to return home, he next became a boy on a small sailing-brig, the *Dorothea*, trading between Hamburg and Venezuela, but the ship was wrecked off the Dutch coast.

After tossing for nine hours in a small open boat in a fierce storm, Heinrich and his eight companions were thrown by the surf on to a bank close to the shore of the River Texel.

In Amsterdam, exhausted and starving, he feigned illness and was taken into hospital, and while there wrote to a shipbroker friend, Mr Wendt in Hamburg, explaining his situation. The letter arrived when Wendt was entertaining friends. A subscription was immediately raised and the delighted Schliemann received the sum of 240 florins (£20). Soon after, through the help of the Prussian Consul-General, he found a situation in the office of an Amsterdam merchant, F. C. Quien, stamping bills of exchange and carrying letters to and from the post office. From Quien he joined the office of an old-established firm of merchants, B. H. Schröder & Co., as 'correspondent and book-keeper'.

From the moment he entered Schröder's office his fortunes began to improve. Before he had been stumbling and floundering; now he had two valuable assets, a post in which he could exercise his talents, and an employer who had the wit to perceive and make use of them. For the shy young amateur antiquarian from Ankershagen, the Homer-loving grocer's assistant, discovered that he had a brilliant flair for business.

He did not come to Schröder's unprepared. While working as a messenger-boy for Quien he had applied himself to the study of modern languages. Out of his annual salary of £32 0s 0d, he devoted half to payments for books and lessons, and lived on the remaining half 'in a wretched garret without a fire, where I shivered with cold in winter and was scorched by the heat in summer.' He learned each language by a unique method of his own, which consisted in reading a great deal aloud, without making a translation, taking a lesson every day, and constantly writing essays on subjects which interested him, correcting these under the supervision of a teacher, and repeating in the next lesson what was corrected on the previous day.

When he applied for a post with B. H. Schröder & Co. they were astonished to find that this pale, awkward youth of twenty-two, with his large head perched on his small body, had command of seven languages. Oddly, however, the seven did not include Greek. Deliberately he left that to the last for fear lest 'the powerful spell of this noble language might take too great a hold on me and endanger my commercial interests.' First he must make money. Afterwards he would be free to pursue the passion of his life.

Within a few months of his arrival Schröder saw that young Schliemann had all the makings of a first-class merchant. He was shrewd, tireless in pursuit of business, and endowed with a prodigious

Heinrich Schliemann

memory and great capacity for detail. Behind these qualities, supplying the drive-force, was a consuming ambition to become rich. Riches he must have, he saw clearly, not for their own sake, not for ostentatious display, but because they could give him security, leisure and freedom to pursue his chosen interests. And, of course, once he had acquired wealth he could return to Mecklenburg and marry Minna.

He was promoted rapidly. At the age of twenty-four he decided to learn Russian and within six weeks was writing business letters in that language and was able to talk in their own tongue to Russian indigo merchants visiting Amsterdam. Schröder's did a large trade as indigo exporters, especially with Russia. Schliemann, no longer a clerk, was sent by his employers to St Petersburg and later to Moscow as their representative. In Russia he throve so successfully that within two years of his arrival he was registered as a merchant in the First Guild and the banks had advanced him credits amounting to 57,000 roubles. Elated with his success, he wrote to a friend of the Meincke family asking him to see Minna on his behalf and ask for her in marriage.

But to my sorrow, I received a month later a heartrending answer, that she was just married. I considered this disappointment at the time as the greatest disaster which could have befallen me, and I was for some time utterly unfit for any occupation and sick in bed. . . . I now saw such a brilliant chance before me; but how could I think of realizing it without her participation?

It was fourteen years since he had seen her.

To a man of Schliemann's type, there was only one way of dealing with such an emotional wound—by work, which, while it could not kill the pain, would at least deaden it. Soon he had become a merchant in his own right, and was approached by one of the richest business men in St Petersburg who offered to put his nephew into partnership with the German, with a backing of 100,000 roubles. For the moment Schliemann declined. He could afford to bide his time.

He continued to amass money, travelling from capital to capital— Berlin, Paris, London, always staying at the best hotels (though in the cheapest rooms), fascinated by the new industrial age which he saw growing up around him. He loved machines and speed fascinated him, though even the new railways were too slow for his restless, impatient spirit. Occasionally he sought solace in the past. While in London on business he would take a few hours off to visit the British Museum. 'I saw the Egyptian things, which interested me more than anything I have ever seen.' Then back to indigo shipments and order books, and the life of hotels, packet-boats and railways. By the time he was thirty he had acquired a huge fortune, and began to consider marriage.

But though shrewd and practical in his business affairs, Schliemann was extremely awkward in his relations with women. He feared—with good cause—that women might now seek to marry him for his money; he was conscious of his plainness, jealous of the handsome young officers who danced attendance on the women whom he favoured. He was always imagining himself in love—then doubting his judgment. 'I only see the virtues and never the failings of the fair sex,' he wrote to his sister. And when, finally, he married Katherina, niece of a business acquaintance, the marriage soon proved a failure. She was intelligent, but practical and unimaginative, quite incapable of understanding his impetuous, romantic nature in which there was still so much of the ardour of a boy. 'You do not love me, and therefore have no sympathy for my good fortune, nor do you share my joys and sorrows, but think of nothing but the gratification of your own desires and caprices,' he wrote to her only eighteen months after the marriage. Yet this unfortunate union survived fifteen years of quarrels, partings, re-conciliations, and violent outbursts of hatred; and Katherina bore him a son and two daughters.

By thirty-three he was master of fifteen languages; in addition to the seven with which he had equipped himself ten years earlier, he now had Polish, Swedish, Norwegian, Slovenian, Danish, Latin, and modern and ancient Greek. Yet he despaired of ever enjoying the life of scholarship and learning which he longed for as a very young man. 'I am lacking in the grounding and fundamentals of learning,' he wrote despairingly. 'I can never become a scholar.' Yet after the week's work in his office he would sit up, on Sundays, from early morning till late at night translating Sophocles into modern Greek. And now at last he could read his beloved Homer in the original.

The vision of his childhood never left him; he was still determined to dig at Troy, and believed that there he would find Homer's city. To this end he studied and memorized the great epics, reading them as history rather than as poetry. Schliemann approached Homer with the same unquestioning faith with which the literalist regards the Bible. If Homer said so, it *was* so. But many years were to pass before he could put his beliefs to the test.

Meanwhile, in 1851, he paid his first visit to America, acquired American citizenship, opened a bank in California during the gold-rush, bought gold-dust and casually scooped another fortune, almost without meaning to. His main purpose in visiting the United States was to settle the financial affairs of his brother Louis, who had died of typhus in Sacramento City; the gold-dust fortune was incidental. Schliemann also caught typhus, and directed the affairs of his bank from a bed in the backroom, while the prospectors queued up with their bags of dust in the front. Although his life was despaired of, he recovered and returned to Europe.

Seven years later he made an extensive tour of the Middle East, travelling across the desert from Cairo to Jerusalem, visiting Petra in Trans-Jordan and learning yet another language—Arabic. On this journey he is believed to have visited Mecca disguised as an Arab, and even had himself circumcised as an extra precaution.

His second visit to America was in 1868, when he was forty-six and already thinking of giving up his business affairs. On his return he made yet another attempt to be reconciled to his wife, after one of their periodic estrangements, even buying and furnishing for her a magnificent house in Paris. But it was in vain. Her family disliked him, and supported her in opposing his plan to give the children a German education. Katherina stayed in Russia and sent only bitter replies to his pleading letters. In despair the unhappy homeless man set off on another of his restless journeys across Europe, journeys which were yielding him less and less delight. But this time he turned to Greece, and set foot for the first time on Homeric soil, on the rocky island of Ithaca, home of Odysseus, the Wanderer.

Peace and delight came to him there. Although he had come to Ithaca at the height of summer, so great was his enthusiasm that, in his own words, 'I forgot heat and thirst.... Now I was investigating the neighbourhood, reading in the *Odyssey* the stirring scenes enacted there, now admiring the splendid panorama.'

And, being Schliemann, of course he had to dig. Visiting the so-called 'Castle of Odysseus' he hired workmen and dug up vases containing human ashes, together with a sacrificial knife and a few clay idols. He went away quite happy, believing he had found the ashes of Odysseus and Penelope and their descendants. From Ithaca he went on to the Peloponnese, paid a brief visit to Mycenae, then crossed over to the Dardanelles and rode across the Plain of Troy. These visits, though brief, had been enough to whet his appetite. From then onwards he began to make plans to retire from commerce and devote the rest of his life to excavation. He had the money, the leisure, and the opportunity. But something very essential was missing—the companionship of the woman with whom he 'could imagine nothing pleasanter than to spend all our lives in digging for relics of the past.'

When he returned to Paris at the end of the year he had at last made up his mind to obtain a divorce. To do so, he decided, it would be best to go to America, where the divorce procedure was simpler than that obtaining in Europe. But, in that winter of 1878, surrounded by gay company but lonely at heart, he remembered an old friend, a priest named Vimpos who had taught him Greek in St Petersburg, and was now Archbishop of Athens. To Vimpos Schliemann opened his heart in what must have been the strangest and most moving letter that reverend gentleman ever received. For in it, Schliemann, the forty-six-year-old millionaire, asked the Archbishop to find him a Greek wife.

I swear to you, by the bones of my mother, that I will direct my whole mind and energies to making my future wife happy. . . . Here I am constantly in the company of witty and beautiful women, who would be very willing to heal my sufferings and make much of me if they knew I was thinking of a divorce. But, my friend, the flesh is weak, and I am afraid to fall in love with a Frenchwoman, lest I should be unlucky once again.

Therefore I beg you to enclose with your answer the portrait of some beautiful Greek woman. . . . I entreat you; choose for me a wife of the same angelic character as your married sister. She should be poor, but well educated; she must be enthusiastic about Homer and about the rebirth of my beloved Greece. It does not matter whether she knows foreign languages or not. But she should be of the Greek type, with black hair, and, if possible, beautiful. But my main requirement is a good and loving heart. . . .

In the spring of the following year, while Schliemann was in Indianapolis waiting for his divorce, Vimpos' reply arrived, enclosing a photograph of a classically beautiful girl of sixteen named Sophia Engastromenos. The German was entranced, but under no illusions. There is a lovely humility in the letter he wrote to his sister concerning his plans.

I intend, if everything goes well, to go to Athens in July. . . . I shall, however, only marry her if she is interested in learning, for I think that it is only possible for a beautiful young girl to love and honour an old man if she is enthusiastic about learning, wherein he is much farther advanced than she.

But in August, when he arrived in Athens, any such doubts were set at rest. Not only was Sophia more beautiful than her photograph had suggested, but she was modest and sweet-natured, besides being able to answer satisfactorily his catechism, which included such questions as: 'In what year did the Emperor Hadrian come to Athens?' and 'What passages of Homer have you by heart?' They were married, and on his honeymoon the bridegroom wrote:

Sophia is a splendid wife, who could make any man happy, for, like all Greek women, she has a kind of divine reverence for her husband. . . . She loves me as a Greek, with passion, and I love her no less. I speak only Greek to her, which is the most beautiful language in the world.

After forty years the dream which had haunted Schliemann at Ankershagen, and which he had wanted to share with his childhood sweetheart, Minna Meincke, was coming true. In the following spring he was making preliminary excavations at Troy, and a year later his eighteen-year-old wife had joined him at his camp near the hill of Hissarlik. Their joint adventure had begun.

3 THE TREASURE OF PRIAM

Passing the lookout and the windswept fig-tree and keeping
some way from the wall, they sped along the cart-track, and so
came to the two lovely springs that are the sources of
Scamander's eddying stream. In one of these the water comes up
hot; steam rises from it and hangs about like smoke above a
blazing fire. But the other, even in summer, gushes up as cold as
hail or freezing snow or water that has turned to ice. . . .

The *Iliad*, Book XXII (147–156)

Those 'two lovely springs', described so minutely by Homer, intrigued
and puzzled nineteenth-century visitors to Troy long before
Schliemann came. For he was far from being the first to seek the site of
Priam's city. From the eighteenth century onwards the inhabitants had
become accustomed to the sight of learned gentlemen from Europe
plunging thermometers into the hillside springs in the hope of finding
the two which Homer had described, but the results had not been very
satisfactory. The only place at which two springs of differing tempera-
tures could be found was the village of Bounarbashi, and even there
the difference was only a matter of a few degrees. None the less, for
some time this village, and the rocky hill of Bali Dagh behind it, were
considered to be the site of Homer's Ilium. Bounarbashi stands at the
southern extremity of the Plain of Troy and the rocky heights behind it
do strongly suggest at first sight the obvious place for a citadel.

But there was another possible site, the hill of Hissarlik, much
nearer the sea, and from 1820 onwards a number of scholars supported
its claim, though it was much less spectacular than the towering Bali
Dagh; nor did it possess the 'hot and cold' springs.

Schliemann, who had been over the ground in 1868, *Iliad* in hand,
had decided against Bounarbashi and for Hissarlik. After all, had not
Homer described Achilles' chasing Hector three times round the wall
of Troy, an impossible feat if the town had been perched on the edge
of Bali Dagh, but feasible at Hissarlik.

In addition to this (he wrote) the distance of Bounarbashi from the Hellespont is, in a
straight line, eight miles, while all the indications of the *Iliad* seem to prove that the
distance between Ilium and the Hellespont was very short, hardly exceeding three
miles.

As for the hot and cold springs, he had tested those at Bounarbashi
and found, not two, but thirty-four, 'all at a uniform temperature of 62
degrees Fahrenheit'.

No, Hissarlik must be the place. Near it, in historic times, had stood
the Hellenic and later Roman town of Novum Ilium—'New Troy'—

Walls of Troy I as visible today

ruins of which still survived. This was the city which the later Greeks and Romans had built on what they believed was the traditional site of Priam's 'sacred Ilios'. Alexander the Great himself had offered at its temple before marching on to conquer the East. Historical tradition, geography, and above all the testimony of the poems themselves all combined to convince the German that under Hissarlik lay Homer's Troy. There it stood, the mysterious mound, rising 162 feet above the scanty ruins of the classical city. Other investigators had scratched its surface, but now, for the first time, Heinrich Schliemann was going to attack it.

From September to November, 1871, eighty workmen, under Schliemann's direction, drove a deep trench into the face of the steep northern slope, and dug down to a depth of thirty-three feet below the surface of the hill. Winter compelled him to give up, but in March he was back again with Sophia, and this time he increased his labour force to 150, and brought with him 'the very best English wheelbarrows, pickaxes, and spades ... provided by my honoured friends Messrs. John Henry Schröder & Co. of London', together with 'three overseers and an engineer, to make maps and plans.' He also built on top of Hissarlik a wooden house, with three rooms and a kitchen.

Remember that when Schliemann began this monumental work he had no previous experience to guide him, nor could he draw upon the experience of other field archaeologists, because nothing on this scale had ever been attempted. At that time there was no recognized technique of excavation. The modern archaeological student, trained,

45

This engraving comes from Schliemann's book *Ilios*, and shows a view looking south east from the Hill of Hissarlik with the excavations in the foreground. Schliemann wrote of the site: 'I beg the reader to accompany me at sunset to the summit of Hissarlik in order that he may convince himself how greatly the Trojans were favoured above other men in the beautiful situation of their city.'

long before he is allowed near a site, in the careful methods which have left even Hogarth and Pitt-Rivers far behind, shudders when he reads of Schliemann's methods. His great trench drove through the successive strata of the mound, and when he came to a building of relatively late date which impeded access to the lower levels which alone interested him, he did not wait, as would a modern excavator, to photograph and record it, but demolished it forthwith.

At a later date, under the guidance of his brilliant young assistant Dörpfeld, he learned to be more patient and scientific, yet ruthless though his methods were at first, there is no doubt that his instinct was right. For as he dug into the mound he discovered that there was not only one Troy but many Troys; walls stood upon earlier walls, and below them older walls still. He could not have hoped to have uncovered the whole of each city in turn before digging down to the next. Believing that the Troy he sought—Homer's Troy—must lie very deep, his only course was to cut down through the strata—like taking a slice out of a 'layer cake'.

His young wife was at his side during the long days when he toiled in the trench, and at night, in their hut on top of the mound her delicate fingers helped him to sort out and classify the fragments of pottery, clay idols, fragments of weapons and tools, which they had sifted from the soil. It was a far more difficult, perplexing and unrewarding task then Schliemann had dreamed of, nor did the climate make it easier. Summer brought dust, flies, and a sultry heat; snakes slid down from the roof of the hut and had to be killed; mosquitoes put Heinrich down with malaria, though Sophia escaped it. In winter a freezing blast from

46

the north 'blew with such violence through the chinks in our house-walls . . . that we were not even able to light our lamps in the evening, and although we had fire on the hearth, yet the thermometer showed nine degrees of frost.'

In the spring of 1873 he wrote, 'The leaves are already beginning to burst on the trees, and the Trojan plain is covered with spring flowers. For the last fortnight we have been hearing the croaking of millions of frogs, and the storks returned a week ago.' And he complained of 'the hideous screeching of the innumerable owls that nest in the holes of my trenches. There is something weird and horrible about their screeching; it is unbearable, especially at night.'

This was in the spring of 1873, and the beginning of the Schliemanns' third season at Troy. By now several huge cuttings and platforms had been driven into the hill and thousands of tons of earth had been removed. There, undoubtedly, were the remains of several prehistoric and later cities—Schliemann discerned seven—but which was Priam's Troy? The excavator knew that the traditional date of the Trojan War, as calculated by the ancient writers, was round about 1180 BC, but in 1873 there was no convenient system of comparative dating by pottery,* and Schliemann had no means of telling which of the cities had been destroyed in the twelfth century. Yet he firmly believed that, somewhere in that bewildering tangle of walls, some built on top of each other, some separated by layers of débris, lay the

---

* He could of course recognize that pottery which was unlike any belonging to the historical periods must almost certainly be prehistoric, but whether early, middle or late he had no means of knowing.

city he had sought so long and painfully. Surely he would recognize it from Homer's own description? He must look for the remains of the Scaean Gate above which the aged King Priam had sat with his counsellors:

Old age had brought their fighting days to an end, but they were excellent speakers, those Trojan counsellors, sitting there on the tower, like the cicadas perched on a tree in the woods, chirping delightfully....

Somewhere, too surely, were the ruins of Priam's Palace, wherein had stood the coffers from which the old king had taken the precious objects to ransom his son's body.

He also weighed and took ten talents of gold; and he took two shining tripods, four cauldrons and a very lovely cup, which the Thracians had given him when he went to them on an embassy....

But did any of the walls he had uncovered look as if they had belonged to the mighty city the poet had described? Only those in the higher strata; and this perplexed and saddened Schliemann, who argued that, as Homer's city was so ancient, it must lie near the bottom of the mound.

As it was my object to excavate Troy, which I expected to find in one of the lower cities, I was forced to demolish many interesting ruins in the upper strata; as, for example, at a depth of twenty feet below the surface, the ruins of a prehistoric building ten feet high, the walls of which consisted of hewn blocks of limestone perfectly smooth and cemented with clay.

And again, during the same excavation, in May, 1872, he had 'brought to light, near the surface, a pretty bastion, composed of large blocks of limestone, which may date from the time of Lysimachus.' Though the bastion was of Homeric proportions, the fact that it was near the surface damned it for Schliemann, who could not conceive that it was earlier than the third century BC. (Lysimachus was one of Alexander's generals, 360–281 BC).

Yet the lower strata were disappointing; much of them consisted of rough, ill-built walls and mean dwellings containing poor pottery and sometimes stone implements. However, the layers were not clearly defined, but overlapped in different parts of the site, so it was not always easy to decide which were the earlier strata and which were the later. In one place, on the south side of the hill, he had made a more promising discovery, a great mass of masonry, consisting of two distinct walls, each about fifteen feet broad and twenty feet high, built close together and founded on the rock at a depth of forty-six feet below the surface. These he called 'the Great Tower' though admitting that 'they may originally have been intended by their builders for a different purpose'.

In the middle of March, 1873, Schliemann began a large excavation to the west of this so-called 'Great Tower'. After digging down through the remains of a late Greek house, then through a layer of débris, the workmen uncovered what appeared to be a well-paved street, seventeen feet wide, running down abruptly in a south-westerly direction towards the plain. This street, the excavator decided, must at one time have led to a large building within the city:

Above Excavations below the Temple of Athene as they appeared in April 1873. Schliemann wrote: 'In order to bring Troy itself to light, I was forced to sacrifice the ruins of this temple of which I left standing only some parts of the north and south walls.' (from Schliemann's *Ilios*)

Right Colossal jars as unearthed in June 1873. Schliemann wrote: 'One of the compartments of the uppermost houses, below the Temple of Athene and belonging to the third, the burnt city, appears to have been used as a magazine for storing corn or wine, for there in it are nine enormous earthen jars of various forms, about 5¾ ft high and 4¾ ft across.' (from Schliemann's *Ilios*)

I therefore immediately set 100 men to dig through the ground lying in front of it in that direction. I found the street covered to a height of from 7 to 10 feet with yellow, red, or black wood-ashes, mixed with thoroughly burnt and often partly-vitrified fragments of bricks and stones. Above this thick layer of *débris* I came upon the ruins of a large building composed of stones cemented with earth. . . .

Nearby, in a north-easterly direction, he brought to light two large gateways, standing twenty feet apart, in front of which lay a mass of calcined rubbish, from seven to ten feet deep, which, Schliemann thought, had fallen from the burning walls of his Great Tower 'which must once have crowned the gates.'

The impatient child in Schliemann was always stronger than the cool-brained archaeologist. He had tried hard to find what he wished to find, and now, after three arduous years, it seemed that his faith had been justified. Without pausing to check his deductions, or to consult the opinions of other scholars, he announced to the world that he had discovered the Scaean Gate and the Palace of Priam.

Many of the professional scholars, particularly the Germans, had been opposed to Schliemann's excavations. For more than a century they and their predecessors had theorized, from the depth of their study chairs, over the probable site of Troy; but not one had gone out to dig there. And now here was this audacious merchant, without academic training, a lover of publicity (which, as scholars, they pretended to hate), hasty and inexact in his methods, ruthlessly tearing down the remains of classical buildings in an insane search for a city which had probably never existed outside a poet's imagination. Worst of all, his naïve belief in the historicity of Homer had led him to announce that he had found the Palace of Priam—a King for whose historical existence there was not a shadow of proof! This was not scholarship, but sensational journalism. Academic pens were dipped in acid. Schliemann, behind his apparent triumph, was secretly discouraged by these attacks. In May he wrote to his brother:

We have been digging here for three years with a hundred and fifty workmen . . . and have dragged away 250,000 cubic metres of débris and have collected in the depths of Ilium a fine museum of very remarkable antiquities. Now, however, we are weary, and since we have attained our goal and realized the great ideal of our life, we shall finally cease our efforts in Troy on June 15th.

Twice in Schliemann's career as an archaeologist events occurred which were strangely like those in the life of Howard Carter, who discovered Tutankhamun's Tomb more than half a century later. The first of these parallels was to occur now. Readers who recall the great Egyptian discovery in 1922 will remember that it was not until Carter had begun what was to have been his farewell season in the Valley of the Kings' Tombs, after six years of unsuccessful digging, that he came upon the intact tomb of the Pharaoh. Schliemann, as we have seen, had decided to end his Trojan excavations and pay off his workmen on June 15th. *One day* before this date, he was standing, accompanied by a few of his workmen, near the circuit wall close to the ancient building which he believed to be Priam's Palace, and north-west of the 'Scaean Gate', when he noticed a large copper object embedded under a layer of red and calcined ruins, above which stood a fortification wall.

The Tower of Ilium, the Gate and the ruins of a large house as they appeared during the excavations in May 1873 (from Schliemann's *Ilios*)

Looking more closely, the excavator's sharp eyes noticed, behind the copper, something bright and gleaming. It looked like gold. . . .

Schliemann glanced at his workmen. They had noticed nothing. Then followed a piece of Odyssean cunning. Keeping quite calm, he called Sophia to him and told her quietly to have the 'Paidos' called—the time of rest. 'Tell them it is my birthday,' he instructed her, 'and that they'll get their wages without working!' When the workmen had dispersed, together with the overseer, Sophia returned and stood near her husband as he crouched beneath the wall in the bright sunlight, digging out from the hard-packed earth object after object of gleaming gold or dull silver.

This required great exertion and involved great risk, (he wrote afterwards), since the wall of fortification, beneath which I had to dig threatened every moment to fall down upon me. But the sight of so many objects, every one of which is of inestimable value to archaeology, made me reckless, and I never thought of any danger. It would, however, have been impossible for me to have removed the treasure without the help of my dear wife, who stood at my side, ready to pack the things I cut out in her shawl, and to carry them away.

Finally when the last object had been transferred to Sophia's red shawl, the two discoverers, feeling like naughty children on some conspiratorial adventure, walked with careful unconcern to their hut atop the mound, locked the door, and then spread out the treasure before them.

The loveliest of all the objects, far outshining the rest, were two

51

magnificent gold diadems. The largest of these consisted of a fine gold chain, intended to be worn round the crown of the wearer's head, and from which hung seventy-four short, and sixteen longer chains, each made up of tiny heart-shaped plates of gold. The 'fringe' of shorter chains rested on the wearer's brow; the longer chains, each ending in a small 'Trojan idol', hung down to her shoulders. Thus her face would be framed in gold. The second diadem was similar, but the chains were suspended from a narrow band of sheet gold, and the side-chains were shorter, and evidently meant only to cover the temples. In the first diadem alone there were 16,353 separate gold pieces, consisting of tiny rings, double-rings, and lancet-shaped leaves. In both articles the workmanship was rare and delicate.

There were also six gold bracelets, a gold bottle, a gold goblet weighing 601 grammes, a goblet of electrum, and a large vessel of silver which contained, beside the diadems, sixty gold ear-rings, 8,700 small gold rings, perforated prisms, gold buttons, small perforated gold bars and other trinkets. Vases of silver and copper, and weapons of bronze, completed the hoard.

But Schliemann's eyes kept returning to the shining diadems. This fifty-year-old merchant who, as a child, had dreamed of Trojan treasure, sat running the golden chains through his fingers, watched by the lovely Greek girl who was his wife. Sophia was twenty now, and her dark beauty had reached maturity; she seemed at that moment the embodiment of the 'white-armed Helen' for whom Greeks and Trojans had joined in battle near this very spot; and surely this was none other than Priam's treasure? So his imagination raced on, as trembling, he placed on his wife's brows the glittering diadems which, he believed at that moment, had once adorned Helen herself.

From now on, let the scholars scoff, he was convinced that Homer would lead him to the treasures of the pre-Hellenic world. 'Since,' he wrote, 'I found all the objects together or packed into one another on the circuit wall, the building of which Homer ascribes to Neptune or Apollo, it seems certain that they lay in a wooden chest, of the kind mentioned in the *Iliad* as having been in Priam's Palace. It seems all the more certain, since I found close to them a copper key about four inches long, the head of which, about two inches in length and breadth, bears a very marked resemblance to the big key of an iron safe.' (This 'key', the copper object which had first attracted Schliemann's attention, was later found to be a bronze chisel.) And he continued: 'some member of Priam's family packed the treasure in the chest in great haste and carried it away without having time to withdraw the key, but was overtaken on the wall by the enemy or the fire, and had to leave the chest behind, where it was immediately covered to the depth of five or six feet with red ash and the stones of the neighbouring Palace.'

Having explained, to his own satisfaction, how the treasure got there, his next problem was to get it out of the country. Admittedly, permission to dig had only been granted him on condition that half of

Sophia Schliemann, wearing the 'Jewels of Helen'

everything he found be handed over to the Turkish government. But now he had these precious things in his hands he could not bring himself to hand over even a part of them to people who he believed would not appreciate their unique archaeological value, but would almost certainly melt them down for the sake of gold. Customs examinations were less rigorous in those days, and without much difficulty the excavators managed to smuggle the whole of the Trojan Treasure away from the Turks to Athens.

But now an aggravating problem arose. He had the treasure, but how could he enjoy the glory of his discovery unless the learned world was told? And if the scholars knew, then so would the Turks. Schliemann made his plans. He announced his discovery, and allowed a number of responsible people to inspect the objects, so that there could be no doubt that he was telling the truth. But when the inevitable happened, and his house in Athens was searched through the agency of the Turkish ambassador, nothing was found. The treasures were safely hidden away in baskets and chests, in barns and stables, in the homes and on the farms of Sophia's many relatives. Schliemann's craft had an Odyssean magnificence.

But for the time being it put a stop to his archaeological work. The Greek Government, sycophantic towards the Turks, gave him no support. Indeed the Director of the University Library denounced him as a smuggler, and even went so far as to accuse him of obtaining his finds, not under the soil of the Troad, but from the antique dealers. The authenticity of his Trojan discoveries was doubted, and when he applied to the Greek Government for permission to dig at Mycenae, in the Peloponnese, difficulties were placed in his way. First he was told that under Greek law no one was allowed to keep Greek antiquities, even for life. 'Alter the law, then!' said Schliemann, a suggestion which was coldly received. He offered to give the whole of his discoveries, including Trojan treasures, to the Greek nation after his death if he could keep what he found during his lifetime. Still the authorities were adamant. Then, in 1874, he made a compromise suggestion offering the same terms, i.e. everything to go to Greece after his death provided he could keep *part* of his finds during life.

Sure that the Government would accept this offer, Schliemann and his wife paid a two-day preliminary visit to Mycenae to survey the site. But so alarmed were the officials at the German's alleged powers as a discoverer of treasure, that a local busybody from Nauplia was sent hot-foot after the couple to examine their luggage and see that they had spirited nothing away. 'This man is a swindler,' said the Director of the Archaeological Service, adding that Schliemann was quite capable of finding treasures at Mycenae (presumably without digging for them) then mixing them with his Trojan discoveries and smuggling them out of the country.

When the official found nothing in Schliemann's suitcase but a few potsherds he apologized, but the great man was furious. He would leave Greece, he threatened. He would dig in Italy, in Russia, where he would be treated with honour and dignity, and his services to archaeology would be appreciated. Sophia, anxious to remain in her own country, pleaded with him to stay, and eventually the Government concluded an agreement which allowed Schliemann to dig at Mycenae under the supervision of the Archaeological Society of Greece, at his own expense, and on condition that he handed over all he found. The sole concession they would grant was exclusive right of reporting on his discoveries for a period not exceeding three years. He had to accept.

However, two years were to pass before he was ready for the attack on Agamemnon's citadel. He had first to fight a lawsuit with the Turks, which he lost, and was ordered to pay 10,000 francs compensation. Instead he sent five times that amount to the Ministry at Constantinople, hoping thereby to win over the authorities into allowing him to continue his Trojan excavations. For the time being there was no response, but Schliemann could afford to wait. Meanwhile his book *Trojan Antiquities* was published, prefaced by the brave but over-optimistic announcement that

if the people are disappointed in their expectations . . . and consider that Troy was too small for the great deeds of the *Iliad*, and that Homer exaggerated everything with a poet's freedom, they must, on the other hand, find a great satisfaction in the certainty now established that the Homeric poems are based on actual facts.

But Schliemann's sanguine belief that he had found the Palace of Priam and the Scaean Gate had aroused the scepticism of professional scholars, and as Schuchhardt said later in his authoritative work on the excavations, 'the final conclusion of sober thinkers was that even if a primeval settlement did exist on Hissarlik, its ruins did not correspond to the great period depicted by Homer. Hissarlik could scarcely have been the capital of the land; and therefore, until further excavations should take place, Bounarbashi, defined by such acute and varied arguments, must still be accepted as Troy.'As we shall see later, the 'sober thinkers' were wrong, though at that time one can hardly blame them for refusing to change their opinions.

Through influential friends in Constantinople Schliemann eventually obtained, in April 1876, a *firman* (permit) to recommence his excavations at Troy, but he had not reckoned with the Oriental genius for organizing delay. For two months he was detained at the town of Dardanelles, under the pretext that the *firman* required confirmation. When at last he was allowed to begin, the local Governor, Ibrahim Pasha, sent along a commissioner to Hissarlik who did all in his power to annoy him. It was just one more example of the petty persecution which, in every age, genius has to suffer from jacks-in-office. Schliemann retaliated by giving up his excavations and writing a violent article to *The Times* to show how the attitude of the Pasha conflicted with the interests of culture. Very soon Ibrahim found himself removed to another province.

But when, in October, 1876, Schliemann received this pleasing intelligence he was no longer interested in Troy. For, in a lonely valley in the Peloponnese, he had just made a discovery so important that it transcended his Trojan triumphs. This time even the most sceptical scholars were forced to take notice. Throughout the civilized world, in university combination-rooms, in learned journals and famous newspapers alike, another Homeric name had become the focus of interest—*Mycenae*.

4 GOLDEN MYCENAE

Watchman:
I pray the gods a respite from these toils,
This long year's watch that, dog-like, I have kept,
High on the Atridan's* battlements, beholding
The nightly council of the stars, the circling
Of the celestial signs, and those bright regents,
High-swung in ether, that bring mortal men
Summer and winter. Here I watch the torch,
The appointed flame that wings a voice from Troy,
Telling of capture; thus I serve her hopes,
The masculine-minded who is sovereign here. . . .

So begins Aeschylus' great tragedy *Agamemnon*—surely one of the most dramatic beginnings devised by any playwright. From his look-out point high above the citadel of Mycenae, the tired watchman gazes down the dark valley to the sea and the mountains beyond. From those distant peaks he waits for the gleam of beacon fires by which the Greeks had arranged to signal to their homelands the fall of far-off Troy.

Nine years have rolled, the tenth is rolling,
Since the strong Atridan pair
Menelaüs and Agamemnon
Sceptred kings by Jove's high grace . . .
Sailed for Troy.

sing the Chorus. Then the beacon is seen shining, and the Watchman hails it wildly.

All hail, thou cresset of the dark! fair gleam
Of day through midnight shed, all hail! bright father
Of joy and dance in Argos, hail! all hail!

Although Aeschelus was writing in the classical period of Greece, in the fifth century BC he took his plots from that ancient Epic Cycle mentioned in an earlier chapter; in particular from the cycle which went by the popular name of 'The Returns'—describing the adventures of the Achaean heroes when they sought to return home after the sack of Troy. Of these 'Returns' the most famous was that of Agamemnon 'King of Men' and Lord of Mycenae who was murdered by the treachery of his Queen, Clytemnestra, and her lover Aegisthos. Warned by the watchman of her lord's return, she laid her plans to destroy Agamemnon, in revenge for his having sacrificed their

---

* Agamemnon and Menelaüs were the sons of Atreus, hence they were often called 'the Atridae'. 'The Atridan' here referred to is Agamemnon.

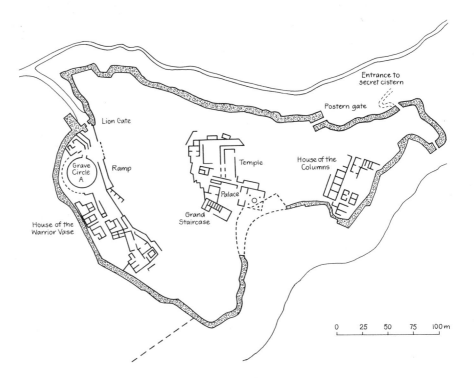

Site plan of Mycenae

daughter Iphigeneia to the gods to obtain fair winds for Troy. On his return the unsuspecting King and his companions were killed at a banquet, though one version of the story states that Clytemnestra slew Agamemnon in his bath.

In the times of the later Greeks and Romans, when the ancient epics were regarded, not as legends, but as authentic history, Mycenae was confidently accepted as the scene of the murders. Although it had fallen into ruin, it still retained its 'Cyclopean' walls and huge empty 'beehive' tombs, which were occasionally visited by Greek and Roman travellers. For example, the Greek historian Pausanias, who lived in the second century after Christ, saw Mycenae and has left a description.

... parts of the wall are still preserved as well as *the gate over which the lions stand**. These also they say are the work of the Cyclopes who built the wall for Proteus at Tiryns. In the ruins of Mycenae there is a fountain called Perseia and underground buildings of Atreus and his sons where their treasures were. There is a tomb of Atreus and there are also tombs of all those whom Aegisthos murdered on their return from Troy after entertaining them at a banquet.... Another is the tomb of Agamemnon, one of Eurymedon the charioteer, and one of Teledamus and Pelops—for they say Cassandra gave birth to these twins and that while they were still infants Aegisthus killed them with their parents—and one of Electra.... Clytemnestra and Aegisthus were buried a little outside the wall, *for they were not deemed worthy of burial within it, where Agamemnon lies and those who were murdered with him.**

I have italicized the last phrase because it was the crux of Schliemann's triumph at Mycenae. He, of course, was minutely familiar with all the epical and classical references to the citadel of the Atridae. He had noticed, for example, that whenever Homer men-

* Our italics

57

tions Mycenae he usually accompanies it with an epithet which has been variously translated as 'rich in gold' ... 'golden' ... and 'opulent'. Homer's conventional epithets—a familiar feature of epic poetry—are extremely well-chosen (Schliemann had had good reason to remember 'windy Troy'). Therefore, if the poet had called Mycenae 'golden' he must have had good reason; and if the gold was still there Heinrich Schliemann would find it. So, in August 1876, he appeared in that remote, windswept valley which slopes down to the plain of Argos, made his headquarters in the nearby village, recruited his workmen, and began to dig.

The main elements of the Mycenaean scene, as Pausanias saw them, as Schliemann saw them, and as we can still see them today, are these:
(*a*) A narrow valley, sloping up from the plain of Argos and the sea which is to the south, to a chain of hills on the north. Through these hills passed roads to Corinth and other northern centres.
(*b*) Near the top of the valley, between two high hills, is a much lower hill, but steep-sided and crowned with the ruins of a massive ring of walls. 'Crowned' in this case is not a cliché, but precisely describes the

Right Interior of the 'Treasury of Atreus'

Opposite Detail of the lions (or griffins?) above the gate at Mycenae way this knob of a hill 'wears' the walls like a crown on a human head. The small area within the walls, steep, but with the top shaved off almost flat, Schliemann regarded as *the Citadel*, or *Acropolis*.

(*c*) On the west side, the ring of walls, which are built of huge unmortared stones, is broken by a magnificent gateway above which stand two rampant lions carved in stone; this is the famous *Lion Gate*.

(*d*) Part of the valley to the south of the Citadel and a large area to the south-west of it contains '*Tholos*' *tombs* sometimes called '*Treasuries*', the largest of which is the so-called '*Treasury of Atreus*'. These, which will be described in more detail in the next chapter, are large, beautiful stone-lined chambers hollowed out of the hillside in the shape of gigantic beehives, each approached by a straight-sided entrance passage called a '*dromos*'. This large area in which the 'Tholos' tombs occur also contained the homes of the humbler Mycenaeans who lived outside the Citadel.

If these elements are borne in mind, the shrewdness of Schliemann's judgment will be better appreciated; because he was not the first man to dig at Mycenae. Lord Elgin had been there before him, and carried off part of the pillared entrance to the 'Treasury of Atreus' which can still be seen in the British Museum; so had Lord Sligo, and a Turkish gentleman named Veli Pasha. But they had all dug in the wrong places.

Although no professional scholars shared Schliemann's belief in the literal truth of the Homeric poems, they took the guidebook of Pausanias more seriously. True, he had visited Mycenae one thousand three hundred years after the traditional date of the Trojan war, when Mycenae was a legend-haunted ruin. Still, there was no reason to doubt that he had been shown tombs, or at any rate sacred areas, which local tradition ascribed to Agamemnon, Clytemnestra and the rest. But when the scholars of Schliemann's day were asked where these tombs could have been, they all located them, in their imaginations, *outside* the walls of the Citadel. How, then, did they square this assertion with the last phrase of Pausanias's description which we quoted above?

Clytemnestra and Aegisthos were buried a little outside the wall, for they were not deemed worthy of burial *within it, where Agamemnon lies and those who were murdered with him. . . .*

Pausanias, said the scholars, could not have meant by 'the wall' the so-called Cyclopean wall crowning the brow of the hill. Why not? Because these walls enclosed only a relatively small area, most of it bare rock and steeply sloping, totally unsuited for a cemetery. No, the wall which Pausanias saw must have been a *second* wall enclosing a much larger area outside the Cyclopean wall, and which had since disappeared. No doubt the tombs which Pausanias saw were the empty 'tholos tombs'—which had been despoiled centuries before this day.

But this explanation did not satisfy Schliemann, who wrote:

that he [Pausanias] had solely in view the walls of the Citadel, he shows by saying that in the wall is the Lion's Gate. It is true that he afterwards speaks of the ruins of Mycenae, in which he saw the fountain Perseia and the treasuries of Atreus and his

Mrs Schliemann supervising the excavations at the Treasury of Clytemnestra (from Schliemann's *Mycenae*)

sons, by which latter he can only mean the large treasury described above, which is indeed in the lower city, and perhaps some of the small treasuries in the suburb. But as he again says further on that the graves of Clytemnestra and Aegisthos are at a little distance outside the wall ... where Agamemnon and his companions reposed, there cannot be any doubt that he had solely in view the huge Cyclopean walls as he *saw*, and not those which he did *not see* ... he could not see the wall of the lower city, because it had been originally only very thin, and it had been demolished 638 years before his time*.... For these decisive reasons I have always interpreted the famous passage in Pausanias in the sense that the five tombs were in the Acropolis.†

It may well have been Schliemann's decision to dig in such apparently barren ground that persuaded the Greek Government to let him dig at all. The Greek Archaeological Society, which advised

* When Mycenae was sacked by the Argives in 468 BC.
† It has since been discovered that there *is* another Grave-Circle *outside* the wall.

61

the Government, was known to be jealous of him, fearing that he might rob them of the glory which should be theirs. But when the crazy foreigner showed that he was going to dig where nothing could possibly be found, they smiled behind their hands and gave him permission. Even so the Society appointed an *ephor*, one Stamatakis, to watch over him and see that he kept to the Society's conditions—that he should employ only a limited number of men at a time, so that the *ephor* could watch what was going on, and hand over everything he found.

He began his excavations in the neighbourhood of the Lion Gate. Sophia was with him of course, and they had under their supervision at first only sixty-three workmen. He chose this area because test-shafts he had previously sunk there showed a good depth of soil, and besides he had struck two Cyclopean house-walls, an unsculptured slab resembling a tombstone, and a number of female idols and cows of terracotta. He had a hard job getting through the Lion Gate, which was obstructed by heavy stones. On the inside, to the left, he found a small chamber 'undoubtedly the ancient doorkeeper's habitation ... only 4½ feet high, and it would not be to the taste of our present doorkeepers; but in the heroic age, comfort was unknown, particularly to slaves, and being unknown it was unmissed.'

Then he began to dig in the area behind the Lion Gate, within the Citadel itself; he unearthed walls, some evidently of late date, which, in his ruthless way, he wanted to clear away to get at the older structure. At this point the battle with Stamatakis, the *ephor*, began. The latter's letters to his superiors are full of pathetic complaints.

A few days ago he found a wall superimposed on another wall, and wanted to put down the upper one. I forbade it, and he stopped. Next morning, when I was not there, he had the wall pulled down and the lower one exposed.

When the *ephor* complained to Sophia she told him sharply that her husband was a learned man who knew what he was doing, that he, Stamatakis, was not a learned man, and would be well advised to keep his mouth shut. More workmen were enrolled, against the rules laid down by the Society, and though this enabled the work to proceed more rapidly, it also meant that Stamatakis could not see what was going on everywhere at the same time. His letters become more and more agitated. . . .

If we find Greek or Roman vases, he looks at them in disgust and lets them fall. . . . He treats me as if I were a barbarian. . . . If the Ministry is not satisfied with me, I beg to be recalled. . . .

But by now Schliemann had made a most significant discovery. At a distance of 40 feet within the Lion Gate, and not far from the encircling Cyclopean wall, he had dug a trench 113 feet square, and had begun to disclose a circle of upright slabs, 87 feet in diameter. The ground within the circle had been levelled in ancient times, and within this space the excavators found an upright stone *stele* like a gravestone. This slab had been carved, but was so badly damaged that the subject of the sculptured relief could not readily be made out. But soon another sculptured gravestone was unearthed ... and yet another.

Above The Grave Circle as Schliemann left it after his excavations in 1877 (from Schliemann's *Mycenae*)

Right The Grave Circle as it looks today

These were in better condition, and clearly showed warriors in chariots.

Soon afterwards, Schliemann found a circular stone altar, provided with a large opening in the form of a well. Schliemann decided that this was intended to allow the blood of sacrifice to be offered to the dead below. He also announced that the scenes of the *stelae* represented. Homeric warriors, that the circle of stone slabs had enclosed the *agora* (town meeting-place) and that below the *stelae*, though perhaps at some depth, must be graves. Under the fierce July sun, with dust in their nostrils and sweat in their eyes, the workmen toiled on. And while Heinrich and Sophia watched their men, the aggrieved little *ephor*, half-dead with fatigue, tried to keep an eye on them all.

Still more gravestones were unearthed, some sculptured with scenes of hunting or battle, or decorative designs; others quite plain. Carefully these were removed as the earth and loose rock were dug away from them; then, as the toiling workmen dug deeper they found still earlier stone monuments, below the level at which the gravestones had stood. By this time they had dug through the thick layer of surface and were down to the solid rock. And then came a thrilling moment for Schliemann and his wife. At one point the edge of a cutting was revealed. Spades cleared away the last remnants of surface soil, and there, without a doubt, was the beginning of a vertical shaft going down into the rock—to what depth they did not yet know. They looked at each other in excitement and triumph. They had found the first of the Shaft-Graves.

Watched anxiously by Heinrich, Sophia, and the *ephor*, the workmen carefully removed the soil, each shovel-full of which was examined for any tell-tale sign. The men were out of sight, fifteen feet below the level of the rock and still digging, when Sophia's sharp eyes caught a bright gleam in the soil. She picked up a tiny object and wiped away the clay. It was a gold ring.

It was too risky to let the workmen dig any further, so they were immediately dismissed. They shambled out through the Lion Gate, chattering and speculating among themselves, and the two discoverers, with the *ephor* Stamatakis, watched them as they moved down the valley road. From now on the three of them had to work alone whenever they came to the final clearing of a grave (for this was only the first of several). They worked on their knees with pocket knives,

Gold cups from Shaft Grave V

64

Golden ornaments from Shaft Grave III

delicately scraping away each layer of soil; and as Heinrich was now in his middle fifties much of this task fell to his young wife.

Those who wish to enjoy the full flavour of Schliemann's Mycenaean saga must read his great book *Mycenae and Tiryns* which is fascinating both in its archaeological detail and its wealth of personal anecdote. Here I can only dwell on the more dramatic moments of those few weeks in the summer of 1876, when the educated world followed Schliemann at Mycenae with as much avidity as a later generation followed Howard Carter at Tutankhamun's tomb. Schliemann and his wife found five graves in all, and Stamatakis a sixth—all contained within the ring of stone slabs which Schliemann had thought was an *agora* but which was in reality a 'Grave Circle' specially built to mark off the cemetery as a holy place.

Each of these graves was a rectangular shaft, varying in depth from approximately three feet to fifteen feet, and in length from approximately nine to twenty feet. In these sepulchres were the remains of nineteen people, men, women, and two small children. Many of these bodies were quite literally laden with gold. To quote Professor Wace's summarizing description:*

On the faces of the men lay golden masks and on their chests golden breast plates. Two women wore golden frontlets and one a magnificent gold diadem. The two children were wrapped in sheet-gold. By the men lay their swords, daggers, drinking cups of gold and silver and other equipment. The women had their toilet boxes of gold and dress pins of various precious materials and their clothes were decked with golden discs ornamented with bees, cuttle fish, rosettes, and spirals.... This was indeed one of the richest archaeological discoveries ever made.

* In his *Mycenae*.

65

Rich it certainly was, but far from barbaric in its magnificence. More remarkable than mere weight of precious metal was the brilliance of the art which the treasures revealed; an art of such vigour and maturity that it could only have been produced by a long-established civilization. Among the most lovely objects were two bronze dagger blades, inlaid in gold with designs in intaglio. One showed a lion hunt, with a wounded beast turning on a group of spearmen carrying huge 'figure-eight' shields. Another showed a conventionalized river-scene, probably the Nile; wild cats slunk through the papyrus-plants which grew beside the winding river, while about fluttered the startled wild-fowl. On both these dagger-blades the artist had shown effortless mastery in fitting his intricate design into the narrow space, and the craftsmanship of the gold inlay work was superb.

Bronze dagger inlaid with scene in gold representing a lion-hunt (notice the figure-eight body shields)

Besides these particular blades there were many others equally beautiful, including a bronze sword-blade with running horses, a dagger-blade with lions, and on the reverse side, gold and electrum lilies. The hilts were richly ornamented with gold leaf, and fixed to the blade by rivets of gold.

In the women's graves were golden diadems, intricately embossed with circles, spirals and conventional patterns; there were gold leaves arranged like stars (for dress ornaments) bracelets, ear-rings, hairpins, and tiny human and animal figures in gold. There were also on bead-

An engraving from Schliemann's *Mycenae* of a gold signet ring from the tomb to the south of the Agora. It shows a scene of worship, with goddesses or women by a tree. Plants are offered and the tree is harvested. A small warrior god hovers. In the centre are a pair of double axes.

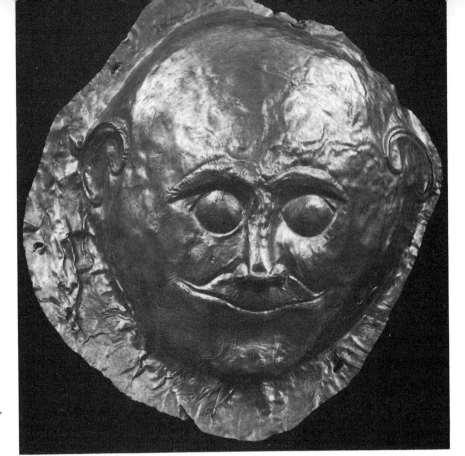

Right Death mask found in the Shaft Graves

Below A gold plate with a butterfly design found in the third Shaft Grave. This is an engraving from Schliemann's *Mycenae* in which he wrote: 'The ornaments of which the greatest number was found were the large, thick, round plates of gold, with a very pretty decoration of repoussé work, of which I collected 701.' The butterfly design in particular was exceedingly frequent.

seals and signet rings, tiny scenes in which women appeared; slim-waisted women with elegantly coiffured hair, and wearing full, flounced skirts like Victorian crinolines; but there the resemblance stopped, as the tight bodices of the women seem to have left their breasts bare.

All these precious things had lain hidden for thirty centuries under that barren hillside, undisturbed by the 'drums and tramplings' of five conquests. The Dorians, the Romans, Goths, Venetians and Turks had come, abided for a little time, then gone their way. But Mycenae had kept its secret for 3,500 years.

Schliemann at the moment of discovery did not realize just how old these objects were. To him they were indisputably Homeric, the triumphant justification of his faith. For him it was a moment of supreme romance, and he revelled in it.

For the first time since its capture by the Argives in 468 BC, he wrote, ... the Acropolis of Mycenae has a garrison, whose watch-fires seen by night throughout the whole plain of Argos carry back the mind to the watch kept for Agamemnon's return from Troy, and the signal which warned Clytemnestra and her paramour of his approach. But this time the object of the occupation by soldiery is of a more peaceful character, for it is merely intended to inspire awe among the country people, and to prevent them from making clandestine excavations in the tombs. ...

His belief in Homer's Troy had led him to discover the 'Treasure of Priam'. Now his faith in the accuracy of Pausanias had led him to the

bodies of Agamemnon and his companions. For such he was convinced they were; nor was he alone in this belief. Even scholars who had been sceptical before now confessed that the German dilettante had a strong case. For when the treasures of the shaft-graves were examined more closely some of them seemed to have an unmistakable connection with the Homeric poems. In an earlier chapter I drew attention to the big Homeric body shield, which Aias held before him 'like a tower' and which tapped Hector's neck and ankles as he walked. On the gold-inlaid dagger-blades the lion-hunters were shown holding just such shields, shaped like an 8 and covering the entire body. Schliemann pointed out another example on a gold signet-ring with a design representing a battle scene.

The third warrior seems to have taken to flight, the rest of the body being hidden by *an enormous shield, of peculiar form, which if the man were standing upright would cover his whole body from head to foot.* (My italics.)

Generations of scholars had been puzzled by these descriptions in Homer of shields for which there was no parallel in classical times, or even in Homer's own period (900–800 BC). Now they were revealed for the first time.

Then in Grave IV Schliemann found a gold cup of most unusual shape; a stemmed goblet with two handles on which were two doves facing each other. From the bottom of each handle a flat side-piece

68

was joined to the round base. Then the discoverer remembered the description of the golden cup into which old Nestor pours Pramnian wine for Machaon and himself (*Iliad* Book XI).

It had four handles. Each was supported by two legs; and on top of each, facing one another, were two doves feeding.

The arguments over 'Nestor's Cup' have continued to this day. The parallel is close, and yet there are important differences, e.g. the cup described by Homer has four handles, and is much larger. But to Schliemann it was the old Pylian chieftain's cup.

The most remarkable parallel of all, and one that no sceptic can disprove, is provided by the Boars' Tusk Helmet. In the Fourth Grave were found sixty boars' teeth 'of all of which the reverse side is cut perfectly flat, and has two borings, which must have served to fasten them to another object, perhaps on horse-trappings. But we see in the *Iliad* that they were also used on helmets....' Later, Schliemann and other archaeologists found many more examples of these ornaments, and also small ivory plaques showing warriors wearing helmets (probably of leather or hide) covered with slivers of boars' tusks, exactly as found in the graves. Now consider the following passage in the *Iliad*. It occurs in Book X, that wonderful night-piece called the Doloneia, in which Odysseus and Diomedes 'of the loud war-cry' disguise themselves and set out to spy out the

Above Cast of an ivory plaque of the 'Boars' Tusk Helmet'

Right The 'cup of Nestor' from Mycenae

Replica of the cow's (bull's) head

Trojan camp. Their comrades lend them arms and armour:

Meriones gave Odysseus a bow, a quiver and a sword, and set a leather helmet on his head. Inside it there was a strong lining of interwoven straps, under which a felt cap had been sewn in. The outer rim was cunningly adorned on either side by *a row of white and flashing boars' tusks.*

Evidently the helmet was a curiosity even in the time of the Trojan War, for the poet says:

This helmet originally came from Eleon, where Autolycus stole it from Amyntor son of Ormenus by breaking into his well-built house. Autolycus gave it to Amphidamas of Cythera to take to Scandaea; and Amphidamas gave it to Molus in return for hospitality. Molus, in his turn, gave it to his son Meriones to wear, and now it was Odysseus's head that it served to protect.

Schliemann had to admit, of course, that he had found many things of a type never mentioned by Homer. Among these were three characteristic types of object which, while Schliemann merely notes them along with others, were very important in relation to later discoveries in Crete. I shall therefore mention them briefly here. First, in the Fourth Grave, Schliemann found—

A *cow's head** of silver, with two long golden horns. . . . It has a splendidly ornamented golden sun, of two and a fifth inches in diameter, on its forehead. . . . There were also found two cowheads of very thin gold plate . . . which have a *double axe* between the horns.

The third and more numerous type of object were *seals*; these were sometimes in the form of signet rings, sometimes flattish beads of semi-precious stone (some scholars refer to them as 'gems') often engraved with tiny, vividly drawn scenes in intaglio. It was mainly these miniature scenes which gave Schliemann and later excavators a clue to the life of the ancient people. Some scenes were manifestly religious; others depicted hunting and fighting. We have noted Schliemann's description of such a scene in which the 'body-shield' occurs. Here he is describing another seal, in which he fancies he sees the fight between Hector and Achilles in Book XXII of the *Iliad*.

The intaglio on the following smaller ornament represents two warriors fighting a deadly duel. The one to the left of the spectator is a tall, powerful, beardless young man with an uncovered head, whose loins only are covered, the rest of the body being naked. He leans with all the weight of his body on his advanced left leg, and with his uplifted right hand he has just plunged his double-edged sword into the throat of his antagonist. . . . On the wounded man's body we see a round shield with a circle of small points, probably intended to represent the glitter of the brass [here he was wrong; the shields were of leather]. . . . I asked whether we do not see here in the young, powerful, handsome man, Achilles, the most beautiful man in the Greek army; and in his antagonist, Hector of the dancing helmet-crest; for, just as we see represented on this bead, Hector was slain by Achilles by a stab in the throat.

Night after night, when the day's excavation was over, and the soldiers' watch-fires gleamed on the Mycenaean Acropolis, Heinrich and Sophia would be poring over that day's discoveries, weighing the heavy golden goblets, admiring the vessels of silver, alabaster and *faience*; scrutinizing through magnifying-glasses those fascinating,

* Subsequently recognized as a bull. See Cretan chapters.

puzzling scenes on the seal-stones, trying to understand this long-dead world which they had re-discovered.

For Schliemann there were no doubts that it was Homer's world he had found—the world of the *Iliad*. Had he not discovered the tombs of Agamemnon, Cassandra, Eurymedon and their companions, slain at that fatal banquet by Aegisthos? Who could doubt it? Eurymedon had been a charioteer; chariots were represented on the grave *stelae*. Pausanias had mentioned five graves; Schliemann had found five graves. Cassandra was said to have given birth to twins who were also killed with their mother; the bodies of two infants, wrapped in gold, were found in one of the graves.

Replica of the gold funeral mask, believed by Schliemann to be Agamemnon's

The identity of the mode of burial, the perfect similarity of all the tombs, their very close proximity, the impossibility of admitting that three or even five royal personages

of immeasurable wealth, who had died a natural death at long intervals of time, should have been huddled together in the same tomb, and, finally, the great resemblance of all the ornaments . . . all these facts are so many proofs that all the twelve men, three women, and perhaps two or three children, had been murdered simultaneously and burned at the same time [the graves showed signs of fires having been lit within them].

It was in this spirit of passionate faith that he excavated the fifth and, for him, the last grave.* And there, as at Troy, he found what he ardently wished to find. Three male bodies lay in the tomb, their richly-inlaid weapons beside them, golden breastplates on their chests and golden masks on their faces. When the mask was removed from the face of the first man his skull crumbled away on being exposed to air; the same thing happened with the second body.

But of the third body, which lay at the north end of the tomb, the round face, with all its flesh, had been wonderfully preserved under its ponderous golden mask; there was no vestige of hair, but both eyes were perfectly visible, also the mouth, which, owing to the enormous weight that had pressed upon it, was wide open, and showed thirty-two beautiful teeth. From these, all the physicians who came to see the body were led to believe that the man must have died at the early age of thirty-five.

Schliemann lifted the gold face mask from the soil and kissed it. And that evening, while the news spread like wildfire through the Argolid that the well-preserved body of a man of the heroic age had been found, the discoverer sat down and wrote a telegram to the King of Greece. It read:

I have gazed on the face of Agamemnon.

We have followed Heinrich Schliemann from the obscurity of a Mecklenburg parsonage to his finest hour in the citadel of the Atridae. In describing his successive discoveries I have tried to be faithful to *his* interpretation of them; to see them as *he* saw them, and not as we now understand them in the light of later knowledge. But this book is the story of a journey in search of truth, and Schliemann, like all pioneers, sometimes lost his way. The time has come, therefore, to call our first halt; to look behind at the ground we have covered and ahead at the hills we have still to cross. We have seen Mycenae through Schliemann's eyes. Now let us look at it for ourselves.

Back, then, to our own time, to the gravelled space in front of 'La Belle Hélène' on the morning after my arrival. On a bench near a low-hanging pepper-tree sits Orestes, looking out towards the Vale of Argos from whence blows the faint smell of the sea. And ahead lies the narrow winding road to Mycenae.

* After Schliemann's departure Stamatakis discovered and excavated a sixth grave, which contained two bodies.

5 PAUSE FOR REFLECTION

Although February was not quite over, the morning was clear and sunny, the air full of the scent of thyme and the tinkle of sheep-bells. At a turn in the road I met a ring of shepherd-boys, in ragged ex-American Army greatcoats, dancing rather solemnly to the sound of a pipe.

Ahead rose the twin hills of Mount Zara and Mount Hagios Elias sharp against the Wedgwood-blue sky; on Hagios Elias archaeologists have found remains of a Mycenaean watch-tower, probably that from which Clytemnestra's watchman saw the beacon fire. Between these two peaks I could see the lower hill on which stood the Citadel, but at that distance it was disappointing. I had expected to see great walls

The entrance to the 'Treasury of Atreus'

73

The roof of the 'Treasury of Atreus'

clearly outlined against the green earth; but this was not Château Gaillard or Ludlow, here was no soft meadowland but naked limestone. The bones of the hill showed through their thin covering, and the spring grass was only a faint mist of green above the grey, so that at a distance walls, rock and surface boulders merged into one.

But near at hand there was wonder. On the left of the road, where it curved round a buttress of the valley, a great stone gateway, three times as high as a man, opened into the hillside, approached by a deep cutting, the sides of which were also of finely masoned stonework. I recognized it, from the triangular opening over the gate, as the largest of the 'Tholos' or 'beehive' tombs, the famous 'Treasury of Atreus'. Entering the cutting, called the 'Dromos', I paused beneath the great doorway and looked up at the lintel.

Carved from a single piece of limestone, it weighs a hundred and twenty tons. Five tall men lying heel to head in a straight line would just cover its length; it is over sixteen feet wide and has a thickness of more than three feet. Yet somehow the Mycenaeans had manoeuvred it on to its stone jambs without cranes or lifting-jacks, and fitted it accurately in position where it has stayed for over three thousand years.

Inside the tomb it was dim, cool, and reverberant; a smooth, circular cave, rising in courses of beautifully cut blocks which curved inward till they met in the centre; exactly like the interior of a huge

74

beehive. This great chamber is nearly fifty feet in diameter at floor level, over forty-five feet high, and seems even bigger when one is inside it. There are numbers of these 'Tholos' tombs in and near the valley, though in most the roofs have fallen in and none are so perfectly preserved as this one. Pausanias and other classical writers called them 'Treasuries' in which it was believed the ancient lords of Mycenae kept their wealth. But from interments found in similar tombs in other parts of Greece, it is now known that they were tombs, comparable to the Pyramids of Egypt. And though Sir Arthur Evans believed that they were older than the shaft-graves, the excavations of Professor Wace and others have shown conclusively that they are

Cyclopean walls at Mycenae

later; that, in fact, they date from between 1500 and 1300 BC.

Before coming to Greece I had read Professor Wace's recent book on Mycenae, the fruit of many years' patient study and excavation of a site which he clearly loves. Indeed I had begun to suspect that his fondness for the place might have led him to over-praise its monuments. But no one standing within that lovely building could help but endorse his judgment on its unknown architect.

Here, first of all, there is a definite plan showing that before a single stone was cut or excavation begun a trained brain had considered the problems involved and found a solution. The plan of the tomb reveals clear thinking and a definite intention as well as bold imagination. Furthermore it reveals that the mind behind the plan had also calculated weights and thrusts and stresses and taken the necessary steps to counteract them. The purpose of the tremendous hundred-ton lintel, the oblique jointing system in the setting of the threshold, the accuracy of the building, all show that an intellect was at work. This unknown master of the Bronze Age who designed and built the Treasury of Atreus deserves to rank with the great architects of the world.

To which I would add a personal observation, for what it is worth. Travel in Egypt and the Near East had familiarized me with many ancient buildings, so that almost automatically I had come to regard any great structure earlier than 1000 BC as oriental. But here, on European soil, nearly a thousand years before the Parthenon, someone had produced a building grand in conception, superb in construction, graceful in proportion, and, to my eyes, unmistakably European in spirit.

Returning to the road, I climbed towards the Citadel. As I drew nearer the walls became more distinct, and I realized with a thrill that I was not to be disappointed. At close quarters the hill on which the Acropolis stands is much more steep than it appears from a distance, especially on the east. The fortress walls, called 'Cyclopean' by the later Greeks who thought that only the Cyclopes (giants) could have built them, almost encircle the hilltop like the *enceinte* of a medieval castle. In all the world there are few sights as stirring as these dark ramparts, built of unhewn, unmortared blocks so huge and heavy that thirty centuries of wind, rain, earthquake, battle and pillage have not been able entirely to dislodge them. There they stand, pierced, on the west side, by the proud Gate of Lions, through which passed Agamemnon and his men on their way to Troy. Then, as now, the wind blew in from the sea, whipping the helmet-crests of the warriors as they marched down the winding valley to the ships, while the women watched them go.

Above the big square portal, with its great monolithic lintel stone, two rampant lions, headless but still magnificent, support a central pillar. This was perhaps a sacred symbol of the Great Earth-Mother, goddess of fecundity and source of all life. The lions are the oldest monumental statuary in Europe. Passing through the gate and over the threshold worn by chariot-wheels I climbed the steep ramp on the left, which wound upwards towards the peak of the Acropolis. After a few yards I paused and looked down at the space on my right, between the ramp and the western wall of the fortress. Immediately below me lay six open square shafts, surrounded by a circle of stone slabs standing to

Opposite The ramp, leading from the Lion Gate to the Palace (the steps are modern)

76

a height of several feet. I was looking at the graves discovered by Schliemann and Stamatakis nearly eighty years ago. Grass and spring wildflowers grew where once lay the royalty of 'golden Mycenae'.

Then a laborious scramble over low walls, through rooms now open to the sky and choked with prickly oak and asphodel, brought me to the eastern limits of the fortress, where a pointed arch in the mighty wall overlooked the ravine. From this place, an obvious lookout point, the Mycenaean sentry had a fine view down the ravine and towards the sea. Only a military people would have chosen such a site; on this side the steep rocky sides of the ravine made it impregnable, while on the remaining sides the huge walls must have been impassable in the days when spears and arrows were the most powerful weapons. How, I asked myself could such a place be taken? Perhaps by surprise or treachery, as in the case of Troy. But properly victualled it could have withstood a long siege.

Water it did not lack. The secret cistern from which the Mycenaean garrison drew its supplies is still there, and, apart from the Lion Gate, this subterranean reservoir makes a greater impression than anything else in Agamemnon's fortress. I found the entrance to it on the north side, not far from the 'postern gate'—a smaller entrance than the Lion Gate, probably used as a 'sally port'. On this side, where the sentries pacing the wall looked northwards up the pass to Corinth, I came to a triangular-headed arch from which a steep flight of steps began to descend into the earth. First they passed obliquely through the great wall, until they were outside the wall and underground. After a short horizontal section the passage turned at right-angles (to the west) and descended by about twenty more steps until it doubled back on itself and plunged steeply into the earth. It was damp, and pitch-black, and I counted over sixty steps as I felt my way downward. Near the bottom I lit a heap of dried sage-brush, and as the flames leaped up saw the glistening, arched walls of the tunnel, and right at my feet a square-shaped stone shaft, filled to the brim with clear water.

This cistern, nearly twenty feet deep, was the secret water supply of the garrison which they could use in time of siege. The water is fed to it by earthenware pipes from the same spring Perseia which the Greek traveller Pausanias saw 1,700 years ago; but the cistern and its approach-tunnel, according to Professor Wace's estimate, were 1,500 years old when Pausanias came here. And the same spring which supplied the Mycenaeans still provides water for the modern village of Charvati.

Returning to the surface, I climbed higher still, up steep winding paths past ruined walls, till I came, breathlessly, to the highest point, the site of the Palace itself, of which, alas, practically all that remains are a few walls of the Great Hall or 'Megaron'. The rest has slipped down the hillside. But it was possible to make out the foundations of the Outer Court, on one side of which was the entrance porch leading to the Megaron itself. Readers of the *Odyssey* will remember that when Telemachus pays a visit to Menelaüs to discover news of his father, he sleeps under the porch:

Above The 'sally port'

Right The entrance to the
secret cistern

And so Prince Telamachus and Nestor's royal son spent the night there in the forecourt of the palace, while Menelaüs slept in his room at the back of the high buildings and the lady Helen in her long robe by his side.

Just such a porch and forecourt lay before the Hall of Agamemnon, Menelaüs's royal brother.

Within the hall itself, now a platform of stone open to the sky, I found the four bases of the pillars which had supported the roof; near these pillars, according to Homer, the King had his High Seat, and between them was the hearth on which the fire burned in winter. It was the floor of this Courtyard and Hall which Clytemnestra adorned with royal purple in honour of her husband's return, according to the story as told by Aeschylus.

Spread purple where he treads!

the Queen commands.

Below The postern gate

Opposite The Grave Circle, Mycenae

Fitly the broidered foot-cloth marks his path
Whom justice leadeth to his long-lost home
With unexpected train. . . .

On the far side of the court are the foundations of a small room which—may one be allowed to fancy—was the bathroom in which the King was done to death? At Knossos, we know, such bathrooms existed. Lured by her flattery of the purple cloths, not suspecting her long-maturing hate, Agamemnon was struck down:

Not with a random inconsiderate blow,
But from old Hate, and with maturing Time.
Here, where I struck, I take my rooted stand,
Upon the finished deed. . . . Here, Agamemnon lies
My husband, dead, the work of this right hand—
The hand of a true workman. Thus it stands.

Among the spring grass and the worn grey stones grew tiny scarlet anemones, like splashes of fresh blood. I had reached the end of the first part of my pilgrimage. Tired after my climb, I sat down and looked around me.

On every side rose mountains. Behind me Mount Hagios Elias stood grandly against the pale sky. Far off to the south, beyond range upon range of intervening peaks, beyond the Bay of Argolis, rose the snow-

Opposite The Lion Gate from inside the citadel, Mycenae

Below The King's Megaron

crested ridge of Mount Parnon, a giant in a land of great mountains. At my feet the land fell away gently in terraces, in which the delicate green of vetch alternated with bands of terra-cotta. Here and there, symmetrical rows of olive-trees marched along the lower slopes, accented in places by the darkly vertical cypresses. And beyond lay the fertile Argive Plain—'Argos, home of lovely women', as Homer described it, when he was not calling it 'horse-rearing Argos'. The air was still, save for an occasional puff of wind which brought with it the song of a shepherd-boy on one of the far-off slopes, or the sound of his pipe. Here was the landscape of the Peloponnese at its loveliest, warmed by the first breath of spring.

Resting there, I reflected on the many developments in Greek archaeology since Schliemann dug there seventy-five years ago. Some of his early views he corrected himself in his own lifetime. Others had to be modified after his death when new knowledge had been gained. Schliemann would have been the first to approve of these changes. He knew that archaeological truths must inevitably be expressed in theories which represent the most feasible explanations from available evidence. But every year, new facts are disclosed, a dated inscription here, a piece of potsherd there, or perhaps the result of a piece of solid research between four study walls. If the theory is soundly based, it still stands. If not, it collapses, or has to be modified. But there is always a gain in truth.

Was Schliemann right in believing that the bodies in the shaft-graves were those of Agamemnon and his companions? Alas, no! Assuming Agamemnon to have been an historical personage, he would have lived round about 1180 BC, the traditional date of the Trojan War (since confirmed by archaeology). But it is now known that the shaft-grave interments were much earlier, roughly between 1600 and 1500 BC. We know this because, since Schliemann's day, discoveries on scores of 'Mycenaean' sites in Greece and the islands have enabled scholars to develop a system of 'sequence dating' principally by means of pottery. It would take too long to explain exactly how this is done, but—at the risk of over-simplification I will try to get as near the truth as possible in a few sentences.

As we shall see later, Mycenae seems to have been the centre of an empire extending over a large part of the Aegean; and many 'Mycenaean', and 'proto-Mycenaean' sites have been unearthed. Where a site has been in long occupation it is possible to trace the development of a culture by studying the pottery and other objects found in successive layers; the lowest obviously being the earliest, and the highest the most recent. For example, if one particular type of pottery is always found within the same strata, on dozens of different sites, and does not appear in lower or higher strata, then it clearly belongs to one chronological period. But how can one apply a date to such a period, when the people of prehistoric Greece left no dated inscriptions which can be read? Fortunately for archaeology some of this early Aegean pottery found its way into *Egyptian tombs*, which

Minoan vase with leaves

can be dated. Once having been able to date certain layers by the presence of pottery found in 'dateable' Egyptian tombs, it was possible to date, very approximately, the objects found in layers above, between and below the dated layers. Even so the dating is inevitably far less precise than Egyptian chronology.

But Schliemann's mistake was revealed long before this system of comparative dating had come into general use. In fact it was discovered by his own assistant, the brilliant young Professor Dörpfeld, who did so much to bring more scientific methods into Schliemann's later excavations. The error might have been detected by the master himself if he had not been so passionately anxious to prove that the bodies had all been buried *at the same time*. He found the corpses lying on beds of pebbles at the bottom of the shafts, covered with a mass of clay and stones which he naturally assumed had been thrown into the graves after the burials. 'The sides of each grave were lined with a wall of small quarry stones and clay, which has been preserved up to different heights; in the fifth grave it still reached seven feet eight inches,' writes Schuchhardt, 'Several *slate slabs* were leaning against this wall; others were lying crossways or slanting over the bodies. Dr Schliemann saw in them *the revetment of the clay walls*.' (my italics). These slate slabs were to prove very important later.

The bodies lay within a few feet of each other, each laden with and surrounded by arms and ornaments. They must all have been buried at the same time, argued Schliemann, since it would have been impossible to dig down through the superincumbent earth to introduce a later burial without disturbing those already lying there. That seemed logical enough.

But in certain of the graves Schliemann found what he described as 'little boxes of stout sheet copper', filled with wood in fair preservation, and fastened all round by a number of strong copper nails. He could not make out what these had been, and finally suggested that they might have been head-rests. They were put into the Museum at Athens with the rest of the treasures.

Years later, when Dörpfeld was working for Schliemann, the young man began to reflect on the still unsolved problem of the shaft-graves. Did the bodies represent a simultaneous interment—or the successive burials of a dynasty? He read and re-read Schliemann's descriptions of the graves as he had found them. Then he noticed the reference to the 'slate slabs' which Schliemann had found leaning against the wall, and which he thought had been 'the revetment of the clay walls'. A thought struck him, and he asked the Doctor a few questions.

'Those slabs,' he asked, 'how were they placed when you found them?'

'Against the sides of the graves.'

'Flat against the sides?'

'No, some were leaning against the side. One was lying across a body.'

When Dörpfeld heard this he became more suspicious. He went again to the Museum and examined those 'little boxes of sheet copper' which Schliemann had thought were head-rests. They were full of

83

decayed wood held in place by copper nails. Then he realized what had happened. Originally those slabs of slate had served to roof the graves, *which had not been filled in with earth*. Baulks of timber had been laid across the lips of each tomb, the ends resting on the ground being strengthened by copper sheaths—Schliemann's 'boxes'. The slabs of slate had rested on top of the baulks, so that originally each grave had been a family vault; in which it would have been quite possible to make a number of separate interments without disturbing the others. Years, perhaps centuries, after the last of the dynasty had been laid in this tomb, the timber baulks had rotted away, and the slabs, pressed down by the earth which had accumulated above, crashed down on to the bodies (which accounted for the crushed condition of several). This had not been noticed by Schliemann, anxious as he was to believe that all the bodies had been buried simultaneously, but the 'boxes' gave the game away.

Later, when more had been learned of Mycenaean and Minoan art, it became clear that the objects found in the shaft-graves did not all belong to the same period; that, in fact, there were subtle differences indicating that the burials had extended over roughly a century. Certainly they were royal, the members, perhaps, of an entire dynasty. But to Agamemnon, had he lived, they would have been as ancient as the Tudors are to us. He himself is more likely to have been buried in one of the great 'Tholos' tombs in the valley; one likes to think he lay in the finest of all, that 'Treasury of Atreus' which is sometimes called the Tomb of Agamemnon.

But what of the tradition cited by Pausanias, who said the tombs lay within the citadel, where indeed they were found? I think the answer is that there was in Pausanias's time a strong local tradition that royal personages lay within the citadel, but it seems to me unlikely that he ever saw their gravestones. The shaft-graves were more than 1,500 years old when he came to Mycenae, and during much of that time it had been a deserted ruin. In all parts of the world neglected tombs have invariably attracted the plunderer. Is it likely that the gravestones could have been visible in classical times and remain unrobbed? But there still lingered in the vicinity of Mycenae an ancient folk-memory of the kings who had been buried there, though their graves, and even their gravestones, were buried under the tons of loose earth and rock washed down from the steep slopes of the Acropolis above.

It was this circumstance which favoured Heinrich Schliemann, as Sir Arthur Evans pointed out later in his introduction to Emil Ludwig's biography of the excavator.

Excavators learn by experience that the best chance—indeed the only chance—of hitting on an unplundered tomb is by digging into a natural talus, such as is formed by the deposit of earth and debris washed down or fallen at the foot of a declivity. But the area in which the Shaft-Graves had been sunk answered to all these conditions. It lay, in fact, immediately beneath the ascending ramp of the Acropolis and its inner wall, dominated by the steep above. And it was thus, happily inspired by the most fruitful version of the old tradition, that he dug with such dramatic results.

Here is the second interesting parallel (the first was the discovery of the Trojan treasure) with the finding by Howard Carter of the Tomb of

Tutankhamun, half a century later. Carter, like Schliemann, found his tomb at the foot of a slope, hidden under the stone chippings thrown down from a later sepulchre excavated at a higher level.

After Schliemann's departure the much-enduring Stamatakis found the Sixth Shaft-Grave, which did something to restore the *amour-propre* of the Archaeological Society of Greece. He also cleared the débris from the 'Treasury of Atreus', leaving it as we see it today. Then came Tsountas (1862–1902), Keramopoullos and Rodenwaldt, all of whom made their contribution to the revelation of Mycenaean civilization. From 1920 onwards British scholarship, represented by the British School at Athens, continued to excavate at Mycenae up to and since the war. These excavations, directed by Professor Wace and published in the Annual of the School, have disclosed facts which were not available to Schliemann or his successors.

For example, Wace has shown that the prehistoric cemetery of which the Shaft-Graves form part originally extended *beyond the line of the Cyclopean walls*, west of the Lion Gate. Between approximately 1600 and 1500 BC princes and princesses of the royal family were buried in that part of the cemetery which now comes within the walls. They seem to have belonged to one dynasty, and were contemporary with these kings of the early Eighteenth Dynasty in Egypt—Amasis and the early Tuthmoses. Mycenae's greatest period was that of the last phase of the Late Bronze Age, about 1400–1150 BC. Of this epoch Wace says:

all the evidence indicates that Mycenae was a strong and flourishing state, the seat of a powerful dynasty with a wide dominion. It corresponds admirably with our idea of the stronghold which was the capital of Agamemnon, King of Men, *primus inter pares* of the Greek princes before Troy and holder of the supreme sovereignty granted by Zeus.

It was during this latter period that the Mycenaeans built the Cyclopean Walls with the Lion and Postern Gates. At the same time the burial place of the earlier kings, held in great veneration, was surrounded by the circle of stone slabs which Schliemann had mistaken for the *agora*. The slope of the ground was levelled off, and within the circle, the gravestones were raised, with the circular well-like altar through which the blood of sacrifice could be poured to the heroes below. As in Egypt it is probable that regular offerings were made to the illustrious dead. Later, when the citadel fell into ruin, soil washed down from the slopes above gradually covered both the Grave Circle and the memorial stones with their sculptured charioteers, sealing them from curious eyes for more than thirty centuries.

Is there still any support for Schliemann's belief that the Mycenaean civilization was the one described by Homer? Answer: yes and no.

The arguments on behalf of the '8-shaped' shield, the boars' tusk helmet, the use of bronze for weapons, and, perhaps, 'Nestor's Cup' are still accepted; indeed they are irrefutable. Even the objection that some of Homer's shields are round can be met by those who support a Mycenaean origin of the poems. It is true that the shields shown on the shaft-grave daggers are large and shaped like a figure-of-eight. But in

The Warrior Vase

the remains of a late Mycenaean house near the Lion Gate was found a fragment of a vase—the famous Warrior Vase—which clearly shows Mycenaean soldiers carrying smaller, *round* shields with a 'bite' out of the bottom. This case is believed to be of the thirteenth century BC—the period of the Trojan War. So, said the believers, the round shields mentioned in Homer do not in themselves prove that he had lived in post-Mycenaean times.

Yet even Schliemann had to admit that there were many elements of Mycenaean life which were quite unlike that which Homer describes. To take a few examples: the Mycenaeans buried their dead—the Homeric heroes burned theirs. The Mycenaeans were a Bronze Age people; Homer understood the use of iron. Mycenaean bronze swords are rapiers designed for thrusting: Homeric swords were sharp-edged for a slashing stroke.

Eventually even Schliemann himself was forced to admit that the Homer who composed the *Iliad* could not have lived at the time of the Trojan War. Yet he had started a controversy which was to rage for more than half a century; nor has it ceased even today. Hundreds of books and articles in many languages poured from the presses of Europe and America, and learned gentlemen fought their wordy battles with the vigour of Achilles and Hector themselves.

But the real significance of Mycenae, and the discoveries which followed soon after at Tiryns, was *not* in their resemblance, or lack of resemblance to the Homeric poems. The indigo-merchant turned scholar had opened up a new world for archaeology. Minds accustomed to the cautious scepticism of Grote suddenly realized that there had existed, on European soil, a high civilization a thousand years older than the Greek. Nor was it confined to Mycenae. Archaeologists who investigated other sites, on the mainland and in the islands, made a significant discovery. In most of the places which Homer described as having sent contingents to the Trojan War, and were therefore important political centres—places such as Tiryns, Orchomenos, Lacedaemon, Amyclae—*there were remains of Mycenaean settlements.* The Catalogue of Ships in the *Iliad* seemed to give a fairly true picture of the political and military structure of Greece in Mycenaean times. In a way it was exasperating. With one hand Homer seemed to betray his devotees. With the other, he magnificently supported them.

Gradually the Homeric side of the question became less and less important as the further excavations proved how widespread and how long-established this ancient culture had been. But who were these people? Where did they come from? What language had they spoken? What could be learned about their religion and customs? Had they a system of writing and could it be deciphered? What was their relationship with other Mediterranean peoples?

These were some of the questions to which archaeologists and historians had to apply themselves during the coming years. Some have remained unanswered. To others partial replies can be given, which I will try to summarize at the end of this book. But for the present we are going back to take up the thread of Schliemann's story after his Mycenaean glory, for he himself was able to follow the trail of discovery a good deal further before it was taken up by others.

6 HERE BEGINS AN ENTIRELY NEW SCIENCE

A few miles from the town of Argos, on the road to Nauplia, stands a village. There is a café with a few wobbly iron tables; a gaol from which, at intervals, a trumpet sounds; a few low houses of mudbrick and terracotta tiles; donkeys, barking dogs and a general air of polite decay. On one side of the road is an arm of the Bay of Argolis. On the other are the inevitable rows of dusty olive-trees, their old, gnarled feet gripping the brown, crumbling earth. Beyond them, to the north, the land rises gradually towards the hills where lies Mycenae.

You climb off the ramshackle bus, walk a few steps along the village street, go past the prison, and there in front of you stands Tiryns—next to Mycenae the mightiest surviving example of a Mycenaean fortress. Although the site has not the romantic setting of Mycenae,

Tiryns

nor the glamour of its legend, the place has a grim splendour which still justifies the name which Homer gave it—'Tiryns of the Great Walls'. From a distance, it rides the peaceful fields like a battleship—long and low and grey, with its Acropolis breaking the outline like a gun-turret. It is 900 feet long, from 200 to 250 feet broad, and from 30 to 50 feet high.

From close at hand all other impressions are crushed by those Cyclopean walls, made of ponderous, unwrought or roughly-hewn blocks, weighing up to ten tons each. The total width of these walls varies from between twenty-five and fifty feet. Some are hollow, and have within them long galleries, vaulted at the top and pierced on the outer side by triangular embrasures which from outside the fortress look like black, gaping mouths. The resemblance to a medieval castle is even more marked than at Mycenae, embrasures resembling gunports; yet Tiryns was built more than 1,200 years before Christ. The apertures were probably intended for archers, whilst the galleries themselves must have served for covered communications leading to armouries, guard-chambers or towers.

If you could have been at Tiryns in 1884, you might have seen, sitting under the shade of a wall and munching cheese and corned-beef sandwiches, two men in shirt-sleeves. The elder, a balding, spectacled gentleman with a high forehead and thick moustache, was talking rapidly and making energetic gestures to his much younger companion, who sat calmly eating, or taking an occasional satisfied gulp from his glass of resinous wine. Now and again he would make a note, or interject a few words into his companion's monologue, then return to his meal.

The older man was Schliemann, now aged sixty-two. The other was Dörpfeld, the brilliant young architect whom Sir Arthur Evans, in later years, described as 'Schliemann's greatest discovery'. It was Dörpfeld who gradually introduced the discipline of science into the older man's investigations, and taught him the value of care and patience in excavation, accuracy in publication, and temperateness in controversy. 'Scientific questions,' he would tell his angry employer, 'cannot be settled by abuse . . . but only by objective proof.' It says much for Schliemann's vision and essential humility that he appreciated Dörpfeld's genius and accepted (with occasional rebellious outbursts) his wise guidance.

Once again Schliemann had followed his ancient authors. Pausanias had described the walls of Tiryns as 'composed of unwrought stones, each of which is so large that a team of mules cannot even shake the smallest one. . . .' (an exaggeration, as the cautious Dörpfeld pointed out). Traditionally the fortress had been built by Proteus. Heracles is also supposed to have conquered it and lived within its walls for a long time—hence he is sometimes called 'The Tirynthian'. In classical times it had, with Mycenae, sent four hundred men to the battle of Plataea. In 1876, just before beginning his Mycenaean excavations, Schliemann had sunk a few test pits here and brought to light 'Cyclopean' house-walls at considerable depth, and a few clay cows and terra-cotta 'idols' similar to those he later discovered at Mycenae.

The Cyclopean galleries at
Tiryns

But that was eight years ago, and now he had returned, not, this
time, with Madame Schliemann, but with a skilled architect, seventy
workmen, and 'forty English wheelbarrows with iron wheels, twenty
large iron crow-bars ... fifty pickaxes, fifty large shovels' and other
formidable equipment. Already, in that summer of 1884, they had
removed hundreds of tons of earth from the middle and upper citadels
and revealed, for the first time, the clear ground plan of an Homeric
palace. Walls, doorways, thresholds, pillar-bases were laid bare, and
carefully measured and drawn by Dörpfeld. The excavations were not
complete yet, but enough had been done to give Schliemann great
satisfaction.

For the plan of the Palace, with its Megaron, porch, courtyards and
adjoining rooms, bore unmistakable resemblances to the Palace of
Odysseus, described in the *Odyssey*. True, that building had been in
Ithaca, but this was so similar to it that it was even possible, if one

allowed for a few discrepancies, to visualize the fight in which Odysseus slew the suitors. Schliemann was in his element. The ageing merchant-scholar with his rapidly-thinning hair and thick spectacles had reason to feel content as he leaned his back against the ancient wall and looked across the sunny plain of Argos. There, on the northern skyline, rose the hills which hid Mycenae, scene of his greatest triumph only eight years ago. But what years they had been!

First there had been his triumphal tour of England in 1877, when thirty learned societies had vied with each other to honour him, and he renewed acquaintance with Gladstone, whom he had first met in 1875. This was an age when it was still not unusual for a Prime Minister to combine statecraft with classical scholarship. Gladstone's interest in Homeric studies was well known, and Schliemann asked him to write a Preface to his forthcoming *Mycenae*. The Liberal leader could hardly refuse, though when he read the German's book he confessed to Murray, the publisher, that he was 'quite worried about it, as I am not the right man for it.' Nevertheless he contributed a lengthy and well-reasoned introduction in which, after cautious consideration of the available facts he came out in support of Schliemann's view; that the shaft-graves had contained the bodies of Agamemnon and his murdered companions.

When Heinrich arrived in England in 1877, Sophia had been ill and unable to accompany him. Convalescing in Athens she read wistfully her husband's enthusiastic letters, telling her that ten societies had asked him to lecture, that yesterday he had had dinner with Gladstone, who had carried off her photograph—'so please bring others with you'—that the London Photographic Society had paid him £40 for permission to take and sell his photograph, and that 'Hodge, the painter, has been after me for weeks to paint me life-size for the Royal Academy.'

Finally, in the summer, she was able to join him, and took her seat, a grave and lovely woman of twenty-eight, on the platform of the Royal Society. There, before a distinguished audience of over a thousand people, they were each awarded a special diploma by the Archaeological Institute. Both made speeches in English, and fashionable ladies listened, fascinated, while Sophia told them how for twenty-five days she and her husband had knelt almost in the soil of the shaft-graves and lifted from it, one by one, the golden treasures of the Atridae.

Those had been heart-lifting moments, moments which almost compensated for the bitter attacks of the critics, attacks which had made him write:

In London. . . . I was received for seven weeks as if I had discovered a new part of the globe for England. How very different it is in Germany. There I met only with abuse. . . .

Criticisms, some fair and unbiased, others prompted by jealousy and malice, were to continue through Schliemann's life, and never ceased to cause him pain. Yet gradually, as the years passed, responsible opinion came to place an ever higher value on the German's discoveries, especially when, in later years, he brought in

Schliemann's house in
University Street, Athens

trained specialists to help him. But the legend of the publicity-seeking
mountebank died hard, and he often had reason bitterly to regret the
too precipitate publication of his early finds.

In the following year, 1878, his English triumphs were crowned by
an even greater joy; Sophia presented him with a son. Seven years
earlier, when he had first begun to dig at Troy, a daughter had been
born to them, whom Schliemann had christened Andromache, after
Hector's wife. But now his dearest hopes were fulfilled. Before the
child was more than a few hours old the entranced father held a
copy of Homer above his head and read aloud a hundred lines from
the poet. That was Schliemann the romantic. Schliemann the
practical revealed himself at the solemn Orthodox christening, when,
just as the priest was about to immerse the infant, his parent darted
forward, plunged a thermometer into the font and checked the
temperature.

In the same year he began to build for himself a mansion in Athens,
on what is now University Street. When completed, a few years later,
it was the most palatial building in the capital, and throughout the
whole of Greece few equalled its magnificence. On the roof marble
gods and goddesses stood against the blue sky. Within were pillared
halls and marble staircases, opulent but chilly, and a particularly
splendid ballroom where guests who cared to examine the frieze of

92

putti round the walls could see that these tiny figures represented the principal activities of the host's life. Here some of the figures were reading Homer and Pausanias; there were others digging and unearthing the rich treasures of Mycenae and Troy; and who was this, a figure in black, with horn-rimmed spectacles gazing across the landscape—why, Schliemann himself!

On walls and staircases, above doors, within and without the house were inscriptions from the ancient Greek authors. Above the great man's study were the words of Pythagoras:

All who do not study geometry, remain outside.

Other walls bore the verses of Homer and Hesiod, while, carved on the front of the palace, in Greek letters, were the words 'Iliou Melathron'—*Palace of Ilios*. Here Schliemann and his wife would receive their distinguished guests from many parts of the world, and on the ground floor, displayed in glass cases, was the golden 'Treasure of Priam' which Heinrich and Sophia had unearthed from beneath the walls of Troy.

But all that was to come later. Meanwhile, as the house was building, Schliemann paid another visit to Ithaca, where he thoroughly explored the island, climbed Mount Aëtos, sunk a few experimental shafts at various places, but found nothing of great interest. Then in September, 1878, he returned to Troy, the difficulties concerning the *firman* having been temporarily solved, though they were soon to crop up again. He recommenced digging near the point at which he had found the 'Treasure of Priam', i.e. the large building west and north-west of the Gate. Less than a month after he had begun excavating he uncovered another smaller treasure of golden objects, contained in a broken terra-cotta vessel 'in a chamber in the north-west part of the building ... in the presence of seven officers of HMS *Monarch*....' Winter rains stopped work at the end of November, so Schliemann went to Europe for a few months, returning to the Dardanelles in February 1879. A month later he was joined by one of the most distinguished scientists of Europe, a man who was to have a strong and beneficial influence on Schliemann during the closing years of his life.

Professor Rudolf Virchow had come out at Schliemann's invitation. They had already corresponded but this was the moment when their association became close and intimate. Virchow, a brilliant doctor of medicine, was almost the same age as the archaeologist. He had gained fame in his thirties as the founder of a new pathological system. Later, impelled by humane and liberal convictions, he had become a member of the German Parliament where he had again distinguished himself as a politician. Mr Emil Ludwig, to whose *Schliemann of Troy* all later writers on Schliemann are bound to be indebted, happily explains the reasons why these two very dissimilar spirits were drawn together.

Both men had in youth stepped beyond the bounds of their calling, and struck out, or at least prospected, by-paths into the world ... both ... had voluntarily and disinterestedly assumed a second burden, the one out of revolutionary sympathy, the other from ambition and an impulse towards higher tasks....

93

... Intrepid, humane, and cool, Virchow was the man to support new discoveries whatever their source. He was distinguished from other German university professors by an unbiased outlook, which always ruled out personal questions about the origin, education, religion, or relationship of an independent mind about whom controversy raged.

It was these qualities which made Virchow such a valuable friend and ally for the impetuous excavator. His cool, scientific brain restrained Schliemann's wilder impulses, while he had the discernment to recognize and encourage the natural genius of the man, untroubled by scruples concerning his un-academic background. And as Virchow was a man of means, he avoided the imputation of being influenced by the millionaire's wealth.

With Virchow came M. Emile Burnouf, Honorary Director of the French School at Athens, and together the three worked throughout the summer season, Schliemann directing the excavations, Burnouf making plans, and Virchow studying the flora, fauna, and geological characteristics of the Plain of Troy, as well as the conditions of the ruins and débris brought to light in the course of the 'dig'.

Schliemann was also able to make several excursions with Virchow into the surrounding country. They went to the discredited site of Bounarbashi and took the temperature of the springs around which so much controversy had raged, and Heinrich was delighted when his friend agreed that the difference in temperature between one spring and another was almost imperceptible. They climbed Mount Ida together, and found the course of the river Scamander which plays such a vital part in the topography of the *Iliad*. By the end of the season the ex-indigo-merchant and the great scientist had become close friends, and when, in the following year, Schliemann published his 800-page volume *Ilios*, it was Virchow who contributed the Preface.

... there stands the great hill of ruins, forming for realistic contemplation a phenomenon quite as unique as 'Sacred Ilios' for poetical feeling. It has not its like. Never once in any other heap of ruins is a standard given by which to judge it.... This excavation has opened for the studies of the archaeologist a completely new theatre— like a world by itself. Here begins an entirely new science.

Virchow, unconcerned, as Schliemann was, with a desperate search for Homeric parallels, could see the greater significance of his friend's discoveries. But Schliemann, who had hollowed out an enormous crater in the centre of the hill, was still perplexed by the seven strata he had uncovered, and of which only the lower layers could, in his view, possibly be Homeric. He now put forward the belief that the Third Stratum (from the bottom), the so-called 'Burned City', was Priam's Troy, but his doubts and perplexities are pathetically evident in the book.

... this pretty little town, with its brick walls, which can hardly have housed 3,000 inhabitants ... could [it] have been identical with the great Homeric Ilios of immortal renown, which withstood for ten long years the heroic efforts of the united Greek army of 110,000 men? ...

Only the absence of any reliable system of comparative dating by pottery prevented him from seeing that his 'Homeric' Troy, i.e. the city which had existed in 1180 BC, was there in front of his eyes. Had he known, he need not have looked at the miserable prehistoric settlement which lay at the bottom of his crater; the walls of Homeric Troy were in the upper layers*—as massive as those of their contemporaries at Mycenae and as satisfying to his romantic imagination. He knew and admired the walls—had he not spared them when digging for deeper remains?—but he thought they were of the time of Lysimachus—a mere 300 years BC.

In 1881, he was persuaded by Virchow to present his Trojan collection to the German nation, but only after strings had been pulled by that adroit politician to ensure for Schliemann the Freedom of Berlin and, among other honours, the *Pour la Merité*. He could not forgive easily the sneers of the German scholars and the scornful press attacks which followed his first discoveries at Troy.

He had spent the 1880 season digging in Greece, where at Orchomenos, another Homeric site, he had uncovered a Mycenaean 'Tholos' tomb which, following Pausanias, he thought was a 'Treasury'. But in the ensuing year he was back at Troy, this time with young Dörpfeld, who had asked for the honour of working for him. Dörpfeld, with his architect's training, was able clearly to distinguish and plan the complicated strata of Hissarlik. Like Virchow, he was also able to exercise a restraining influence on Schliemann, and prevented him from rushing into print with a very inexact plan of the excavations. 'Only by means of a correct plan,' he advised, 'shall we be able to silence our adversaries completely.' Gradually the old lion was being tamed—for the good of science, and for his own good—and yet, one suspects, at the cost of much of his earlier enthusiasm.

Sophia did not accompany him during these later seasons at Troy, where, in the first years of their marriage, they had found the ancient gold. Sometimes she paid him brief visits; when he was alone he missed her greatly, and would write from his hut on the Trojan hill:

I burn four candles, but the room is still dark, whereas your eyes would light it up. Life without you is unbearable.

Still struggling with the eternal problem of the Trojan strata, he was prevented for the time being from making further investigations by the Turkish Government, which had now thought of a new way to annoy Schliemann. Not far from Hissarlik was a decrepit fort of no interest to anyone, save, perhaps, the Turkish Army. The Government decided that the archaeologist must be a spy, and forbade him to make further plans. Schliemann returned to Athens and again enlisted the help of his powerful friends—German, British and American—to work through their Embassies in Istanbul for the downfall of the obstructive Turkish officials. He even suggested that Bismarck should appoint another German Ambassador to Turkey as the current one was insufficiently active on his behalf! In the meantime he made a sentimental journey to his childhood home at Ankershagen, taking

* Dörpfeld later identified Homeric Troy as the Sixth Stratum from the bottom. This has been accepted until Professor Blegen dug at Troy immediately before the Second World War. Blegen recognizes nine layers or strata, of which No. 7A is believed to be the Ilios of the Trojan War.

95

Sophia and the children with him. The miller who had recited Homer was still alive, and had to be introduced. So was Minna Meincke, now a fat and tearful old woman.

Then, as we have seen, came two seasons' work at Tiryns, where he made a discovery which, while it pleased the scientific side of his nature, dealt yet another blow to his faith in his Third Stratum. Within the citadel of Tiryns he and Dörpfeld uncovered the foundations of a 'Megaron' or hall, which, with its pillared porch and courtyard, was so like that described in the *Odyssey* as to be unmistakably Homeric. This was great news, but it raised a difficult problem. For at Troy, in the *Sixth* Stratum—the layer which Schliemann had considered to be of the third century, Dörpfeld had excavated a similar Megaron. For a moment Schliemann was on the brink of discovering the truth—that one of the upper layers *did* represent Priam's Troy.

Priam's Troy ... but what about 'Priam's Treasure' which he had found far below in the Second Layer—the ornaments which his imagination gave to Helen herself—these wonderful golden diadems which had hung on the brow on his young wife on that memorable day in 1872? If this Sixth Layer was Priam's city, then the treasure he had found could never have belonged to Priam, but to some nameless barbarian who had lived centuries before him. For a time he would not commit himself, but tried to dismiss the problem from his mind.

One fact was clear; the pottery and other objects found at Tiryns were so like those found at Mycenae as to make it certain that the two cities were inhabited by the same race. But who were they? Schliemann believed them to have been Phoenicians. Others disagreed. Meanwhile the learned world examined and re-examined the precious things from Mycenae, Tiryns and Troy—or if they could not get to the objects themselves, they pored over the hundreds of steel engravings in Schliemann's bulky volumes. Theories were advanced and demolished, new theories put forward in their place. One *savant* said that the so-called 'gold mask of Agamemnon' was a Byzantine mask of Christ. Other scholars, while paying tribute to Schliemann's intuitive genius, asserted that the objects were far older than Homer or even the Trojan War.

One such believer was a young Englishman of thirty-one who came to see the Schliemanns in Athens in 1882. Recently married, he had come to Athens with his wife and obtained an introduction through his father, a well-known antiquarian whom Schliemann had met in England. The Englishman listened politely while Schliemann talked of Homer, but seemed only mildly interested; what interested him most were the golden objects from Mycenae, especially the tiny engraved bead-seals and signet rings which he examined minutely through his keen though short-sighted eyes. These objects—so unlike the art of classical Greece, which he disliked—fascinated him. In some ways they reminded him of Assyrian or Egyptian gems, and yet there were designs which included the octopus which was undoubtedly Aegean. It was puzzling.

The young man's name was Arthur Evans.

Opposite above: Gold Mycenaean goblet

Opposite below: Minoan pottery vase

96

In 1886, when he was sixty-four, Schliemann, restless as ever, was still seeking fresh Homeric sites to explore. Where could he go now? He had torn open the mound of Hissarlik. Mycenae had yielded up its gold. Orchomenos had been dug. Where else? There was 'hundred-cities Crete' the domain of King Minos, of whom the historian Thucydides had written:

Minos is the earliest ruler we know of who possessed a fleet, and controlled most of what are now Greek waters. He ruled the Cyclades, and was the first colonizer of most of them, installing his own sons as governors. In all probability he cleared the sea of pirates, so far as he could, to secure his own revenues.

Of course, Thucydides had only been repeating a legendary story, but Schliemann had great faith in legend and folk-tradition. And Homer had sung of the valiant spearman Idomeneus, leader of the Cretan contingent at the siege of Troy.

... the men from Knosses, from Gortyn of the Great Walls, from Lyctus, Miletus, chalky Lycastus, Phaestus, and Rhytion, fine cities all of them. . . .

Also, the *Odyssey* contains many Cretan stories. In 1883 Schliemann applied to the Turkish Government, who then ruled Crete, for permission to dig there. Naturally his request did not have an easy passage, but three years later, after he had finished his work at Tiryns, he arrived in Crete.

Sir John Myres once told me that when he visited Crete as a young man, with Arthur Evans, there was a story that when Schliemann had been directed to the site of Knosses—legendary capital of King Minos—he had sunk upon his knees and sent up a prayer to Idaean Zeus offering thanks for safe guidance to the spot. This profoundly shocked the devout Moslems and was one reason why the German enthusiast had such difficulty in obtaining permission to dig in the island. Sir John does not vouch for the truth of the story, but it accords well with Schliemann's known character.

A few miles from Herakleion, in a valley rising towards the mountainous interior of Crete, rises the mound of Kephala, traditional site of Knossos. Here, in 1877, the Spanish consul had sunk five shafts and established the existence of a building 180 feet long and 140 feet broad, but at very great depth. This was the site which Schliemann now sought to buy. The negotiations were complicated, and there are several conflicting stories about them which are unimportant to our story. But the owner of the site refused to agree to the sale of part of his land. If the millionaire wanted it he must buy the whole estate—with all its olive-trees—for 100,000 francs. This was too much. Schliemann knew that in any case he would have to hand over all he found to the Turkish authorities, so he returned to Athens, leaving the peasant owner in suspense.

Meanwhile England saw the great archaeologist again, when he came to London to answer, in public debate, the criticisms of the English architect Penrose, who asserted that Tiryns was of much later date than Schliemann had claimed. The Englishman was defeated and had the grace to apologize. Next Schliemann made two trips to Egypt, the second in 1881, with Virchow. When in the following year, the

Opposite Portrait of Sir Arthur Evans with the 'cupbearer' fresco behind him

Cretan landowner offered the site for 40,000 francs, Schliemann was pleased but wary, especially when he was informed that there was no need for him to visit the island to clinch the deal. A deposit would be enough. This was sufficient to bring out all the old merchant's commercial cunning. He arrived unexpectedly in Crete, and discovered that the owner of the land was trying to cheat him—there were 1,612 fewer olive-trees than had been stipulated. True, the site of Knosses was still included, but this time Schliemann the business man triumphed over Schliemann the archaeologist. He broke off negotiations and never reopened them.

A year later, after an operation on his ear in Halle, Germany, he was hurrying across Europe to be home for Christmas. It was a bitterly cold winter, and the doctors had warned him against travelling. But Schliemann longed to be home in his great house in Athens with Sophia and the children. Although often in pain, he continued his journey, getting out of the train at intervals, finding a local doctor who would treat him, and then continuing on his way. Much of his life had been spent in ships and trains; travel was a tedious necessity, but he had the German's sentimental love of Christmas. He *must* be home in time.

At Naples the pain returned, so ferociously that he was forced to cable Sophia asking her to postpone the Christmas celebrations until his return. He saw a doctor, and obtained some relief. Then, feeling better, he decided to visit the ruins of Pompeii about which his father had spoken to him sixty years ago in Ankershagen. The weather was cold, and on his return Schliemann again felt the return of that fierce pain. Next day, Christmas Day, when he was on his way to the doctor, he collapsed in the street, paralysed and unable to speak. Police took the unknown foreigner to hospital, but as no money could be found in his clothes he was refused admission.

Eventually the doctor who had treated him was traced through a paper in the sick man's pocket, and Schliemann, still unconscious, was moved to an hotel, where a surgeon discovered that the inflammation had spread from the ear to the brain. The next day, Boxing Bay, while doctors in an adjoining room debated what should be done, Heinrich Schliemann quietly died.

His journey was ended. But his discoveries—the full significance of which he had not understood—had launched other minds on a voyage which even Schliemann could hardly have imagined. One of these minds—perhaps the greatest—was that of the young Englishman who had been so absorbed by Schliemann's Mycenaean treasures when he and his wife had visited him eight years before. Many years later, when in the full tide of his own triumph, Sir Arthur Evans wrote of his great predecessor:

I had the happiness ... to make his acquaintance on the fields of his glory, and I still remember the echoes of his visits to England, which were his greatest scenes of triumph. . . . Something of the romance of his earlier years still seemed to cling to his personality, and I have myself an almost uncanny memory of the spare, slightly built man—of sallow complexion and somewhat darkly clad—wearing spectacles of foreign make, through which—so fancy took me—he had looked deep into the ground.

7 THE QUEST CONTINUES

Out in the dark blue sea there lies a land called Crete, a rich and
lovely land, washed by the waves on every side, densely peopled
and boasting ninety cities. . . . One of the ninety towns is a great
city called Knossos, and there, for nine years, King Minos ruled
and enjoyed the friendship of almighty Zeus.

So Homer makes Odysseus describe Crete, in that famous passage
from the *Odyssey* in which the 'Cunning One' pretends to Penelope
that he is the grandson of Minos. Homer had almost certainly visited
Crete, for, with one of those topographical details of which he is so
fond, he tells us, on the same page, that his hero

. . . put in at Amnissus, where the cave of Eileithyia is—a difficult harbour to make;
the storm nearly wrecked him.

I visited that cave shortly after I landed in Crete with the de Jongs.
Piet de Jong, former architect to Sir Arthur Evans, was Curator of the
Palace of Minos at Knossos, to which he and his wife were returning
after their overseas leave. We had met in Athens, after my return from
Mycenae and Tiryns, and they had kindly invited me to stay at the
Villa Ariadne, Sir Arthur's former home at Knossos which he had
later given to the British School at Athens. De Jong is a quietly-spoken
Yorkshireman of about fifty, with a lean, tanned face and steady eyes;
he is a little taciturn until he has decided whether he likes you or not,
but kind, friendly, and willing to give the benefit of his vast practical
knowledge of the Palace to anyone whose interest goes a little deeper
than tourist-level. His wife, Effie, is a Scotswoman, as voluble and
vivacious as he is shy; witty, observant, and wickedly intelligent, she
has an unending stock of stories, about archaeology and archaeologists, about Crete and the Cretans, and about Sir Arthur Evans, the
great scholar and excavator of the Knossian Palace, whom they both
knew well and greatly admired.

As we flew south over the many-islanded Aegean, I felt that I was
regretfully leaving the ghost of Heinrich Schliemann behind. At
Mycenae and Tiryns I had almost felt his physical presence, so vividly
is his personality associated with those places. But in Athens I said
farewell to his lively shade, appropriately enough outside his fantastic
palace, *Iliou Melathron*, which stands in University Street, opposite
the airline company's office where I had waited with the de Jongs for
the airport bus. Schliemann's marble statues still fret the Athenian
sky, though now they look down on a street crowded with shining
American motor-cars and the noisiest tramcars in the world. And even

Evans in 1867

as our aircraft soared above the beach of Phaleron I remembered that he used to bathe there before breakfast in the coldest weather, even when he was quite old ('Go for walks! Bathe!' he would say to fat, red-necked men, 'or you'll die of apoplexy!')

Now I was passing into the orbit of another personality, as strong as that of Schliemann, but much more sophisticated and complex. When Sir Arthur Evans died, in 1941, at the age of ninety, he had done that which no one man had ever been able to achieve before—written, alone, a new chapter in the history of civilization. Yet, in a sense his work was complementary to that of Schliemann. He built on foundations which Schliemann had laid; and for all their many differences in character and temperament, they were in three ways alike. Both were rich men. Both were egotists of genius, accustomed to getting their own way and using their wealth to achieve great ends. And both became archaeologists in middle-age,* after successful careers in other fields. As the plane droned on over the sea I looked through my notes and began to recall what I knew of Evans's career.

* Although Evans had been keenly interested in archaeology since his early youth he did not excavate on a large scale until he dug at Knossos.

100

Arthur Evans was born in 1851, the year in which twenty-nine-year-old Heinrich Schliemann was buying gold-dust from the 'forty-niners' of California. The child grew up near the sedate little town of Hemel Hempstead in Hertfordshire, at a place called Nash Mills. Here stood the long-established paper-manufacturing work of John Dickinson & Company. John Evans, Arthur's father, had married his cousin Harriet Ann Dickinson, whose father, John Dickinson, was then head of the firm.

The Evans and the Dickinson families were closely linked by marriage, and both had produced a number of distinguished scholars; the tradition of learning in the family was strong. Arthur's great-grandfather, Lewis Evans, had been a member of the Royal Society; so had his great-uncle, John Dickinson. His own father, John Evans, was a distinguished geologist, antiquary and collector, Fellow and Treasurer of the Royal Society, and, to quote Sir John Myres, 'a leading member of that group of men—including Lubbock, Tylor, Francis Galton, and Pitt-Rivers—who established the new studies of anthropology and prehistoric archaeology on a scientific basis in this country.'

Arthur grew up in an atmosphere heavy with Victorian scholarship. In his father's study at Nash Mills were cases of flint and bronze implements; his father's scholarly friends met often in the comfortably ugly house beside the river, to talk and discuss and prepare their papers for presentation to the learned societies. In the summer Arthur and his two brothers, Lewis and Norman, went on excursions with their father, flint-collecting in Britain or France. Of the three brothers, Arthur had more in common with Lewis than with Norman, who was gay, irresponsible and charming, and who eventually quarrelled with his father and went for a time to America. But both Lewis and Arthur inherited their father's scholarly interests, and early in life Arthur acquired the habit of collecting. Coins especially fascinated him, and in this study he was helped, to some degree, by a physical handicap. In *Time and Chance*, Dr Joan Evans's sensitive portrayal of her half-brother, occurs this passage:

Evans was extremely short-sighted, and a reluctant wearer of glasses. Without them, he could see small things held a few inches from in eyes in extraordinary detail, while everything else was a vague blur. *Consequently the details he saw with microscopic exactitude, undistracted by the outside world, had a greater significance for him than for other men.'* (Our italics.)

It was this seeming handicap of short sight which eventually led Arthur Evans to Crete, and enabled him to reveal and interpret a civilization as highly developed as that of Egypt. Evans was able to do this because of his minute, almost microscopic vision of the tiny Cretan bead-seals and signet-rings, the study of which brought him at last to the Palace of Minos. But that comes later in the story.

It would be a mistake, however, to imagine the young Evans as a timid, myopic youngster, interested only in anthropology and numismatics. True, he was short in stature and near-sighted, and at Harrow he took no interest in games (he lampooned the 'hearties' in his own satirical magazine—*The Pen-Viper*—which was suppressed after publication of the first number). But he had a wiry, energetic frame, swam and rode well, and enjoyed strong physical effort provided it did not take the form of organized games, which bored him. He loved travel—especially 'travelling rough'—and throughout his youth and early middle age delighted in long, adventurous journeys, mainly on foot or on horseback, in the more primitive parts of eastern Europe. He had courage, obstinacy, a hot temper, and a determined will.

At Harrow he tied with Frank Balfour for the Natural History Prize, for which Huxley was assessor. At Oxford, where he was a member of Brasenose College, he read history, and varied his Long Vacations between adventurous trips to eastern Europe and periods of intensive study in—of all places—Broadway Tower, in Worcestershire. This extraordinary 'Folly' of one of the eighteenth-century Earls of Coventry stands on the north-western fringe of the Cotswold Hills, overlooking seven counties. Arthur shared the upper part of the Tower with a friend, while the caretaker and his wife, who lived below, looked after the two young men.

It is typical of Evans that, recognizing how similar was his father's mind to his own, he set about being as different from him as possible. They were both antiquarians, and they were both collectors. But as he grew older, Arthur's antiquarian interests diverged boldly from those of his father, and when in later life old John Evans left him his enormous and bulky collection of Stone Age implements and weapons, the younger man was more embarrassed than grateful. His chief interest at the time was in the Balkan countries, an interest which grew into an ardent passion after his first visit to Bosnia and Herzgovina* in 1871.

It is not an exaggeration to say that Arthur Evans fell in love with the South Slav countries. The landscape, especially the glorious Dalmatian coast, the architecture—the fascinating mixture of cultures—Roman, Byzantine, Venetian, Moslem—above all, the tough, liberty-loving people, all took his young heart. At this period Bosnia and Herzgovina were under the heavy, brutal hand of Turkey. There were Balkan insurrectionary movements, bloody repressions, lootings, burnings, tortures—flights of refugees—the same sickening pattern with which our own age has made us familiar. But to young liberal intellectuals of Evans's type such outrages were a challenge to action. Arthur (he was then twenty) became a convinced Liberal, a follower of Gladstone—whom his Conservative father detested—and a champion of the oppressed minorities of eastern Europe. He signalized his arrival in Paris by buying a magnificent black cloak lined with scarlet silk, but as the smoke of the Franco-Prussian War had hardly blown away, he took the advice of a friendly *douanier*, who warned him that if he wore it he might be shot as a spy. He put the cloak away; but it came in useful later.

In the following year he spent his vacation mountaineering in Roumania with his brother Norman, and from there moved into Bulgaria. Next year, 1873, he toured some of the Scandinavian

---

* Incorporated after the First World War into the new state of Yugoslavia.

102

countries—Sweden, Finland, and Lapland. He was not impressed, because, as Joan Evans comments:

To feel at home in strangeness he needed to find there a complex civilization, and a sense of the historic past. In Lapland no ghosts walked. . .

—though perhaps it would be fairer to say that they were not ghosts with whom Arthur Evans felt any sympathy.

Eighteen-seventy-four saw him back in his lofty eyrie in Broadway Tower, looking down on the rich summer wealth of the Vale of Evesham, and working hard for his Finals. Next year he obtained a First in Modern History, after which he went to Göttingen for a further year's study, before applying himself to the problem of earning a living. He had no interest in paper-making; an academic career seemed the only alternative. He tried for vacant Fellowships at Magdalen and All Souls, but failed to get either, partly, perhaps, because his intransigent nature and unpopular opinions were not acceptable to the more conservative elements of Oxford society. For by this time Arthur Evans was developing into an *enfant terrible*, steeped in Balkan politics.

He had returned to Bosnia with his brother Lewis. At Brood they had both been arrested as Russian spies, a situation in which Arthur's pugnacity did not help matters. He was in Bosnia during the insurrection of 1875; he was in Sarajevo when Herzgovina revolted against Turkey. Both Moslem and Christian insurgents liked him and treated him well, but his letters home were full of biting criticism of the British Government's lukewarm attitude to the cause of Balkan freedom. It was not unnatural that British and other European statesmen were reluctant to jeopardize the peace of Europe for the sake of the oppressed peoples of Bosnia and Herzgovina, however heroic and deserving. But the young firebrand who had lived among these peoples, seen their sufferings and identified himself passionately with them, had no patience with the subtleties of Great Power diplomacy.

He produced a book on Bosnia and Herzgovina, sent a copy to Gladstone (who acknowledged it) and was delighted when the G.O.M. quoted his evidence on Turkish atrocities. Next year, 1877, the Great Powers again shuffled the cards and Evans's unhappy Bosnians found their country occupied by Austria. C. P. Scott, the great editor of the *Manchester Guardian*—pro-Gladstone and anti-Turk—appointed Arthur as Special Correspondent in the Balkans, based on Ragusa. This was a job after the young man's heart. He set off enthusiastically with a sum of money and goods for the refugees, contributed by British sympathizers.

The next few years were the peak years of Evans's youth, which should be read in full in Joan Evans's *Time and Chance*. Here we have only time for the highlights. We catch glimpses of Arthur exploring, at some personal risk, the country occupied by the insurgents; plunging depths of sordid horror in the infested refugee-camps; seeking out and interviewing Desptovitch, the insurgent leader, in his stronghold; swimming a flooded river, naked, with notebook and pencils stuck in his hat; wearing his red-lined cloak inside out when visiting a Moslem stronghold (trying to look as Oriental as possible) and sending back dispatch after brilliant dispatch to his delighted editor. Later these 'Letters to the *Manchester Guardian*' were published as a book.

Nevertheless, in the midst of his political and journalistic activities, he found time to excavate Roman buildings, explore medieval castles, copy out old Bosnian inscriptions and to add, as a postscript to an adventure-packed letter home, 'tell Pa I've got a new flat celt.' Archaeology and numismatics still retained their hold upon him. After his adventures in the hinterland he returned to Ragusa more in love with the Balkans than ever. He soon became a familiar, eccentric figure in that lovely city. Because of his short sight he carried throughout his life a stout walking-stick, to which his family gave the name 'Prodger'. Ragusans soon became familiar with Evans and Prodger—the 'mad Englishman with the walking-stick' who was believed to carry with him a bag of gold. . . .

Then began a personal conflict between the young journalist and Holmes, the British Consul at Sarajevo, who advised his Government not to accept stories of Turkish atrocities. Evans went out to get evidence—it was on one of these dangerous journeys that he swam an icy river, swollen with rain and melting snow, to visit an insurgent outpost. Soon the *Guardian* began to receive fully-documented evidence of burned-out villages, and lists of victims' names; evidence which even the British Consul could not discredit. Evans won his battle.

Then war broke out between the Turks and Montenegro. Again the young correspondent went out on his journeys, sometimes on foot, sometimes on horseback, always returning with vivid dispatches. While in the Montenegrin highlands covering this story Evans heard that an old Oxford friend, Freeman, the historian, was visiting Ragusa for a short time with his two daughters. Arthur greatly admired Freeman, who had taken a leading part in organizing Balkan relief in England. In his anxiety to get to Ragusa before the Freemans left he rode non-stop for seven hours, just missed the steamer at a vital ferry, took a small boat and rowed himself across the sea-channel, took a horse on the other side and rode all through the next day to reach Ragusa.

'He has acquired,' wrote Evans's sister about this time, 'a slightly *insurgent* expression.' . . . Margaret Freeman, who had not seen the young scholar since she knew him several years earlier in Oxford, met a lithe, active, bronzed young man—'not,' wrote his sister cautiously, 'without charm'. Margaret fell in love with him, and in February, 1878, when both were back in England, they became engaged. Characteristically (Margaret was also a scholar) the two celebrated their engagement by going to see the exhibition of antiquities from Troy, brought to London by Dr Heinrich Schliemann.

We were about half-way between Athens and Crete. Our aircraft rumbled drowsily on above the wintry blue of the Aegean. A tiny ship drew a broadening line of white across the misted, sunlit water. Schliemann, like Homer, had travelled to Crete in a ship. But Evans— had Evans flown? I turned in my seat to ask Piet de Jong.

'Oh yes, he liked flying. He used to fly regularly even as far back as the 'twenties, when flying wasn't as safe and as commonplace as it is now. He'd try anything new——'

'And in any case sea travel always made him horribly ill,' added Effie, 'so that a long sea-trip was agony for him. But flying never upset him.'

I showed them the passage in my notes describing Evans's famous walking-stick—Prodger. They both smiled at the recollection.

'That stick of his,' laughed Piet, 'it was a part of him. It was like a staff of office—you just can't imagine Sir Arthur without it. I tell you,' he went on, leaning forward to emphasize his point, 'I've been walking down Piccadilly with Sir Arthur in the middle of the day, when the place was crammed with cars—and he's seen a friend on the other side of the road—or a window with something which interested him, and, by gum, off he's gone, slap-bang into the middle of the traffic, waving that darned stick over his head and *expecting* the cars to give way to him! And they did, too.'

'Just as if he was in Herakleion,' added Effie.

'He was something of an autocrat?' I asked.

'Call him that if you like. . . . No, not really. But he was a kind of benevolent despot, a Grand Seigneur—some of the Cretans were afraid of him. But he loved Crete.'

'Of course,' Piet went on, 'we only knew him well in later life, when he was rich and established, and settled in his ways. But even as a young man I think he must have had an iron will. And he *loved* a fight. Look at the way he fought the Austrians on behalf of his beloved Bosnians—until he was deported. And then what does he do but go home and begin another fight—with the University authorities over the Ashmolean Museum. And all that was long before he came to Crete.'

'He was like Schliemann in that way,' added Mrs de Jong. 'They both had successful careers long before they took up excavation.'

She and her husband returned to their books. I looked down for a while, half-hypnotized by the endlessly moving pattern of waves which creased the surface of Homer's 'wine-dark sea'. . . . Then, with an effort, I turned again to my notes, to the world which Arthur Evans knew when he was young.

8 PRELUDE TO CRETE

After his marriage to Margaret Freeman in 1878, Arthur took his bride to his beloved Ragusa. They bought a particularly beautiful Venetian house, the *Casa san Lazzaro*, and made their home there. He still continued to act as correspondent for the *Manchester Guardian*, but devoted himself principally to the history, antiquities and politics of the Southern Slav people and their countries.

Meanwhile he continued to archaeologize. We see him excavating burial mounds, buying Greek and Roman coins, studying Dalmatian history, and rhapsodizing, in lyrical letters to his family, over the superb Venetian buildings of Ragusa, and the Illyrian landscape. But Margaret, though as devoted to him as he was to her, could not accommodate herself to Ragusa. She had no taste for the picturesque, and dirt worried her. The climate, the strange food, the flies, fleas and mosquitoes, all distressed her until eventually her health broke down. And there were other troubles. In 1880 she returned home to undergo an operation, in the hope that it would enable her to bear children; in this it was not successful.

In the following year a fresh insurrection broke out against the Austrians. Immediately Evans left for the insurgent citadel at Crivoscia, seat of the rebellion, and soon readers of the *Manchester Guardian* were again reading dispatches from his brilliant pen, in which every Austrian reverse was delightedly acclaimed.

It was no secret that Evans and his English friends, passionately believing in the insurrectionary movement, were hoping for a rising of all the Slav peoples. This was too much for the Austrian authorities at Ragusa. Evans became a marked man. His house, his wife, his servants, were watched, and when it became evident (for he had little skill in subterfuge) that meetings were taking place at the *Casa san Lazzaro* between people known to be sympathetic to the insurgents, Evans and his wife were given notice to quit. When he took no action he was eventually arrested and lodged in Ragusa gaol. On April 23rd, 1881, he was examined, found guilty, released and immediately expelled, with his wife. They arrived back in England to be met by a relieved and delighted family. One of them wrote:

Arthur has been capering in and out of the house all day, bearing Prodger and visiting the raspberries.

Another letter says:

He has had a lesson which will keep him at home—I hope.

But any hope which the more timid members of the family

entertained, that Arthur would at last 'settle down,' were soon dashed. Restless, dissatisfied, he longed to go abroad again, knowing that his heart was in Ragusa, but for the time being he knew he must find a niche in academic Oxford.

But travel, study, and a questing, adventurous mind had made Arthur Evans difficult to accommodate in a conventional university professorship. He was an archaeologist but he had no sympathy with the way archaeology was taught at Oxford, nor with the 'classical' outlook of such men as Jowett, the Vice-Chancellor. Thus, as he wrote gloomily to his friend Freeman, who shared his views:

> ... there is going to be established a Professorship of Archaeology, and I have been strongly advised to stand. I do not think I shall, unless I see any real prospect of getting it; and to say the truth I see very little. To begin with, it is to be called the Professorship of Classical Archaeology, and I understand that the Electors, including Jowett and Newton of the British Museum (who prevented me from getting the Archaeological Travelling Studentship of old) regard 'archaeology' as ending with the Christian Era. Anyhow, to confine a professorship of archaeology to classical times seems to me as reasonable as to create a chair of 'Insular Geography' or 'Mezozoic Geology'. . . .

Freeman, in a sympathetic reply to this letter, advised him to apply, while warning him that 'they will have some narrow Balliol fool, suspending all sound learning at the end of his crooked nose, to represent self-satisfied ignorance against you, but I would go in just to tell them a thing or two.'

The chair eventually went to Percy Gardner, a 'classical' archaeologist after Newton's own heart.

At the end of April 1883, Arthur and Margaret set off on a tour of Greece. It was during this trip that they called on the Schliemanns, as described in an earlier chapter. Evans was fascinated by the Mycenaean gems, arms and ornaments found in the shaft-graves, but not because he shared the German's view that they were Homeric. To the Englishman they seemed far older. There was something in their style—neither Hellenic, or Egyptian, nor Oriental—to which his fastidious mind immediately responded. He spent hours examining them, while Margaret talked to Sophia Schliemann.

For Arthur Evans, as will have been noticed in his comments on the university authorities, refused to make the conventional obeisance to 'classical' Greek art. He detested the type of narrow academic mind, fundamentally unaesthetic, which would not admit of other standards. His mind was free-ranging, individual, and sensitive, and to him the so-called 'Mycenaean' art—vigorous yet controlled, aristocratic in spirit, yet humane—had a far greater appeal. It satisfied yet puzzled him. Where had it originated? To what culture or group of cultures was it related? This problem seemed to his sophisticated intelligence far more important than old Heinrich's endeavours to relate Mycenaean art to the world of Homer. It was a problem to which he was to return again and again during the coming years, though more than a decade was to pass before he discovered the answer.

He visited Tiryns and Mycenae—scene of Schliemann's triumphs, and was fascinated—especially by the Lion Gate with its headless lions supporting that strange central column—so different from Greek 'classical' architecture. Where had it originated—at Mycenae? In Greece? Or elsewhere? Evans wondered....

Returning to Oxford the Evanses set up house in Broad Street, enlivening the sombre Victorian rooms with bright Dalmatian fabrics which reminded them of the sunlight and colour of Ragusa....

Next year Arthur obtained a university appointment at last—but one which seemed, at first sight, to hold little promise for his ardent, impetuous spirit.

He became, at the age of thirty-three, Curator of the Ashmolean Museum. In 1884 this Museum, founded in the seventeenth century by Elias Ashmole, had been so neglected, abused and mutilated by later generations that it had almost ceased to have any practical value. In fact, its condition accurately reflected the indifference with which archaeology was regarded by Vice-Chancellor Jowett and other high officers of the University. 'After long neglect,' writes Sir John Myres, 'stripped of its coins and manuscripts by the Bodleian, and its natural history collections for the New University Museum; it was embarrassed with architectural casts collected by the "Oxford Society for the study of Gothic Architecture"; there was disorder and neglect within; it was enclosed by other buildings which precluded enlargement; and it had a rival in the University Galleries since Ruskin's tenure of the Slade Chair of Fine Art.'

But to Arthur Evans all this was a challenge. He set about, in his combative spirit, to fight for the Ashmolean as a revived centre of archaeological studies. The Bodleian had taken the coins, had they? Right, then they must hand them back. Old Tradescant's gallery had been gutted and turned into an Examination Room, had it? Then, he, Arthur Evans, would restore it to its original function; not only that, but he knew a distinguished collector of Renaissance art, Drury

The Ashmolean Museum

Fortnum, who was only waiting to hand over his magnificent collection to the University—if suitable accommodation was provided for it. And what could be more suitable than the Tradescant Gallery?

He found the death-mask of old Tradescant rolling about in the dust of the Ashmolean's cellar, together with that of Bethlen Gabor. He restored them both to a place of honour. Finally, he drew up detailed plans for a revived and glorified Ashmolean, improved, modernized, restored. In high spirits he went to Jowett to obtain his approval of the plans. But the Vice-Chancellor asked to be excused. He was very busy. He had not time to look at the plans because he was about to leave Oxford for a month. In any case, he pointed out, the University could not afford to spend money on the Ashmolean at present because much was needed for the new professorships. Arthur returned to the house in Broad Street, fuming.

The family held its breath. There was going to be a fight, and Arthur dearly loved a fight. 'I can see him,' wrote a relative, 'snuffing up the tainted breeze and pawing like a war-horse. . . .'

The struggle was long and hard. Evans, reluctantly compelled to become a politician, disciplined himself to wait, manoeuvre and bargain. Drury Fortnum again offered his collection to Oxford with a handsome endowment, provided the University would consider the creation of a Central Museum of Art and Archaeology *under the Keeper of the Ashmolean*. The governing body of the Museum was easily won over, but Jowett held out until at last, finding himself in a minority of one, he was forced to agree. Evans's report was adopted. He celebrated the occasion by giving a party for two hundred guests in the limelit Upper Gallery of the Museum.

Even then he had to struggle for years to obtain adequate funds for the revived and reconstituted Ashmolean. But university politics and administration bored him, and he sought relief, whenever possible, in archaeological research (at Aylesford he dug a late Celtic urnfield) and in foreign travel with his wife. They visited the Crimea, Yalta, Kertch, Batum, Tiflis, Greece and Bulgaria, on the frontier of which they were arrested on suspicion of being spies, and Margaret wrote, 'I don't know what I should have done without my "bug-puzzler". . . . In two nights we killed 221 plus 118 plus 90 equals 429. . . .' This was in the year 1890. One wonders if the young girl students of today—trousered or not—would equal Margaret's equanimity, if faced with a similar situation.

Arthur's other interest was in numismatics—the study of ancient coins—in which he brought imagination to bear on what might appear to the layman to be an arid study. For example, his recognition, on tiny Sicilian coins, of artists' signatures so small that only his microscopic sight could detect them, enabled him to establish a chronological test of styles and of political relations between Sicilian cities. It was this feeling for *style*, in all its subtle ramifications, which enabled him, in later life, to interpret the details of Minoan civilization as revealed in the miniature seals of Crete.

'It is,' writes Sir John Myres, 'a peculiarity of Ashmole's Keepership that its conditions of residence are so liberal that travel is possible and presumed; on the other hand the Keeper is expected to give occasional public lectures on the progress of studies which concern the Museum. For a man of Evans's qualifications and temperament it was the ideal post, and it is to the years of his Keepership that the greater part of his learned output belongs. But between the earlier and later activities 1894 marks a crisis; for it was early in that year that he first visited Crete.'

While gathering material for this book I had the good fortune and privilege to meet Sir John Myres—now in his eighties—in Oxford, and was able to settle a question which had puzzled me for some time; how Sir Arthur Evans, whose background was mainly in the Balkan countries and whose principal interest lay in numismatics, came to be so closely associated with Crete.

'For more than a generation,' Sir John told me, 'Continental opinion had attributed most of the characteristic features of Greek civilization to Egyptian and Mesopotamian influences. But in about 1890 there was a reaction, and in 1893 Solomon Reinach brought out a book called *Le Mirage Oriental* which made a formal challenge to all Orientalizing theories. Reinach contended that the West had, throughout, shown a large measure of originality and genius of its own. Evans, as shown from his studies in Celtic archaeology which he had just completed, was greatly impressed with this alternative point of view.'

'At that time,' Sir John went on, 'I was still an undergraduate, while Evans was usually travelling abroad, and I didn't actually meet him until I had finished my examinations. I first met him at a party in North Oxford. We had a little talk, and I told him of my project of going to Greece and doing some work on prehistoric civilization there.

'He encouraged me to go ahead, and said that he would see me when I came back. And in July and August, 1892, I went to Crete, travelling over a good part of the west of the island.'

Sitting with Sir John in his study in his quiet, old-fashioned house near the Woodstock Road, watching his fine, white-bearded face (like an old Norse king), I could not help thinking of the 'young black-bearded Ulysses' with whom Arthur Evans, only ten years older himself, grubbed for Mycenaean fragments beneath the 'Pelasgian' wall of the Athenian Acropolis in 1892. Of the young Myres, Evans wrote home to his wife:

I am glad to find Myres here, who is at once Craven Scholar *and* Burdett Coutts, and is combining geology and archaeology in a useful way. We worked at Mycenaean rings, grubbed under the 'Pelasgian' wall of the Acropolis, picked up fragments of pre-Mycenaean vases. Heard Dörpfeld lecture on his discovery of the fountain of Enneakrounos; but he has been finding it at different spots for months....

Tempora mutantur . . . Schliemann's brilliant assistant was no longer the power he had been.

In the following year Margaret died. Her health had never recovered completely after her breakdown at Ragusa. Typically, she was accompanying her husband on one of his Mediterranean journeys. It was at Alassio that she was suddenly seized with violent spasms of pain and died within a few hours, holding Arthur's hand.

'I do not think anyone can ever know what Margaret has been to me,' he wrote to his father. 'All seems very dark, and without consolation. . . . I will try to call up her brave, practical spirit, but one must have time to recover strength.'

But 1893, a tragic year for Arthur Evans, was also a turning-point in his life. His stay in Athens in February and March had confirmed his interest in Mycenaean art. Working over the tiny objects from Schliemann's discoveries at Mycenae and Tiryns, he had an intuition of discovery.

In that year, while searching among the trays of the antiquity dealers in Shoe Lane, Athens, he and Myres came across small three- and four-sided stones drilled along the axis, engraved with symbols which seemed to belong to some *hieroglyphic* system. Of course, most antiquarians were, by this time, familiar with Egyptian *hieroglyphic* writing, but that such a system had once existed in Europe seemed inconceivable. Yet here, in these tiny seals and signet rings, seen under Evans's intense, microscopic gaze, there appeared to be tiny symbols which *might* represent writing. Evans asked the dealer where these seals came from.

'From Crete,' he was told.

He pondered for a long time on this problem. He had already considered Crete, which, as a convenient stepping-stone, practically equidistant from Europe, Asia and Egypt, might have provided a stage in the diffusion of a hieroglyphic script. He had considered the possibility that some of the Ancient Egyptian reliefs depicting invaders of the Nile Valley might represent among them peoples of the Aegean islands. He had already met the gentle, lovable Italian archaeologist Frederico Halbherr, who had begun to excavate Cretan sites a year before. Then there was Stillman, an American journalist, and Joubin, of the French School at Athens. They also had wished to dig in Crete but had been prevented by the Turkish authorities. Yet, with care and patience, and the discreet use of cash, something might be accomplished. . . .

In the spring of 1894 Arthur Evans set foot in Crete for the first time.

From the moment he landed at Herakleion he felt at home. At Ragusa he had loved Venetian architecture. Here, at Herakleion, the Lion of St Mark was carved on the battlements of the great Venetian wall which surrounded the city. There were noble Venetian buildings, and, since Crete was still under Turkish rule, mosques stood side-by-side with Christian churches. There was a blending of European and Oriental races. There was a dramatic landscape of jagged limestone peaks, precipitous ravines, valleys of an idyllic greenness of spring, beaches of white sand gleaming through a sea of deep, translucent blue. And above all, there was an all-pervading, impermeable sense of history. Cretans, Hellenes, Romans, Franks, Venetians, Turks—all had left their mark on the island.

Homer had known it. Here was the legendary home of King Minos and his daughter, the Princess Ariadne, who gave to the hero Theseus the precious thread which guided him to her arms after he had slain the

Minotaur. Zeus, King of Gods, had been born here. On the north of the island rose snow-capped Mount Ida, where, it was said, one could still find the sacred cave in which he was born. And immediately behind the port of Herakleion, on the north, lay Mount Jukta, legendary tomb of the god. Why, said the inhabitants, if you only looked at the mountain from a certain angle and in a certain light, you could see the recumbent profile of Zeus himself!

Like Schliemann, Evans made his way to the legendary site of Knossos, a few miles from Herakleion. Here, surely, thought Evans, he might find further examples of his bead-seal 'pictographs'—and much more. Perhaps he might find engraved tablets like the Egyptian 'Rosetta Stone', with a bilingual inscription which might give the clue to the primitive Cretan language.

A Cretan gentleman, appropriately named Minos, had already dug trenches at Knossos and revealed massive walls, and a store of huge *pithoi* (stone jars). This was more than enough to whet Evans's appetite. Boldly announcing that he was acting on behalf of the 'Cretan Exploration Fund' (at that time non-existent) he acquired a share of the site from the local Moslem landowner. This was not much use to him at all, except for the vital fact that, under Ottoman law, it gave him a veto on excavation by anyone else. Five years later, when the Turkish forces left Crete, and Prince George of Greece became High Commissioner of the Powers—Great Britain, France, Italy and Russia—Evans returned, acquired the freehold of the remainder of the site, and prepared to dig. This time the Cretan Exploration Fund actually came into existence, with Prince George of Greece as patron; 'the British School of Archaeology at Athens was also associated with the work,' writes Myres, 'in the person of its Director, D. G. Hogarth, whose experience of excavation on a large scale was invaluable; subscriptions came in, and digging began in the winter.'

Even before the first spade was thrust in the soil of Knossos, Evans was already convinced that in Crete, whose landscape, traditions and people had won his heart, he would find the clue to that earlier, pre-Hellenic world to which Schliemann's finds at Mycenae had pointed the way. In the years before he began to dig he returned to Crete again and again, exploring, alone and with his friend Myres, the length and breadth of the island. On one occasion, Sir John told me, they climbed up on to the Lasithi highlands, and explored the great sanctuary cave of Zeus at Psychro. 'From there,' he went on, 'we travelled along a great Minoan prehistoric road, with embankments, bridges, and forts, and came back by another route, visiting many villages, and inquiring everywhere for engraved seal-stones. These were greatly valued by the Cretan women as charms when they were nursing their babies—they called them "milk-stones".'

These 'milk-stones'—of which many fine examples can be seen today in the Ashmolean Museum, are lens-shaped, usually round, but sometimes oval, and are perforated from side to side for suspension from a thread. The ancient Cretan people wore them either round their necks, or on their wrists, like the modern identity bracelet. And that, in fact, appears to have been their function—the ancient

Examples of milkstones, and their impressions

equivalent of an identity card. Each was engraved with a design, usually pictorial, but often with hieroglyphic signs. They were the owner's badge, which he could put on his property as a mark or seal; these tiny seals, with their miniature scenes, fascinated Evans, and his search for them led him into the remotest parts of the island; and everywhere he found signs of a once-flourishing civilization, remains of palaces and cities, many of them in the wildest and most inaccessible places. But hardly anywhere did he find evidence of Hellenic or 'classical' remains. He was able to write, even before he dug at Knossos:

The great days of Crete were those of which we still find a reflection in the Homeric poems—the period of Mycenaean culture, to which here at least we would fain attach the name 'Minoan' ... (after Minos). Nothing more continually strikes the archaeological explorer of its ancient remains than the comparative paucity and unimportance of the relics of the historic period. ... The golden age of Crete lies far beyond the limits of the historical period; its culture not only displays within the three seas a uniformity never afterwards attained, but it is practically identical with that of the Peloponnese and a large part of the Aegean world.

In March, 1899, Evans returned to Crete in the middle of one of the worst storms in human memory. He brought with him D. G. Hogarth, who was eleven years younger than himself, but much more experienced in the technique of excavation, and Duncan Mackenzie, a soft-spoken Scotsman with 'a brush of red hair, an uncertain temper, a great command of languages and great experience in keeping the

113

records of an excavation.' Losing no time, they recruited Cretan workmen and set them to work digging in the mound of Kephala at Knossos.

Almost at once a great labyrinth of buildings was revealed. By March 27th Arthur Evans was able to note in his diary: 'The extraordinary phenomenon—*nothing Greek—nothing Roman*—perhaps one single fragment of late black varnished ware among tens of thousands. Even Geometrical (seventh century BC) pottery fails us—though as *tholoi* (tombs) found near the central road show, a flourishing Knossos existed lower down. . . . *Nay, its great period goes at least well back to the pre-Mycenaean period.*'

Evans had come to decipher a system of writing, but before a month had passed he knew that he had discovered a civilization.

D.G. Hogarth with Sir Arthur Evans

Evans and Mackenzie
watching workmen at the south
dump

9 ISLAND OF LEGEND

The ancient cave of Eileithyia is a black hole in the bare hillside a few miles east of Herakleion. Though quite near the road which twists up into the hills, the low, beetling entrance to the cave is half-hidden by a fig-tree, so that without our driver's help I doubt if we should have found it.

The three of us, the de Jongs and myself, sat on the slope above the cave, looking down the bracken-covered slopes to where the waves broke on the beach, far below. So calm was the afternoon that their murmur reached us, like a soft whisper; so clear the atmosphere that the islet of Dia—a nymph, favoured by Zeus, whom angry Hera had turned into a sea-monster—looked only a stone's throw from the height where we sat.

A small river, the Amnissus, came in from a side valley and emptied itself unobtrusively into the Aegean. Thousands of years ago there had been a port at its mouth, which Odysseus had known—'he put in at Amnissus, where the cave of Eileithyia is'—but it had silted up long ago, and Herakleion had long since taken its place as the principal harbour of northern Crete. But the sacred cave of the nymph Eileithyia—protector of women in childbirth—was still there, and when Piet and I explored its depths with a bundle of burning brushwood, a colony of bats squeaked and fluttered in the dark crevices of the roof. The last time I had seen the creatures in such numbers was inside the Pyramid of Snofru, in Egypt, five years ago. But just so Homer had seen them, some 2,700 years ago, and compared them to the gibbering shades of the slain Suitors whom Hermes drove down to the gloomy halls of Hades:

He roused them up and marshalled them . . . and they obeyed his summons, gibbering like bats that squeak and flutter in the depths of some mysterious cave when one of them has fallen from the rock roof, losing hold of his clustered friends. . . .

Odyssey, Book XXIV.

There are many such sacred caves in the limestone hills of Crete—and they still bear witness to the crowds of pilgrims who came there centuries past. Their rocky floors are littered with broken scraps of pottery—remains of the votive vessels left by the worshippers. Near the sacred stalagmite—a dwarf piller in the depths of Eileithyia, round which de Jong pointed out to me the remains of a sanctuary wall—there were scores of such potsherds. He picked one up and held it towards the light of the burning brushwood. 'Roman,' he commented—and threw it away. He searched again in the mud of the cave bottom and produced a fragment of a thin-walled goblet such as I had seen at Mycenae.

'Mycenaean,' he said. I put the sherd in my pocket as we scrambled out into the sunlight again.

In such an atmosphere it is easy to slough off the present. The plane from which we had landed an hour or so before, the Greek soldiers at battle-practice near the airport, the jostling, noisy, dusty, friendly shops of ramshackle Herakleion, where Effie had been greeted like an old friend; all these were forgotten, and other memories began to steal

The cave of Eileithyia at Amnissus

in to take their places. The story of the unfortunate Dia brought to mind the other myths and legends which cling to this lovely island, the largest in the Greek archipelago. Crete has been for 3,000 years a meeting-place and a battle-ground of cultures—Minoan, Hellenic, Roman, Frankish, Venetian, Turkish—and yet, lying far, far to the south in the deep, dark sea, almost equidistant from Europe, Asia and Africa, it still keeps its atmosphere of remoteness.

Schliemann, when he dug at Troy and Mycenae, had been guided by an unsophisticated belief in the literal truth of the Homeric poems. His intention to dig in Crete may have been prompted by the same belief, for Homer mentions Crete many times, especially in the *Odyssey*. But Arthur Evans, as we have seen, had been drawn to the island first by scientific curiosity rather than by belief in legend. He had traced to Crete the mysterious hieroglyphic writing—neither Egyptian nor Babylonian—and his ambition was to interpret that writing, and to prove his thesis that 'Throughout what is now the civilized European area there must have once existed systems of picture-writing such as still survive among the more primitive races of mankind.' At the same time he was thoroughly familiar with the stories which Homer and the classic authors had told about Crete, and as these legends have a great bearing on what follows, it is worth while to recall some of them.

The oldest tradition was that of Zeus, the Father-God of the Greeks, who was said to have been born in a cave in southern Crete. Some said this cave was in the central peak of Mount Ida, others that it was on a lower but still majestic easterly mountain, Lasithi, called by the old Cretans, Dicte.

Rhea, wife of Cronos, bore him several daughters—Hestia, Demeter, and 'gold-shod' Hera—but whenever she bore a son the jealous Cronos swallowed the child, with the intent, says the poet Hesiod,

... that no other of the proud sons of Heaven should hold kingly office amongst the deathless gods. For he learned from Earth and starry Heaven that he was destined to be overcome by his own son, strong though he was, through the contriving of the great Zeus.

So, when she came to bear Zeus, Rhea had to devise

some plan ... that the birth of her dear child might be concealed. ... So they sent her to Lyctus, to the rich land of Crete, when she was ready to bear great Zeus, the youngest of her children.

And Hesiod goes on to tell how Earth

took him in her arms and hid him in a remote cave beneath the secret places of holy earth on thick-wooded Mount Aegeum.

To Cronos Earth gave a stone which, mistaking it for his new-born son, the god

thrust down into his belly; wretch! he did not know that in place of the stone his son was left behind, unconquered and untroubled. ...

It was thus, said the Greeks, that Zeus was able to survive, to overcome his father and reign as King of Gods.

Another long-established tradition concerned Minos, King of Crete, said to have been 'the son of Zeus', or, in another version, his friend and chosen companion. Minos, it was said, was a mighty lawgiver and founder of the first great naval power in the Mediterranean. There were no records or monuments to support such a belief, but the spoken tradition was strong, and accepted, as we have seen, by historians such as Thucydides.

The traditions relating to Minos are various, and in some ways conflicting. All agree that he controlled a mighty fleet which ruled the Eastern Mediterranean. In some he was respected as a great lawgiver.

118

But there were also traditional memories of Minos the Tyrant, embodied in that most imperishable of legends, the story of Theseus and the Minotaur. The legend is worth quoting, as related by Apollodorus.

King Minos had, through conquest, become overlord of Athens and as tribute demanded each year twelve noble Athenian youths and maidens whom he could sacrifice to the Minotaur. This was the monstrous progeny of Minos's wife Pasiphae, a nymphomaniac whom only a bull could satisfy. It was kept by Minos in a Labyrinth—designed by his chief craftsman, Daedalus, beneath his great Palace at Knossos. So tortuous was this maze, with its many twisting passages, blind alleys and false turnings, that no man, having once entered, could ever hope to find his way out again unaided. And within it lurked the Minotaur, waiting to devour its victims. Every year, according to the legend, twelve of the flower of Athenian youth, men and maidens, met their death in this way.

Then came the year when the hero Theseus, son of old Aegeus, lord of Athens, was numbered among those to be sent to Crete—but, writes Apollodorus:

some affirm . . . he offered himself voluntarily. And as the ship had a black sail, Aegeus, (the father) charged his son, if he returned alive, to spread white sails on the ship. And when he came to Crete, Ariadne, daughter of Minos, having falling in love with him, offered to help him if he would agree to carry her away to Athens and have her to wife. Theseus having agreed on oath to do so, she besought Daedalus to disclose the way out of the Labyrinth.

Daedalus the Smith, another great figure of legend, was a combination of artist, craftsman and engineer whom Minos employed as a kind of Master of the King's Works. It was Daedalus who had made for Pasiphae the dummy cow within which she hid herself when she wished to allure the bull.

What methods the 'brown-haired Ariadne' used to persuade the ingenious smith to give her his help are not mentioned, though they may be imagined. At any rate her wiles were successful, for, says Apollodorus:

at his suggestion she gave Theseus a clue [thread] when he went in. Theseus fastened it to the door, and, drawing it after him, entered in. And after having found the Minotaur in the last part of the Labyrinth, he killed him by smiting him with his fists; and, drawing the clue after him made his way out again. And by night he arrived with Ariadne and the children [presumably by this the writer means the rest of the twelve Athenian men and girls destined for sacrifice] at Naxos. There Dionysus fell in love with Ariadne and carried her off; and having brought her to Lemnos he enjoyed her, and begot Thoas, Staphylus, Oenopion and Peparthus.

In his grief on account of Ariadne, continues the poet, Theseus forgot to spread the white sails on his ship when he stood for port; and Aegeus (his father) seeing from the Acropolis the ship with a black sail, supposed that Theseus had perished; so he cast himself down and died. . . .

But that was not the end of the story. King Minos, when he learned at the connivance of Daedalus in his daughter's escape, imprisoned the guilty engineer, with his son Icarus, in the Labyrinth. Then followed the invention of the first flying machine, 3,000 years before Leonardo da Vinci. . . .

Daedalus constructed wings for himself and his son, and enjoined his son, when he took flight, neither to fly high, lest the glue should melt in the sun and the wings should drop off, nor to fly too near the sea, lest the pinions should be detached by the damp. But the infatuated Icarus, disregarding his father's instructions, soared ever higher, till, the glue melting, he fell into the sea called after him Icarian, and perished. . . .

Daedalus, a practical mechanic, made no such mistake. He had suffered enough already through his indulgence towards the King's dark-haired daughter and her handsome though none too intelligent Athenian wooer. He flew on, unscathed, to the court of King Cocalus, in Sicily. But, says Apollodorus:

Minos pursued Daedalus, and in every country he searched he carried a spiral shell and promised to give a great reward to him who should pass a thread through the shell, believing that by that means he should discover Daedalus.

Minos evidently knew human nature. Anyone who has encountered the vanity and self-satisfaction of certain modern scientist-engineers will recognize the cunning with which the King baited his hook.

Having come to Camicus in Sicily, writes Apollodorus, to the court of Cocalus, with whom Daedalus was concealed, he showed the spiral shell. Cocalus (Lord of Sicily) took it, and promised to thread it, and gave it to Daedalus.

Such a challenge was irresistible to Daedalus. But he seems to have a contempt for the lay mind akin to that with which the modern engineering draughtsman regards the glossy young gentleman from the sales department. He knew well that his new lord, Cocalus, would have been as incapable of working out mathematically the curves and convolutions of the shell as was Ariadne's handsome but stupid lover in memorizing the twists and turns of the Labyrinth. So, just as he had provided Theseus with the clue of thread which even he could not misunderstand, so he gave to the King of Sicily a method of threading the shell which was brilliant in its simplicity.

Cocalus took it, and promised to thread it . . . and Daedalus fastened a thread to an ant, and, having bored a hole in the spiral shell, allowed the ant to pass through it. But when Minos found the thread passed through the shell, he perceived that Daedalus was with Cocalus, and at once demanded his surrender. Cocalus promised to surrender him, and made an entertainment for Minos. . . .

And then follows one of the most mysterious records in the chronicle:

but after his bath Minos was undone by the daughters of Cocalus. . . .

But why? and how?

Both history and legend are silent here. Whatever the means of his death, the great King of Crete passes into oblivion, done to death by the young daughters of the King of Sicily. . . . And a legendary chapter in the pre-history of the eastern Mediterranean ends, as mysteriously as it began. . . .

The sun sank behind the headland to our left as we drove back along the rough, twisting road, through Herakleion with its narrow, ancient streets, and out again past the sombre Venetian ramparts to the winding valley-road which leads towards Knossos. It was strange to see that name, 'half as old as Time', attached to one of the ramshackle Cretan buses which rattled past us in a cloud of dust.

The houses were left behind. The valley-sides grew steeper, and a small stream accompanied us on our left, crossed by many old, arched bridges. For several miles the road rose and fell, until, on one of its downward slopes Mrs de Jong pointed to a cluster of houses at the bottom of the hill.

'That,' she said, 'is our village—and these,' pointing to trim ranks of vines which climbed the slopes, 'are our vineyards.'

'My wife means,' interjected her husband, 'that these are the vineyards belonging to the School. The land surrounding the Palace was given by Sir Arthur to the British School of Archaeology at Athens, and we look after it.'

The car stopped in front of a pleasant limewashed cottage behind a stone wall.

'But where is the Palace?' I asked.

'Away to the left, behind those trees,' said Piet. 'You'll see it in the morning.'

'You'll be wanting a bath, I expect,' said his wife. 'Here's Manoli'— greeting a dark-faced, smiling Cretan servant with a flood of Greek. 'He'll show you to the Villa. Your room's all ready for you.'

'Villa?' I asked. 'Is that a hotel?'

'No, no, no,' replied Mrs de Jong. 'The Villa Ariadne is Sir Arthur's old home. He built it in 1912 as a permanent base for his work, and to entertain his friends. He used to spend every spring and summer at the Villa for many years. Then, when he got too old to come out regularly, he handed over the house to the School, as a rest-house for students. This'—indicating the creepered, comfortable cottage—'is our house—we call it the *Taverna*. But you'll be staying at the Villa—up there. Do you see it?'

She indicated a stately façade behind a screen of palms and oleander-trees. A little path wound up the slope between clusters of bougainvillaea. Although I had left England locked in the grip of February frost, here it was already comfortably mild, and I sensed the coming of spring.

'Is anyone else staying there?'

'No,' said Mrs de Jong. 'February is too early for students. You'll have the whole place to yourself. But don't worry—there are no ghosts, or only friendly ones! Look, Piet, what a wonderful *moon*.' She chattered on without pausing for breath, finally calling out to me, 'Dinner's at eight!' as I followed Manoli, through the scented dusk, to the Villa Ariadne.

121

10 A CHALLENGE ACCEPTED

Crete is a long, narrow island much wider from east to west (160 miles) than from north to south (35 miles at its broadest point). The country is ribbed by bare, almost treeless mountains of great magnificence—the highest is 7,882 feet—which runs approximately east and west, in line with the island's longest dimension. But here and there deep gaps break the mountain-chain from north to south. They begin as shallow troughs near the coast, and become progressively steeper as they cut into the mountains. In one of these valleys, at a point near the north coast a few miles from Herakleion (formerly called Candia) lies Knossos.

When Evans began to dig there in the first year of our century he saw before him:

(*a*) a valley, fairly shallow, and running roughly north and south, with the town of Herakleion behind him—to the north;

(*b*) a modern road following the western, i.e. the right-hand side of the valley (looking south);

(*c*) to the east, left of the road, a large, fairly level-topped mound called *Kephala*, falling away steeply on the eastern, i.e. the left-hand side, into a deep gully at the foot of which ran the river Kairatos;

(*d*) ahead, to the south, another steep-sided gully cutting off the mound of Kephala from the valley road to the south, which crossed the gully by a bridge.

Thus one must think of the site of Knossos as roughly a quadrangular mound, bounded on two sides—the east and south—by steep downward slopes, the remaining sides being more or less on a level with the surrounding terrain. It must *not* be imagined as a lofty citadel crowning a steep hill, as at Mycenae. (To all who find topographical description as boring as I do, may I plead that if they grasp the orientation of the site—steep-sided to the south and east, flatter to the west and north—they will find the following chapter more comprehensible and, I hope, enjoyable.)

Virchow, writing of Schliemann's discoveries at Troy thirty years earlier, had stated: 'Here begins a new science'. Now Evans, who at forty-nine was almost of the same age as that of Schliemann when he dug at Troy, was to make another tremendous contribution to that science. Yet when he and his Scots assistant and their original thirty workmen sank the first shaft into the mound, they had only a vague idea of what it might hold. They knew that substantial walls existed at one point—the Cretan amateur, Minos Kalokairinos, had struck them years before. There were also, they knew, some huge jars of baked clay, called *pithoi*—rather like those in which Ali Baba found the Forty Thieves. Apart from these facts there were only myths and legends from the dim beginnings of European history.

Yet almost from the start of the excavations the great mound began to reveal its secrets—not material treasures of gold and precious stones such as Schliemann found at Mycenae—but evidences of a mature, sophisticated art, a skill in engineering and an architecture of such splendour, subtlety and refinement as could only have been produced by a civilization of great age. The style was, in the main, that which had hitherto been called 'Mycenaean' because at Mycenae had been found the first objects of that strange pre-Hellenic style, neither Egyptian nor Oriental—which had so fascinated Evans when Schliemann showed him his treasures. And yet there were differences. There was a suavity of style, an assurance, even a hint of decadence in Cretan art. Above all there was an impression of tremendous age, and of long-continued, uninterrupted development which just did not fit with the stern citadel of Mycenae—that baron's stronghold frowning from its hill-top.

And yet—here at Knossos were the familiar 'Mycenaean' features—the bell-like crinoline skirts of the women depicted on seals and frescoes, even the now famous eight-shaped shield which Schliemann had triumphantly declared to be Homeric. But Homer (between 700-900 BC) now appeared almost modern compared with

Map of Crete

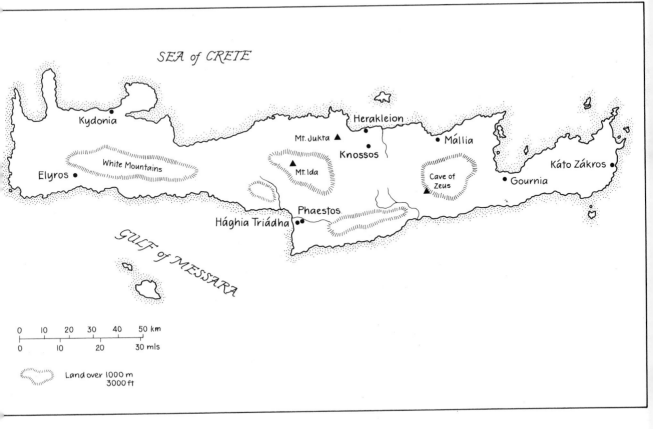

Above left Linear B tablets, as they were found at Knossos

Above right A Linear B tablet

these people! The treasures of the shaft-graves of Mycenae dated from some 1600 BC. Yet it now became increasingly clear that those kings and queens with their golden breastplates and rich jewellery must have come long *after* the builders of the first Palace of Knossos.... Evans and his companions patiently followed Ariadne's thread, but each discovery seemed to bring with it new, unsolved mysteries. The Labyrinth seemed to have no end....

It gradually became clear that the mound of Kephala concealed a great Palace, some six acres in extent—or rather the remains of several Palaces, not neatly stratified one beneath another but to some extent jumbled together, as later builders had utilized some of the buildings of their forefathers, while completely gutting and re-building others. But everything testified to long and comparatively uninterrupted habitation. Human beings had lived continuously on that spot, and on the surrounding hillsides, for more than a score of centuries. Meanwhile Arthur Evans, perhaps at first a little bewildered by the magnitude of his discovery, continued to search for his hieroglyphics, and found them.

We have found, he announced in a letter written at the time, a kind of baked clay bar, rather like a stone chisel in shape, though broken at one end, with script on it and what appear to be numerals. It at once recalled a clay tablet of unknown age that I had copied at Candia, also found at Knossos ... also broken. There is something like cursive writing about these....

Evans had found what he had come to find. More men were engaged, until over one hundred were digging into the mound under the careful direction of Evans, Duncan Mackenzie and a new arrival, Theodore Fyfe, architect of the British School of Archaeology at Athens. Evans was one of the first archaeologists to employ a professional architect always on the site; others usually contented themselves with bringing one in at the end to make plans. But Evans kept a series of first-class architects in constant attendance; first Theodore Fyfe, then Christian Doll, and finally Piet de Jong.

124

Although the architectural revelations of Knossos astonished Evans, his main interest, at first, was in the prehistoric picture-writing which he had come to find. As more of these precious clay tablets came to sight, bearing the same mysterious hieroglyphic writing which he had recognized on the tiny seal-stones, he wrote delightedly to his family:

The great discovery is whole deposits, entire or fragmentary, of clay tablets analogous to the Babylonian but with inscriptions in the prehistoric script of Crete. I must have about seven hundred pieces by now. It is extremely satisfactory, as it is what I came to Crete seven years ago to find, and it is the coping-stone to what I have already put together.

Later, he wrote to his father:

With regard to prehistoric inscriptions, 'the cry is still they come'. I have just struck the largest deposit yet, some hundreds of pieces. . . .

And the Athens correspondent of *The Times* wrote on August 10th, 1900:

. . . the most important discovery is the prehistoric Cretan script, which proves that writing was practised. . . .

This was also Evans's view at first. But, gradually, as the full glory of the Palace was unveiled, he began to realize that whether or not he

Evans, Fyfe and Mackenzie

succeeded in deciphering the mysterious script, there had come to him an opportunity which had never before been granted to one man, the opportunity of writing, almost single-handed, the history of the first two thousand years of European civilization. He accepted the challenge, and was equal to it.

On April 5th came a remarkable discovery—the finding of the first picture of a 'Minoan'—one of the mysterious people who had inhabited the Palace of Knossos more than 1,500 years before Christ. (It was Evans who invented the name Minoan, after Minos, the legendary ruler of Crete). This was a great day for the discoverer, and his diary reveals his excitement.

... Early in the morning the gradual surface uncovering of the Corridor to the left of the 'Megaron' near its south end revealed two large pieces of Mycenaean fresco.... One represented the head and forehead, the other the waist and part of the figure of a female (later recognized to be a male) 'figure holding in her' (his) hand a long Mycenaean 'rhyton' or high, funnel-shaped cup.... The figure is life size, the flesh colour of a deep reddish hue like that of figures on Etruscan tombs and the *Keftiu* of Egyptian paintings. The profile of the face is a noble type; full lips, the lower showing a slight peculiarity of curve below. The eye is dark and slightly almond shaped.... The arms are beautifully modelled. The waist is of the smallest ... it is far and away the most remarkable human figure of the Mycenaean age that has yet come to light....

How Schliemann would have loved to have seen that fresco!

The discovery of this figure, the first example of a well-preserved painting of a man of that far-remote age, contemporary with the Middle Empire of Egypt—caused a great sensation in Crete and beyond. The world's press printed news of its finding, and the local inhabitants of Knossos were equally impressed, though they were convinced that the figure was that of a Christian saint. At night a guard was set.

At night (wrote Evans in his diary) Manoli set to watch the fresco, believed by him to be Saint with halo. Has troubled dreams. Saint wrathful. Manoli wakes and hears lowing and neighing. Something about, but of ghostly kind....

The figure seemed to have formed part of a mural representing a procession of young men, each carrying a tall, conical 'rhyton' in some ceremonial observance. The figure, with its broad, bronzed shoulders, curling black hair, artificially slim waist encircled by a tight girdle, and muscular thighs, was clearly stylized; yet here, clearly, was the first representation of a young Cretan of the prehistoric age which human eyes had seen for at least two thousand years. Egyptologists were particularly excited, for here, in his own *locale*, was clearly represented one of the so-called *Keftiu*, the 'people of the islands', which can be seen on the walls of Ancient Egyptian tombs bearing tribute to the Pharaoh or his officers. Those familiar with Egyptian inscriptions had known for many years of the 'Island People' from the 'Great Green Sea' with whom the Pharaohs were alternately at war and at peace. Their pictures had been seen in Egyptian tombs, recognizable by their blue and gold loin-cloths of non-Egyptian shape, and by the handsome vessels they carried—vessels of a recognizably non-Egyptian type. Now, for the first time, these *Keftiu* were revealed in their own land—and, sure enough, among the pottery which Evans and his

Opposite The cupbearer frescoes

assistants dug up from the depths of Kephala were fragments of vases, 'rhytons' and other ritual vessels such as could be seen clearly depicted in the tomb paintings of Egyptian Thebes.

Were these, then, the mysterious *Keftiu*? ... Were they Cretans?

Then came the dramatic discovery of the so-called 'Room of the Throne'. Evans had begun excavating on the west side of the mound. First he had discovered, on what was evidently the ground floor of the Palace, a long corridor off which led a series of magazines or store-chambers, each containing great earthenware storage jars for oil (the *pithoi*), and under the floor beneath, narrow, stone-lined *cysts*—small chambers, like modern safe-deposits, which, from the fact that fragments of gold-foil were found among them, seem to have been used for the storage of precious objects. All the lower part of this west

Right Examples of the 'Keftiu' or sea-peoples found on the walls of the Tomb of Rekhamara in Egypt, with their non-Egyptian vessels and loin-cloths

Opposite Minoan vase with Octopus design

128

side of the great, rambling building seems to have been used, at any rate during the later period of the Palace's history, for official quarters; one imagines a kind of Cretan Whitehall, full of clerks and civil servants of varying degrees of importance; here was kept the royal wealth (of which oil formed an important part) and here lived those responsible for its collection and safe keeping.

Then there lay, to the east of the corridor and magazines, a large central courtyard, on top of the mound. Buildings of varying sizes surrounded it, but it was much longer on its east and west sides than on the north and south. On the west side of this courtyard was what seemed at first to be the eastern entrance to the palace (though it was not). And here, quite early in the excavations, Evans and his friends found the Room of the Throne.

They thought at first that it was a bath chamber. First there was an antechamber opening on to the central court. Beyond that was a further chamber, with seats on three sides, overlooking a rectangular pit, with broad steps leading down into it. At first it looked very much

Opposite Tapering pillars in the Palace of Minos, Knossos

Below The West Magazine with storage jars

like a bath, until it was discovered that there was no provision for the
escape of waste water. But it was the room above and overlooking the
so-called 'bath' which most interested Evans and his colleagues,
Duncan Mackenzie and Theodore Fyfe. Here is Sir Arthur's diary
entry for April 13th, 1900.

The chief event of the day was the result of the continued excavation of the *bath
chamber* [our italics]. The parapet of the bath proved to have another circular cutting
at its east end, and as this was filled with charred wood—cypress—these openings
were evidently for columns. On the other side of the north wall was a short bench like
that of the outer chamber, and then separated from it by a small interval a separate
seat of honour or Throne. It had a high back, like the seat, of gypsum, which was
partly embedded in the stucco of the wall. It was raised on a square base and had a
curious moulding below with crockets (almost Gothic).

This room, which, in his report to *The Times*, Evans named 'The
Council Chamber of Minos' was recognized later to have had a religious
purpose. But there in its original position stood—and still stands —the
noble throne of Minos—the oldest in Europe by 2,000 years.

The more Evans and his staff explored the site the more extensive
and complicated it became. 'Discovery followed discovery,' wrote
Joan Evans. 'An Egyptian statue of diorite, a great paved area with
stairways, a fresco of olive sprays in flower, another of a boy' (later
discovered to be a monkey) 'gathering saffron, a fresco of people in
solemn procession, *a great relief in painted stucco of a charging
bull. . . .*'

It was this latter discovery which gave Evans the greatest excitement. Already he had seen, among the objects which Schliemann
found in the Mycenaean shaft-graves, a fine silver head of a bull, with

a rosette between its horns. Now at Knossos, here was the animal again, in a magnificent stucco relief, which evidently had once adorned the north portico of the Palace. Not only there, but in other places, in frescoes and reliefs, and frequently on seals, appeared the Bull. Inevitably the legend of Theseus and the Minotaur returned to Evans's mind. 'What a part these creatures play here!' he wrote.... 'Was not some one or other of these creatures visible on the ruined site in Dorian days, which gave the actual tradition of the Bull of Minos?'

Later came the most remarkable of all the discoveries made at Knossos—the remains of a spirited fresco depicting—without a shadow of doubt, a young man in the act of *somersaulting over the back of a charging bull*, while a young girl, similarly dressed in 'toreador's' costume, waited behind the animal's flank to catch him. Soon other examples of the same scene came to light—proving that among these ancient people there had undoubtedly existed a form of sport in which the bull played a prominent part. In none of these scenes was any contestant shown carrying a weapon, nor was the bull killed. But again and again—in wall-paintings, on seals, in a delicate ivory statuette—the same incredible scene was repeated, the slim, agile figure of the youthful 'bull-leaper' in the act of somersaulting over the horns of the charging beast. Had there been, after all, some

132

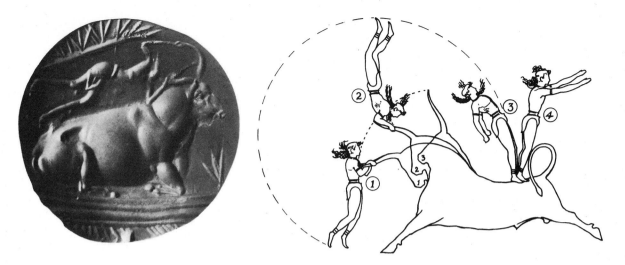

kind of ritual sacrifice? Were these young men and girls the Athenian hostages who, according to tradition, were sent each year as tribute to the Minotaur?

Who were these people? Were they 'Mycenaean'—contemporary with the people whose bodies Schliemann had found in the shaft-graves at Mycenae? Or were they even older? Although the civilization revealed at Knossos was akin to that of Mycenae, every indication pointed to it being far more ancient, and that what had been regarded hitherto as 'Mycenaean' was in fact derived from Crete (although the Mycenaeans were not necessarily of Cretan stock). In an attempt to establish just how long civilization had existed at Knossos, Evans sank test pits deep into the mound of Kephala. The strata thus revealed proved beyond doubt that there had been almost continuous human settlement at Knossos from the Neolithic period (i.e. the New Stone Age—which ended at about 3000 BC)—up to and including the penultimate development of Cretan civilization—the period to which Evans later gave the name *Late Minoan* III—it ended in approximately 1200 BC. There were evidences of one or two breaks, but none of long duration. Civilization had not been a primitive beginning, a long process of growth, a blossoming, and a decay. Then Evans understood why this had been possible. In that remote age when sea-power did not exist, Crete, isolated in a waste of waters, had been safe from invasion. The nearest power, Egypt, had no great naval strength. Contact between Egypt and Crete had been cultural and commercial.

Gradually Crete had built up naval power. Everywhere Evans and his associates found evidence of the close ties between the lords of Knossos and the surrounding ocean. On walls and pillars, on painted frescoes and engraved seals, appeared the trident—emblem of sea power. The makers of the lovely Cretan pottery, especially in its middle and late stages of development, repeatedly used marine emblems and as decorative motifs—the sea creatures such as the octopus, the dolphin, the sea-urchin, and the starfish. The Palace of Knossos itself, unlike the grim fortresses of Mycenae and Tiryns, was almost unfortified. It did not need walls—the ocean was

Opposite Restored fresco of the bull leaping sport showing the acrobat somersaulting over the bull's back. The 'toreador' on the right is a girl

Above left Seal stone showing sideways bull leap

Above right How the acrobats performed the bull leaping feat sufficient protection. Again it seemed that the ancient tradition was true, of King Minos—founder of the first great naval power in the Mediterranean. Was Crete, then, the starting point of Aegean civilization? Was this the answer to the riddle to which old Heinrich Schliemann had sought an answer?

Arthur Evans believed that it was, and determined to prove it. Already, in one of those bold imaginative flights which distinguished him from the mere scholarly pedant, he had written to *The Times* in August of that year:

.., the realms of the legendary Minos, the great conqueror and law-giver who at the close of his temporal reign took his seat on the dread tribunal of the netherworld, the abode of Daedalus, the father of architecture and plastic arts, the haunt of the mysterious Dactyls, the earliest artificers in iron and bronze, the refuge of Europa, and the birthplace of Zeus himself, Crete was in remote times the home of a highly developed culture which vanished before the dawn of history ... among the prehistoric cities of Crete, Knossos, the capital of Minos, is indicated by legend as holding the foremost place. Here the great law-giver (Minos) promulgated his famous institutions, which like those of Moses and Numa Pompilius were derived from a divine source; here was established a ... maritime empire, suppressing piracy, conquering the islands of the Archipelago, and imposing a tribute on subjected Athens. Here Daedalus constructed the Labyrinth, the den of the Minotaur, and fashioned the wings—perhaps the sails—with which he and Icarus took flight over the Aegean. . . .

It was fortunate for the world that this great opportunity—of digging down to the very roots of European culture—came to a man who combined with a scholar's patience and devotion to truth, intuition, sensibility and poetic imagination. Partly by chance, but chiefly through good judgment, Evans had found in middle life a task for which he was supremely fitted. But—he knew well—he must tackle it in his own way, unhampered by committees and official bodies, and responsible to no one but himself. At first the excavations

Dolphin fresco in the Queen's megaron

134

Amphora with an octopus design

had been partly financed by the 'Cretan Exploration Fund' but the expense of excavating such a site was very great, and now that the South African War had broken out there was little money to spare for archaeology. There was a suggestion of making a fresh appeal for funds under the direction of George Macmillan, of the famous publishing house, hereditary friends of the Evans family. But Arthur Evans made his own views quite clear when he wrote to his father in November, 1900.

135

The Palace of Knosses, he wrote, was my idea and my work, and it turns out to be such a find as one could not hope for in a lifetime, or in many lifetimes. That the Fund should help me is another thing. If you like to give me the money personally that also would be quite acceptable. But we may as well keep some of Knossos in the family! I am quite resolved not to have the thing entirely 'pooled' for many reasons, but largely because I must have sole control of what I am personally undertaking. With other people it may be different, but I know it is so with me; my way may not be the best but it is the only way I can work....

John Evans knew his son's temper and agreed. Fortunately he was a rich man. From this point onwards the cost of the monumental work of excavation, reconstruction and publication of the Palace of Knossos, work which continued intermittently for more than thirty years, was borne first by John Evans, and afterwards entirely by Arthur Evans himself, from his private fortune. It is difficult to arrive at an accurate estimate of the total cost, but was probably in the region of a quarter of a million pounds.

But it was not only Evans who was making great discoveries in Crete in the spring of 1900. While Evans dug at Knossos, another British archaeologist, working on the other side of the island, succeeded in penetrating into one of the most awe-inspiring sanctuaries in the world; the birth-cave of Zeus.

11 THE BIRTH-CAVE OF ZEUS

But Rhea was subject in love to Cronos and bore splendid
children, Hestia, Demeter, and gold-shod Hera and strong
Hades, pitiless in heart, who dwells under the earth, and the
loud-crashing Earth-Shaker, and wise Zeus, father of gods and
men, by whose thunder the wide earth is shaken. These great
Cronos swallowed as each came forth from the womb of his
mother's knees with this intent, that no other of the proud sons
of Heaven should hold kingly office amongst the deathless
gods. . . .

So the poet Hesiod had written, some seven hundred years or more
before Christ, setting down in stirring verse the traditions which he
had inherited from a far earlier age.

Some years before Arthur Evans had finally obtained the concession
to dig at Knossos he had explored the mountain of Lasithi, called by
the ancients Dicte, where, it was said, Zeus was born. Now, in the
spring of 1900, although Evans was absorbed in his new-found Palace
of Knossos, he had not forgotten the great cavern in the mountainside,

Inside the Dictean Cave

far up on the heights of Lasithi. There, in 1896, he had discovered an inscribed libation table, although fallen rocks had prevented him from penetrating deeply into the cave. But now there arrived on the scene the redoubtable D. G. Hogarth, then Director of the British School of Archaeology in Athens, and well-seasoned (as Evans was not) in excavation in the Middle East. In May, 1900, while Evans and Mackenzie worked on the mound of Kephala, Hogarth made a determined attack on the Dictean Cave, or as it is sometimes called, 'the cave-sanctuary of Psychro'. He had every advantage on his side, for at last peace had come to the island, and the local inhabitants, who had previously been suspicious of foreigners, were now favourably disposed to the British, who had helped to deliver them from the Turks.

Hogarth, like Evans, was a man of imagination and sensibility. When he began to explore the birthplace of Zeus he was zestfully aware of its mythological associations. In his article in the *Monthly Review*—January to March, 1901—he wrote:

Thither the pregnant Queen [Rhea] was sent by the kindly Earth Mother at the first, and thence she set forth by night to lay her new-born babe on the neighbouring hill. That babe grew to be the Immortal One [Zeus] before whom old Time himself was forced to bow, and in later days still resorted to his birth cave. For thither, as Lucian tells us in his best manner, he led the maiden Europa, flushed and half-suspecting, and there the son [Minos] whom she conceived that day, sought his Father, when, another Moses, he would give a Law to the Cretans. While the Cretans waited above, so runs the story, Minos descended into the grot, and, reappearing at last with the Code, gave out that he had got it from the hands of Zeus himself. . . .

This was the sacred cave, never fully explored, which Hogarth and his assistants were now to examine. He knew how privileged he was, for, as he wrote:

. . . the upland fastnesses of Crete have not, these many centuries past, been any place for the scholarly explorer; and the Lasithi region, which excluded the Venetians and only once admitted the Turks in arms, has remained less known than any part of the classic world. Indeed, jealous and nervous officials on the coast, jealous and arrogant hillmen in the inner country, have kept most of Crete virgin soil to our own day.

He had had predecessors of course. Frederico Halbherr, the great Italian archaeologist and friend of Evans, and Dr Joseph Hazzidakis, the head of the *Candiote Syllogos* (Cretan Archaeological Society) had made tentative attempts to penetrate the cave. They had recovered, from the local peasants, certain bronze objects, such as miniature 'double axes' (the symbol of Zeus), knives, and other weapons, but inside the cave they could do little or nothing, so deep was the cumber of fallen rocks in its upper hall.

Then at last came the liberation of the island, and, as Hogarth writes 'in May, 1900 . . . I left Mr Arthur Evans to his fortunate labours in the Knossian Palace of Minos, and betook myself to Psychro with a few trained men, stone-hammers, mining-bars, blasting powder, and the rest of a digger's plant.'

Then he describes the Cave.

There is a shallow hall to the right and an abysmal chasm to the left, the last not matched in Crete for grandeur, nor unworthy of a place among the famous limestone grottoes of the world. The rock at first breaks down sheer, but as the light grows dim, takes an outward slope, and so falls steeply still for two hundred feet into an inky darkness. Having groped thus far, stand and burn a powerful flashlight. An icy pool spreads from your feet about the bases of fantastic stalactite columns on into the heart of the hill. Hall opens from hall with fretted roofs and the same black, unruffled floor, doubling the torches you and your guides must bear. An impassable labyrinth before, where rock and water meet; behind and far above a spot of faintly luminous haze. Fit scene for Minos' mysterious colloquy with his father Zeus, and the after-cult of a Chthonian god. . . .

To me, one of the most engaging qualities of the great nineteenth-century archaeologists such as Hogarth, is their vigorous literary style. Hogarth, Petrie, Evans, Breasted; they could all *write*. But they were also men of action and decision, as Hogarth makes clear in his next paragraph.

Our blasting charges made short work of the boulders in the upper hill, and luckily the threatening roof held good. Crowbars and stone-hammers finished the powder's work. . . . Then the real dig began. . . .'

He is very amusing on labour recruitment. He believed in mixing the sexes because, he states, 'the men labour the more willingly for the emulation of the women . . .' but this method, applied successfully in Cyprus and Turkey, seemed at first to be a failure in Crete.

At first the Lasithi maidens were very coy, watching from a distance two girls, already trained at Knossos, diligent at their sieves. But, on the third morning, a more cosmopolitan villager, who had fought—or looted—as a volunteer on the French side in 1870, sent up an aged wife and daughter to help his son, and the ice was broken. The laughing mob brandished grain-sieves and demanded all to be written (recruited) at once, and with their sisters, cousins, and aunts, who brought up the mid-day meal, they made the terrace before the Cave the gayest spot in Lasithi. . . .

With this picturesque labour force Hogarth made one of the most sensational discoveries in Crete. There were, as he described, two chambers within the sacred grotto. In the Upper Hall, part of which had already been plundered by the local peasantry, there were found small objects of bronze, such as small 'double axes', knives, bracelets and so forth, and remains of Hellenic pottery, all originally proffered as votive offerings to the god. But these were fairly late in date; i.e. they belonged to 'classical' Greek or Roman times, from about 500 BC onward. But then came the exploration of that 'abysmal chasm to the left' which had been inaccessible until Hogarth arrived with his blasting powder and mining-bars.

The men clambered down, he writes, unwilling and not expectant, to their final task in the dank abyss, regretting the warm sunshine into which they could often emerge from the shallower upper wall; and the girls moaned not a little at the sight of the clammy mud in which they must now stand and search. . . .

The reluctant diggers worked lower and lower into the darkness, till their distant lights showed like glow-worms to the men above, and began to grope in the mud left exposed by the water. And then something wonderful happened.

A zealous groper, wishing to put both hands to his work, stuck his guttering candle into a slit of a stalactite column, and therein espied the edge of a bronze blade, wedged vertically. Fished out with the fire-tongs from the camp above, this proved a perfect

139

Votive offerings from the
Dictean cave

'Mycenaean' knife. But, except by human agency, it could hardly have come into the crevice....

Quickly the word was passed round, and the workers, men and girls, ceased groping in the mud of the pool and began to search in the crevices of the stalactites—those pendulous columns of glistening limestone which hung from the roof of the cave—the products of aeons of natural growth. And there they found, wedged in the crevices, hundreds upon hundreds of votive offerings, knives, miniature double-axes, women's ornaments, *fibulae*—all offerings to the god, placed there by worshippers who had penetrated to that gloomy hall two, three, perhaps four thousand years ago. It was the Holy of Holies. It was the innermost sanctuary of Zeus himself, unseen by man for, perhaps, two millennia....

In this most awful part of the sacred grotto, wrote Hogarth, it was held most profitable to dedicate, in niches made by Nature herself, objects fashioned expressly for the God's service, like the axes or statuettes, or taken from the person of the worshipper, as the knives, pins, and rings. The fact does honour to the primitive Cretan imagination. In these pillared halls of unknown extent and abysmal gloom undoubtedly was laid the scene of Minos' legendary converse with Zeus. For the lower grot suits admirably the story as the rationalizing Dionysius tells it—the primeval king leaving his people without and descending out of their sight, to reappear at last with the credit of having seen and talked with God himself. That here is the original Birth Cave of Zeus there can remain no shadow of doubt. The Cave of Ida, however rich it proved in offerings when explored some years ago, has no sanctuary approaching the mystery of this. Among holy caverns in the world, that of Psychro, in virtue of its lower halls, must stand alone....

140

12 AND STILL THE WONDER GREW

Hogarth had proved that yet another of the ancient traditions had a solid basis. Meanwhile, Evans and Mackenzie continued to dig at Knossos until, on June 2nd, 1900, they had to cease. The weather had become unbearably hot, and besides, the valley had proved malarial. However, by February, 1901, Evans was back in Herakleion (then called Candia) where he rented a Turkish house as a permanent base. Every day, writes Joan Evans,

Evans, Mackenzie and Fyfe used to ride out to Knossos on mules, through a tunnel-like gate over the town moat, past the lepers congregated to beg outside. . . . Arthur Evans loved to go fast, even on a mule, and was always envious of Halbherr's fine horse, until he finally acquired a fast Turkish cob of his own.

By this time Evans had begun to realize the magnitude of the task ahead of him. Here was the work of a lifetime, something which could not be hurried or scamped. He was also conscious of the world publicity which had been focused upon him since his first report in *The Times*. Old John Evans, an antiquarian himself, was almost overjoyed at his son's achievement, and in that year, 1901, managed to get out to Crete himself, although he was then seventy-seven years of age. Together father and son made a strenuous and adventurous journey across the island to Gortyna, where Frederico Halbherr, the Italian archaeologist who had always been a staunch friend of Arthur Evans, warmly welcomed them. Halbherr was beginning to excavate another Minoan palace at Phaestos, in the south, second only to Knossos in size and beauty, and even superior to it in the splendour of its site. Further to the east, at Gournia, two American scholars, Miss Boyd and Mr R.B. Seager, were excavating a Minoan town. Later, Halbherr unearthed the beautiful 'Royal Villa' of Hagia Triadha, and French scholarship was to make its contribution by excavating the small but very rich 'Palace' at Mallia.

But Arthur Evans's greatest discoveries in 1901 took place after his father had returned to England in April. He began to find tiny clay seals which his phenomenal eyesight enabled him to interpret. . . . 'Out of five different impressions, but overlapping one another in design, I have been able to reconstruct a wonderful religious scene; a goddess on a sacred rock or peak with two lions in heraldic attitudes on either side of it, her temple behind, and a votary in front...' Even the layman can appreciate the fascination of this discovery, for the two lions on this tiny seal are identifiable with those flanking the Lion Gate at Mycenae, and the Goddess in her typical Minoan dress stands above

them. It is not impossible that once such a figure surmounted the central pillar between the Mycenaean lions. Later, as we shall see, Evans was able to make a profoundly imaginative interpretation of Minoan religion and its Mother-Goddess, who may well have been Rhea, the mother of Zeus.

It was also in the early part of this second season that he discovered the beautiful inlaid gaming-table, set with crystal and ivory mosaic, and gold settings, which may once have whiled away the leisure hours of King Minos himself. 'It gives,' write Evans, 'an extraordinary idea of magnificence....'

Architecturally the Palace continued to reveal fresh marvels. Evans now began to excavate the east side of the central courtyard where the ground fell away steeply towards the river Kairatos. And here he revealed the Grand Staircase, the most impressive architectural achievement of that four-thousand-year-old civilization which has come down to us. More important still, he not only revealed it, but, by the most skilful and imaginative restoration, saved it from inevitable destruction.

It is evident, he wrote, that we are only just coming to the real centre of the Palace buildings. We have now a hall with two column-bases approached by a quadruple flight of stairs. Two of these, under the others, have had to be tunnelled out. A gallery with a wooden colonnade ran round the west side of this room in two stages. Beyond the hall is a larger room, only partly excavated, with more column bases. It will probably prove to be the principal *megaron* (hall) of the Palace.... Above the stairs are traces of a further higher flight having existed, and in parts we find evidence of two storeys above the basement. It is altogether unexampled and unexpected.

It now became clear to Evans that, while the buildings around the upper courtyard, on top of the mound, were used mainly for official purposes, the spacious domestic quarters of the Royal Family were built much lower down—on a platform cut out of the steep eastern slope, overlooking the river-valley. Hence the need for this monumental staircase, originally of five flights, of which three still exist. The Grand Staircase, as Evans named it, and the suite of noble apartments to which it leads, are themselves a monument to the skill of Evans and his architectural team. As they dug into the shelving hillside they had to support, strengthen and partially restore these high, toppling walls which otherwise would have collapsed into a heap of rubble. How they did this will be described later.

As the work went on more and more fragments of painted frescoes came to light, but most were so small that restoring the original picture was like solving a complex jig-saw puzzle—with the added complication that much of the puzzle was missing and had therefore to be guessed. Yet this was just the kind of imaginative reconstruction which Evans loved, and he also had the wisdom to engage a remarkable Swiss artist, M Gilliéron, who possessed an extraordinary gift for patiently fitting together the tiny fragments, sensitively and accurately restoring what was missing, and then making accurate reproductions which were then hung, as nearly as possible, in the position of the originals. The latter were removed to the doubtful security of the Candia Museum. All the objects found were, of course, the property

Above Design taken from a clay seal found in Crete showing a goddess flanked by two lions which are identifiable with those surmounting the Lion Gate, Mycenae

Opposite The Grand Staircase (second extant flight leading down from the level of the Central Court)

142

of the Cretan authorities, except for a few articles of which duplicates existed. These Evans was able to take to England; they can be seen, with some of Gilliéron's lovely fresco reproductions, at the Ashmolean Museum, Oxford.

Evidently, during the period of its greatest glory, the corridors, porches, and rooms of state of the Palace of Minos had glowed with rich and sensuous colour, delicate blues and greens and russet painted on smooth plaster. The Minoans may have copied this method of decoration from the Egyptians, but in style there is no resemblance between the stiff, highly conventionalized art of most Egyptian wall-paintings, and the refined, fastidious naturalism of the Minoan frescoes. I say 'with *most* Egyptian wall-paintings' advisedly, because there is one—and only one—period of Egyptian art which does show remarkable similarity to that of Crete. This was the famous 'heresy period' under the Pharaoh Akhnaten, when for the first and only time the rigid, hierarchical conventions of Egyptian art suddenly broke down, and the royal artists, (it is believed under the direct guidance of

Right Gold Double Axe from the cave of Arkadochori, in Crete. Many Double Axes have been found in sanctuaries usually of bronze and of considerable size

Opposite Lustral Bath, Knossos

144

Akhnaten himself) painted human beings, birds, beasts and flowers, as they saw them and not according to an accepted religious tradition.

The significance of this departure is that it occurred round about the year 1400 BC—the generally accepted date on which final disaster—earthquake or foreign attack, or both—struck the Palaces of Crete, including Knossos. It is tempting to believe—though it is by no means proved—that refugee Cretan artists may have fled to Akhnaten's court round about this period.

Some of the frescoes represented human scenes; others were charming decorative motifs, often drawn from nature—flowers and grasses, with butterflies flitting among them. The symbol of the Double Axe which we encountered among the Mycenaean grave treasures, occurred frequently, and so did our old friend the figure-of-eight shield. At Mycenae Schliemann had found it represented on tiny seals and signets, but here it was employed, full size, as a wall decoration. It was now possible to recognize clearly how the shield was made—of a bull's hide—just as Homer said—and strengthened with cross pieces, presumably of wood. In one of the rooms of state, which Evans named 'The Hall of the Double Axes', he believed that actual

Opposite The Grand Staircase, Knossos

Below 'Hall of the Double Axes': outer hall with replicas of a wooden throne and figure-of-eight shields

Fresco, restored by Gilliéron,
of Minoan court ladies at a
public function

shields had hung on the wall as part of the decoration; so he had replicas made—of painted metal—and hung in place.

But the most fascinating of all these coloured frescoes were those representing Minoan men and women—especially women. When these were first discovered and restored by Gilliéron they caused wonder and astonishment throughout the world. And no wonder—for they were quite unlike the classical Greeks, unlike the Egyptians, unlike the Babylonians, unlike any ancient people whose painted or sculptured representations had survived from the remote past. As far as the Minoan women were concerned—in their dress, manner, and style of hair-dressing, the nearest comparison which the astonished scholars could make was to the fashionable beauties of their own time—1900! One *savant*, on first seeing them, broke into the incredulous exclamation: *'Mais, ce sont des Parisiennes!'*

An examination of the restored frescoes will explain his astonishment. These highly-bred Minoan ladies are evidently attending some court function—perhaps the reception of some foreign ambassador, or, more likely, a display of that strange, sinister sport in which the young 'bull-leapers' exhibited their desperate skill. The figures are shown on what seems to be a 'grand-stand' and in the background are sketched, in the economical method of a modern cartoonist, a tightly packed crowd of faces, with black hair, white dots for eyes, and white collars. The prevailing colours are rust-red and buff. In the centre of the 'grand-stand' is what Evans believed to be the shrine of the Minoan goddess, distinguished by the 'horns of consecration' which decorate its roof (another allusion to the Bull). But on either side of this central shrine are groups of ladies, much more carefully drawn.

146

Here is Evans's detailed analysis of these scenes.

... on either side of the miniature shrine are groups of ladies seated and chattering, gaily dressed in the height of fashion, with elaborately coiffured hair, engaged apparently in gay chit-chat and ignoring what is going on before them. ... At a glance we recognize Court ladies in elaborate toilet. They are fresh from the coiffeur's hand with hair *frisé* and curled about the head and shoulders; it is confined by a band over the forehead and falls down the back in long separate tresses, twisted round with strings of beads and jewels ... the sleeves are puffed, and the constricted girdles and flounced skirts equally recall quite modern fashions. A narrow band appears across the chest which suggests a diaphanous chemise, but the nipples of the breasts are indicated beneath these ... give a *décolleté* effect. The dresses are gaily coloured with bands of blue, red and yellow, showing white stripes and at times black striations. ...

... The lively nature of the conversation between No. 3 (the lady to whose coiffure the net belongs) and her neighbour at once strikes the eye. The latter points her statement by thrusting forward her right arm so as almost to lay her hand on the other's lap while her confidante raises hers in amazement—'You *don't* say so!' ... These scenes of feminine confidences, of tittle-tattle and society scandals, take us far away from the productions of Classical Art in any age. Such lively genre and rococo atmosphere bring us nearer to quite modern times. ...

As one by one these marvels were told to the world in Evans's vivid reports to *The Times* and various periodicals, and were supplemented by the comments of other visitors, the full grandeur of Evans's achievement—and the immensity of the task which lay ahead of him—became apparent. When he returned to England in June, 1901, recognition of the importance of the Cretan discoveries was general and immediate: Fellowship of the Royal Society (June 6th, 1901), honorary degrees at Edinburgh and Dublin (also in 1901), and diplomas from foreign societies.

Then, following this up, Evans announced, in an address to the British Association in Glasgow, his proposed solution to the difficult problem of dating the successive Knossian strata. It was a bold masterly solution, and though in later years Evans himself had to modify and extend it, in the main his principle of dividing Minoan culture into three broad periods of development—Early, Middle and Late Minoan, synchronous with the Old, Middle, and New Empires of Egypt, is still accepted to-day. To devise such a system was in itself no small achievement for one man, but Evans recognized that in the years ahead of him it would be his task to build a structure of sound knowledge from an amorphous mass of stone, pottery, and fragmented frescoes; and, like an honest builder, he had first to see that his foundations were firm.

13 INTO THE LABYRINTH

In 1902, when Evans returned for his third season's digging at Knossos, trouble arose over finances. Already he had spent some £4,500, more than half of which was his own money, but the rest of which had been raised by the Cretan Exploration Fund. For the benefit of those unfamiliar with the financing of archaeological work, it should be said that it is usual for funds to be raised by a society or group of societies interested in the project; most of the subscribers are people of moderate means, but there are also Universities, museums and other learned institutions with more ample resources. But these people naturally want to see that they are getting value for their money, especially the museums which, in the early days, could sometimes expect a proportion of the finds for their own collections.

At this point a sharp disagreement broke out between D. G. Hogarth, Director of the British School at Athens, who had excavated the cave-sanctuary of Zeus, and Evans, with whom Hogarth was now working in close collaboration at Knossos. Hogarth, as a professional archaeologist, naturally took a salary and expenses. Evans, who was 'comfortably circumstanced'—to put it mildly—could not understand this; to him it seemed like making money out of religion. On Hogarth's side—and they were both men of strong character—there was irritation at Evans's *de luxe* methods of excavation—especially the expensive reconstruction of buildings, which, while greatly benefiting the lay visitor to the site, went far beyond what was archaeologically necessary. There was plain speaking on both sides, of which the following letter from Hogarth must serve as example:

These expensive methods are yours in digging, as in collecting and in ordinary life. You are a rich man's son, and have probably never been at a loss for money. At the other pole to you stands Petrie—I see advantages in the methods of both. If you spend much more in proportion than Petrie, you produce far worthier results in published form, and one feels that nothing has been spared to obtain expert accuracy. One can't feel that with Petrie's rough plans and illustrations; *nor again does he leave a site so that it is a gain for the spectator.* *

The drawback of your method is that it does not appeal to people's pockets. All P.'s 'cave-man' plan of life has been deliberately adopted to convince the subscriber that every penny goes into the earth. There is no doubt that unless you sue *in forma pauperis* public subscription will not follow you. That you cannot do. You are well known as a collector of rare and costly things, and as your father's son, and the public will not be convinced. I am not talking in the air, for I am continually chaffed about the 'princely' way things are done in Crete, and I have lately heard that reports of our Cretan houses, brought back I suppose by the big tourist parties, have decided some

* Our italics.

old subscribers not to pay up again. For those houses I am, I know, as much responsible as you.... In a less degree the same difficulty dogs me—I and my wife do not look like P. and his wife. But to live by public subscription we should have to!...

In the same letter from Hogarth occurs a passage which sums up the whole problem, and explains why Evans eventually decided to shoulder the whole financial burden of excavation himself, to the lasting benefit of all visitors to Knossos.

Restorations like the Throne Room are not a question of methods, *but of the gratifying of a desire to reconstruct tangibly what must otherwise only be imagined.* But you justly admit that it is a luxury which everyone cannot pay for, and perhaps others (the subscribers to the Excavation Funds) can hardly be expected to pay for.

From that date—1902—onwards for thirty years, Arthur Evans devoted his life to the excavation and, in part, reconstitution of the greatest Minoan Palace in Crete; and he also produced, over a number of years, a work of literary scholarship which, in the long run, will probably outlast even the stronghold of Minos himself. For in this fevered world which we have inherited (and how Evans hated it!) no monument of stone, however ancient, beautiful or revered, is safe; all, equally, are at the mercy of 'a boy in a bomber'. But perhaps even after the holocaust of an atomic war, there may survive, in some remote place, the great volumes of Evans's *Palace of Minos*. And if that should happen, our surviving descendants can, if they wish, know as much about the prehistoric civilization of the Aegean as we do, though not one stone of the Palace itself should remain.

In a book of this scope it would be impossible, and, indeed impertinent, to try to explain in detail all that Evans and his professional colleagues on other sites—such as Halbherr, Hogarth, Boyd, Seager, Marinatos—achieved in Crete during the first twenty years of our century. All I can hope to do is to direct the reader's attention to the books which tell the whole story, and, in a few brief extracts, to give a taste of their quality. The full list will be found at the back of this book, but as a starting-point for anyone wishing to learn more about the Minoan civilization, there are four outstanding works which have given me pleasure—not only for the information which they contain, but because they are extremely well written. First, of course, comes Evans's own *Palace of Minos*—but this is monumental, and before approaching it I would recommend three smaller works. These are John Pendlebury's *The Archaeology of Crete*, Joan Evans's *Time and Chance* (especially useful for Evans's family background and early years) and *Crete, the Forerunner of Greece*, by B. M. and H. W. Hawes.

Without reflection it is easy to fall into the mistake of imagining that only one archaeologist—Evans—discovered the prehistoric civilization of Crete. True, he was the master-discoverer; he had the finest site, and most money to spend on excavation, but from 1900 onwards, when peaceful conditions made investigation possible, a succession of scholars explored and excavated in the island. Soon it became clear that there were many scores of 'Minoan' sites only awaiting the spade. Halbherr, at Phaestos in the south, excavated a palace second only to Knossos in size and grandeur.

Nearby, at Hagia Triadha, he revealed a 'Royal Villa' with superb frescoes, and here some of the finest examples of Minoan art were found, including the famous 'Harvester' vase, a fine sarcophagus, and the steatite 'rhyton' with boxers.

Miss Boyd and Mr R. B. Seager found at Gournia, in the east, the extensive remains of a Minoan town. Here Evans had given the clue. He had told Miss Boyd that there were Iron Age tombs on the heights, two thousand feet above the isthmus, and while excavating them in 1900 she became convinced that there had once been a Bronze Age settlement somewhere in the vicinity. A year later, with the help of Cretan peasants, she and her colleague Miss Wheeler found the site. . . .

Within twenty-four hours thirty men were at work . . . cutting down the carobs and digging trial trenches. . . . In less than three days they had opened houses, were following paved roads, and were in possession of enough vases and sherds, bearing octopus, ivy-leaf, double-axe, and other unmistakably Minoan designs, to make it certain that they had found an important settlement. . . .

Gournia is especially interesting because, unlike the princely palaces of Knossos and Phaestos, it seems to have been an artisans' town where, perhaps, were produced the superb examples of pottery and faience which have been unearthed in the Palaces. To quote just one paragraph from the Hawes book, *Crete, the Forerunner of Greece*, originally published in 1909:

In a well-built house on the top of the ridge a whole carpenter's kit lay concealed in a cranny. Was it deliberately hidden under the corridor floor by its owner, when the ships of the destroyers hove in sight? In an adjoining room a horizontal black streak in the earth showed where there had been a wooden board, now long burned or rotted away, and on this housewife's shelf fourteen loom-weights of clay and stone were ranged in order. Other houses contained vats for washing oil, standing on stone benches, with the amphorae and stamni before them to catch the liquid, just as they were left 3,500 years ago. . . .

An interesting contrast to the Court ladies of Knossos. . . .

Boyd and Seager at Gournia, Halbherr at Phaestos, Carr Bosanquet and Dawkins at Praesos and Palaikastro . . . Hazzidakis and Zanthoudides, at point after point the rich soil of Crete yielded its archaeological treasures to the questing Edwardian scholars. Articles appeared in newspapers and learned journals, theories were propounded, supported, and demolished. Meanwhile Evans, securely possessed of the finest archaeological site on the island, became the leading authority on Minoan civilization to whom other workers gladly came for advice and help.

It is very important to understand his dating system, which was sound and scholarly. To the layman it is usually difficult to appreciate how an archaeologist can 'date' a site when no written records or positively dated monuments are available. We have already seen how at Troy, Mycenae, and Tiryns, Schliemann and his successors had not been able to fix even an approximate date to their discoveries; they knew that the lowest layers or strata of a long-occupied site must clearly be the oldest; but that was about all. This gave ammunition to those who wished to discredit the German's discoveries—one 'auth-

Facsimile of the steatite 'Hagia Triadha' rhyton showing the boxers

ority' for example, even claimed that the Mycenaean graves were post-Christian. Yet without positive proof of date it was impossible to disprove even such absurd theories as this one.

How then were Evans, Hogarth, Halbherr, and the other archaeologists in Crete able to establish accurate dates? The answer is—through the *Egyptian* objects found on the sites.

It was fortunate for archaeology that the Minoans had had cultural and commercial contact with the Egyptians from very early times—Evans believed from the pre-Dynastic period. Those who have read something of Ancient Egyptian history will know that it is divided into Thirty Dynasties, beginning in about 3200 BC and ending with the start of the 'Graeco-Roman period' in 332 BC. The period of 2,500 years from the first to the end of the twenty-fourth dynasty (712 BC) is divided for convenience into three main periods of development, the Old, Middle and New Kingdoms: it is worth while trying to memorize these as they help in understanding how Evans dated the Minoan civilization.

At the beginning come the First and Second Egyptian Dynasties (*circa* 3200–2780 BC). The almost legendary figure of Menes was the founder of the First Dynasty; he combined for the first time the hitherto separated Kingdoms of Upper and Lower Egypt. There were, however, Egyptian kings before him, as Amelineau and Petrie discovered, but the period before 3200 BC is called for convenience *Pre-Dynastic*.

Then came the first of the three great epochs into which Egyptian history is divided—the *Old Kingdom* (2780–2100 BC). This period includes that of the great Pyramid Builders who ruled from Memphis in Lower Egypt. It covers eight Dynasties, from the Third to the Tenth.

Next comes the *Middle Empire* (2100–1700 BC) covering the Eleventh to the Thirteenth Dynasties. This has been called Egypt's 'Feudal Age', and was one of considerable expansion both to north and south. At the end of this period a time of weakness and anarchy was followed by an invasion and occupation of Egypt by Asiatic monarchs known as the *Hyksos* or *'Shepherd Kings'* who controlled Egypt for about a hundred-and-fifty years until thrown out by a resurgent Egypt.

Then followed the period of Egypt's greatest imperial expansion, the first part of the so-called *New Empire* (1555–712 BC). Only the first three Dynasties, from the Eighteenth to the Twentieth, need concern us, as after that the ancient civilization of Crete passed into oblivion. But this was the period of Egyptian history of which most is known. It was the age of Tuthmosis III, the 'Napoleon of Egypt', who raised its military glory to its highest point, of the powerful Amenophis III, and his fascinating, enigmatical son Akhnaten, who began a religious revolution, nearly lost an Empire, and may well have welcomed Cretan artists to his court. The following two Dynasties, the Nineteenth and Twentieth, saw a succession of powerful kings, several of whom bore the famous name Ramesses, one of whom, Ramesses III, is recorded on Egyptian temples as having won a great victory over the

151

'sea-peoples' who tried to invade Egypt round about the year 1200 BC. It was to have been a land invasion supported by naval forces. The land-armies moved down from Syria, while their navies accompanied them along the coast; but somewhere between Syria and Egypt Ramesses met and defeated both, and the invasion never took place. This episode, as we shall see, has great relevance to the history of the Aegean civilization—especially of Mycenae. After 1090 BC—the end of the Twentieth Dynasty—the rest of the history of Egypt does not affect our story.

In an early stage of the excavations Evans had discovered in the Knossian Palace 'an Egyptian statue of diorite' which was identified as belonging to the Twelfth Dynasty, and as the work went on, at Knossos and at other Minoan sites, other examples of undoubted Egyptian manufacture were discovered. In themselves these little objects—a clay statuette, perhaps, or a tiny bronze figure of the god Amun—were valueless, but their importance to the scholars was inestimable. Why? At the certain risk of being accused by scholars of vulgarity, I am going to compare these Egyptian *trivia* with the vital clues which the hero discovers in a detective story—the few threads from the suit of the murderer, detected under the nails of the dead man, or—an even more exact parallel—the fact that, when Mr X was seen leaving the victim's house, Mr Y happened to notice that it was *exactly* eleven-thirteen p.m. . . .

Let us suppose that Evans finds—as he did—an Egyptian statue of the Twelfth Dynasty (2000–1790 BC) embedded in one of the *strata* of the Palace of Knossos. He then *knows*—beyond a shadow of doubt— that no object found in that stratum—pottery, *faience*, architectural remains—can possibly be *earlier* than 2000 BC. Of course the statue might be—by some odd chance—a survival from an earlier age, so that the closing date of the Twelfth Dynasty (1790 BC) might not be the latest possible date for the archaeological strata in which the clue was found. But if, at Knossos, or at another Minoan site, other Egyptian objects of the same Dynasty are found in strata containing Minoan objects of similar type—then it is safe to assume that such objects belong to a period between the years 2000 and 1790 BC. As the work went on, at Knossos, Phaestos, Gournia, Mallia, other dateable Egyptian objects came to light, and with each of such discoveries it became possible to establish earliest and latest dates for the Minoan pottery and other objects among which the Egyptian articles were found.

A moment's reflection will make clear the tremendous significance of such finds. If, for instance, Eighteenth Dynasty Egyptian objects were always accompanied by Minoan pottery, faience, painted frescoes and architecture of a particular kind, then, logically and naturally, *all* 'Minoan' objects of a similar type, wherever they were found—in Cyprus or in the Cyclades, must belong broadly to the same period (allowing for the fact that time must elapse before a fashion, originating in Crete, could spread to the outer fringes of the Minoan Empire).

By such methods Evans and other archaeologists in Crete were able to establish that some of the Minoan deposits dated as far back as the pre-Dynastic period of Egyptian history (i.e. before 3200 BC).

Then the Egyptologists came to the aid of their colleagues working in Crete. In Egyptian tombs it was customary to bury numerous articles needed by the dead man in the Underworld—furniture, clothing, and vessels for food and drink. (We have already noted the pictures of the mysterious 'Keftiu' on the walls of Egyptian tombs). Now Egyptologists began to examine afresh the objects found in Egyptian tombs, *especially pottery*. Among them was pottery, not of Egyptian provenance, which could now be identified unmistakably with the Minoan ware now being brought to light in Crete. So another check on dating could be made. And as these finds both in Egypt and Crete were examined, re-examined, discussed and co-related, so, gradually, Arthur Evans was able to draw up his Grand Design—his chronological system of dating Minoan objects and similar objects found in the other islands of the Aegean and the mainland.

For, as the work proceeded archaeologists came to recognize that this civilization, which Evans believed originated in Crete, spread to other Aegean islands and even further eastward to Cyprus, and the coast of Asia Minor, and northward to the mainland of Greece. In all these areas pottery was found similar to, though not identical with, that found in Crete. Whereas at the beginning of Evans's digging his finds were regarded as Mycenaean, progress showed that there were real differences from what was found at Mycenae. A need arose for a set of terms which would differentiate the characteristic cultures of the different areas of the Aegean. Hence 'Minoan' came to be used to describe prehistoric Cretan objects, 'Cycladic' for the islands and 'Helladic' for the mainland. I introduce these technical terms only so that readers who wish to follow this subject further (as I hope they will) will not be confused by the varying names used by scholars to describe this prehistoric civilization of the eastern Mediterranean.

Incidentally, non-archaeologists sometimes laugh at the attention which experts pay to what appear to be uninteresting fragments of pottery. But the archaeological value of pottery is precisely that *it has no intrinsic value*. Objects of gold and silver, or even of bronze and iron, will be stolen. But who cares about heaps of broken fragments of pots, vases, and cups? They remain scattered, unheeded, on ancient sites for thousands of years—as I have seen them in Egypt as well as Greece. But to the modern archaeologist they provide a definitive method of dating a site. One no longer needs intuition or judgment to achieve this; any young student who has gone through his course can do it. Even I—amateur as I am—reached a stage when I could pick up a fragment of a Mycenaean goblet and say nonchalantly 'ah—Late Helladic III' without causing raised eyebrows among my archaeological friends.

Evans's achievement was to mark off the *three great periods of Minoan civilization which could be correlated with the three great periods of Egyptian Civilization*—the Old Kingdom, the Middle Empire and the New Empire. He wrote in *The Palace of Minos*:

For this considerable space of time, extending over some two thousand years, the divisions here adopted into three main sections, the 'Early', 'Middle' and 'Late' Minoan, each in turn with three periods of its own, will not be thought too minute. It allows, in fact, for each period an average duration of nearly two centuries and a half, the earlier periods being naturally the longer. This triple division, indeed, whether we regard the course of Minoan civilization as a whole or its threefold stages, is in its very essence logical and scientific. In every characteristic phase of culture we note in fact the period of rise, maturity, and decay. Even within the limits of many of these periods are such distinct ceramic phases that it has been found convenient to divide them into two sections (a) and (b).

The three main phases of Minoan history roughly correspond with those of the Early, the Middle and the earlier part of the New Kingdom in Egypt....

Now, at last, it was possible to establish dates for the discoveries of Schliemann and Dörpfeld at Troy, Mycenae, Tiryns, Orchomenos and elsewhere. For it was recognized that some of the pottery, arms, jewels, and ornaments, etc., found in the shaft-graves at Mycenae, and at Tiryns, were demonstrably Minoan in type, though some were pretty certainly made by mainland craftsmen following a Cretan model. Thus it was established that the treasures found in the Mycenaean shaft-graves were dated from a late period of Minoan civilization, *circa* 1600 BC—proving that they were far older than the Trojan War, and could not possibly have belonged to Agamemnon and his companions.

And yet, in the scale of Minoan civilization they were *late*—very late; only two hundred years before the final catastrophe which overtook Knossos in 1400. Yet Crete could boast a highly developed civilization more than a thousand years earlier than that.... Deeper and deeper went the bewildered but fascinated archaeologists, groping among the very roots of European prehistory. And in the lead, his torch held aloft to penetrate the darkness of the labyrinth, strode Arthur Evans.

14 THE VILLA ARIADNE

I sat before a blazing fire in the big, comfortable drawing-room of the Villa Ariadne. Manoli, after piling on more sweet-smelling logs, had gone to bed. The de Jongs, who had joined me for dinner, had returned to their cottage. It was two hours since I had watched the yellow light from Piet's torch moving slowly down the winding path until it disappeared behind the cypresses. Now my hosts too were in bed and probably asleep, and I fancied that I alone was awake. In fact I had never felt more intensely awake; the slightest creak from the wainscoting, the intermittent fluting of some creature in the dark garden outside, made me start.

A view of the Villa Ariadne taken at the time Evans was living there

On my knees lay one of the heavy volumes of Evans's great work *The Palace of Minos*, richly bound in blue, with the head of the Minoan Priest King embossed in gold on the cover. I had read them before, in far-off London, but to hold them in my hands now, while sitting alone at night in Evans's former home, with the Palace itself waiting in the darkness outside, produced an excitement which was almost too intense. I tried to concentrate on the page before me, but fancied movement in the garden outside brought me to my feet. It was nothing; just the moving shadow of one of the cypresses, but I had to go to one of the tall sashed windows and look out.

There was a full moon, and the palms stood quite still and black against the luminous sky, the edges of their leaves tipped with silver. About five hundred feet away stood a statue of the Emperor Hadrian, blanched by the moonlight. Evans had found it in the ruins of a Roman villa near the Palace—it had probably formed part of the garden ornament of some Roman official—had dug it up and made it serve the same purpose in *his* garden. There stood the Emperor, the man who had built the great Wall from the Tyne to the Solway in my own country, looking rather splendid on his plinth with his toga draped gracefully over one arm. And yet . . . *Hadrian* . . . really, the man was almost my contemporary compared with the Minoans! When he made his tour of the Roman Empire in—when was it, AD 120–125?—the last pale flame of Cretan civilization had guttered out more than a thousand years before. Hadrian had lived some 1,800 years before our time. Yet 1,800 years before Hadrian's time Crete had known a civilization in many respects finer than that of Rome.

I went back to the fire and then noticed, for the first time, the formidable head of the Minoan Bull—a plaster cast—which hung on the wall to the right of the fireplace. It was black, with gold horns, white nostrils and bright, red-rimmed eyes, and as I moved around the room, taking out books from the shelves, examining pictures and ornaments, those little red eyes seemed to follow me. . . .

Filled with a strange restless elation I left the drawing-room to explore the rest of the empty Villa. I moved from room to empty room, switching on the naked electric lights which gave to much of the house a severe 'institutional' appearance. A curious, dry, antiseptic smell permeated the air, and my footsteps gave back ringing metallic echoes, for Sir Arthur, who planned the Villa Ariadne, had built it of concrete on a steel framework as a protection against earthquakes. Here and there lay cardboard boxes filled with fragments of broken potsherds left by the students of the British School at Athens. Other plaster cases of treasures found in the Palace hung on the distempered walls; in the hall was a fine copy of the 'charging bull fresco'—a massive relief of a red bull with lowered head hurtling across a pale blue ground. And nearby, in incongruous contrast, hung pleasantly sentimental landscapes of a type which I had seen in many ex-German messes during the war—relics of the occupation when the Villa was the headquarters of the German High Command.

Returning to the first floor I found the library. Here were hundreds of books bearing on almost every aspect of Aegean and Egyptian

The Bull's head rhyton found
at Knossos

archaeology. Some were new to me. Others were old friends. Greedily
I took down book after book and, staggering under my load, returned
along the echoing corridor to the warm, firelit drawing-room. There I
sat on the rug before the fire, spread the books around me on the floor,
took out my notebook, and tried once again to focus my mind on the
story of Arthur Evans and his colleagues from the point at which I had
left them—in 1903.

From 1903 onwards Evans divided his time between Oxford and
Knossos. He would come out to Crete in late winter or early spring,
work until the summer heat made further excavation impracticable,
and return to England in summer or autumn. A few years earlier he
had given up his home in Holywell, Oxford, bought sixty acres of land
on Boars' Hill, outside the city, and built himself a house there. He
called it Youlbury, after the piece of heathland which it overlooked,
and, in his leisure hours in England, exercised his imagination by
creating a romantic landscape garden, 'trying,' in the words of a
relative, 'to make his bit of Berkshire look as much like Bosnia as
possible.' As an illustration of his intense love of natural beauty, the
following quotation from one of his letters is typical. . . .

157

... In the woodland fringe of the opposite Cotswold and Chiltern hills splendid is the impression left by the acres of rose willow-herb spread along the slopes. But no sight surely in Nature's wild garden can excel the view near at hand of Hen Wood in May with its dreamy haze of bluebells, stretching between the oaks, wherever a vista opens, as though some mirage had reversed the blue of heaven; or, as a child once put it, 'as if a bit of the sky had fallen down'.

Denied children himself, he loved to have them around him; he adopted Lancelot Freeman, the young son of Margaret's brother. One child at Youlbury made a good excuse for inviting others, and the big house above the 'dreamy haze of bluebells' was rarely without the sound of children's voices. He also bought a car, at a time when it was adventurous to possess one, and loved to go long journeys in it, preferably as fast as possible.

Soon he had decided to build another Youlbury for himself in Crete. Now that he could foresee many years of work ahead of him, the Turkish house he had taken in Candia was no longer practicable, being too far from Knossos. So in 1906 Christian Doll, who had succeeded Theodore Fyfe as his architect, built for him the Villa Ariadne. It embodied many of Evans's own ideas; basement bedrooms for coolness in summer, and steel and concrete construction for strength. Around it he formed a pleasant Mediterranean garden of palms and cypresses and purple-flowered bougainvillaea. This became his spring and summer residence for many years, from which he ruled his domain like a Grand Seigneur. The Villa was both his home and his workshop. Here he entertained fellow scholars such as Halbherr, besides the many distinguished visitors attracted to Crete by the fame of his discoveries; and here, in the evening after the day's work, he would sit with Doll, Duncan Mackenzie, Hogarth and others, planning, discussing, arguing, and preparing for the enormous task of 'publishing' the finds.

The layman might think that the principal justification for excavation is the uncovering of the site itself. To the archaeologist such work is almost valueless unless every part of the site has been 'published'— i.e. fully described, with every object down to the smallest fragment of pottery, with indications of their position and relation to other objects; and with a complete set of photographs, plans and drawings. Even a modest site belonging to a known culture, e.g. Egyptian or Babylonian, may take years to publish adequately; but Evans was faced with the accumulation of more than two thousand years' continuous habitation of one place, embodying the extensive ruins of several palaces, and belonging to an unknown civilization which he could interpret only in the light of his own intuition and judgment.

In 1908 his father, John Evans, died at the age of eighty-five, leaving Arthur the bulk of his fortune. Only a few months later the death of a cousin brought to him the Dickinson estate. At fifty-seven, Arthur Evans found himself a richer man than even his father had been.

One of Evans's greatest disappointments was that he never succeeded in deciphering the mysterious Minoan script which had first attracted him to Crete. After more than thirty years of wrestling with the problem, he eventually had to write in *The Palace of Minos*:

... the widespread hopes of its early interpretation were not verified.... According to every indication—such as that supplied by the local and personal names of pre-Hellenic Crete, and even the appreciable verbal survival in Greek itself—the root affinities of the original language lay on the Anatolian side [i.e. in Asia Minor. L.C.]. The phonetic value of the signs themselves was itself unknown, and though light on them might be obtained from the early Cypriote syllabary, even this ... only exists in a limited degree.... All I have been able here to attempt—after copying over 1,600 documents of which the whole or some material part has survived ... is of a most preliminary nature.

He decided that the numerous clay tablets, which had so excited him when he found them near the western store-rooms of magazines, were merely inventories. '... it appears that the documents in an overwhelming degree refer to accounts and lists of persons and possessions'—and he managed to decipher the numerals. And John Pendlebury, the brilliant young scholar and friend of Evans who was Curator of Knossos in the thirties, had to admit in his *Archaeology of Crete* that

what the language of the Minoans was is as yet impossible to say except that it was not Greek ... it would be a profitless task to guess at it. The material is there and is arranged. We can only hope for a bilingual clue; perhaps one day a bill of lading in Egyptian and Minoan will one day be found at Komo. Even then it may turn out to be a dead language which has left no descendant behind to help in its decipherment.*

Some of the material is contained in Evans's book *Scripta Minoa* which he published in 1909, after optimistically persuading the Clarendon Press to cast a complete fount of Minoan type.

Unable to decipher the writing—which in any case, he suspected, might not include historical records, Evans was forced to interpret the Minoan civilization through its buildings, its art, and above all, through the tiny engraved seal-stones and signets found in such abundance—and of which he had now amassed a large collection. 'Complete in themselves,' he wrote, 'these little intaglio types often serve as an epitome of more fully elaborated works of the great Art, whether in relief or painting, only fragmentary remains of which have been preserved.' Here again his microscopic sight, and his feeling for style and stylistic development, trained through long years of numismatic study, aided him greatly. It is in this imaginative, yet exact and scholarly interpretation of tiny objects that Evans's genius appears most clearly.

For example, what did the Minoans believe? What deities did they worship? Evans discovered, chiefly through the tiny scenes on the bead-seals, that there appeared again and again a female figure, sometimes alone, sometimes with acolytes and adorers, who was clearly a goddess. Sometimes she stands on a peak, with lion supporters. Sometimes she is bareheaded, occasionally—in seals and statuettes belonging to the later, more sophisticated 'Palatial' period—she wears the fashionable dress of the Minoan court lady, with tight-waisted bodice, naked breasts, and a crown or tiara. Evans called her the 'Minoan mother goddess'. Occasionally she is accompanied by what appears to be a male deity, but he is never in a position of

* 'Linear B' deciphered in 1952, see page 210.

equality; he may be considered her son. A delightful ivory statuette of this 'boy-god' is now in the Ashmolean Museum. Could this mother-goddess*, thought Evans, be associated with Rhea, and was the boy-god her son, Zeus?

On other seals and later-discovered statuettes, the Minoan Goddess was shown holding a snake in each outstretched hand, or in other instances the snakes were wreathed tightly around her arms. Among primitive peoples today the snake is often revered; anthropologists and students of primitive religion have observed that the cult of the snake is often associated with the propitiation of an earth-deity. After close study of Minoan scenes, together with those from other ancient cultures in which snake cults were practised, Evans suggested that the Minoan Snake-Goddess was the Mother-Goddess in her aspect as 'Lady of the Underworld'; the reason for this insistence on the propitiation of the Earth became clear to him later, as we shall see.

We have mentioned the 'Room of the Throne' in which was a chamber rather like a cathedral chapter house, with a throne in the middle of the broadest wall, flanked by stone benches on each side. It fronted and overlooked a rectangular pit, approached by flights of steps, which at first the excavators took to be a bath, but which Evans later decided was a 'Lustral Area'—i.e. a place in which some ritual of anointing took place. As he dug in other parts of the Palace more of these 'lustral areas' came to light. All were elaborately built. All were approached by pillared flights of steps, none of them had been built to retain water, nor was there any provision for the release of waste water—which the Minoans, expert hydraulic engineers, would certainly not have omitted had the mysterious pits been baths. Then from other parts of Crete came reports of similar 'lustral areas'—Halbherr found them in the Palace of Phaestos, and there were others at Mallia. Had they, mused Evans, some connection with the earth-cult? He became more and more convinced that they had a religious purpose, and that, indeed, much of the Palace, especially the western half, was devoted to a religious cult. In fact Minos—or a race of kings who may have borne that name—had probably been priest-kings.

Unlike their cousins the Egyptologists, the archaeologists of Crete had no written documents to guide them; nor had the Minoans been as obliging as the Ancient Egyptians and used the walls of their temples to preserve pictures and written records of historic events. They seemed quite uninterested in recording triumphs, battles, treaties and conquests, as had the Egyptians and the blood-lusting Assyrians.† Instead they painted delightful scenes from nature, flowers and birds and trees, processions of noble youths like the Cup-bearer and the even lovelier fresco of the Priest King discovered near the south-east entrance—scenes of public ceremony, sport or ritual at which the Court ladies prinked and chattered—and, again and again, on corridor walls, in miniature statuary, and on the tiny bead seals—the *Bull*.

* Some scholars disagree with Evans. Professor Nilsson, for example, believes that the figures which Evans thought represented one goddess actually represent several, each with her own attributes.
† This is all the more remarkable as the Minoans were in contact with Egyptians for more than a thousand years.

161

Above right The entrance to the Lustral Bath

Right West wing of the Palace with '*pithoi*' and the 'Horns of Consecration'

Opposite Restored fresco of the Priest King

163

Had the Bull, too, some religious significance? Evans noted that on the seals and signets, on the fresco paintings and elsewhere appeared the conventionalized symbol of the bull's horns. Sometimes it appeared as a frieze above the roof of a shrine of the Mother Goddess. At others it appeared in conjunction with that other familiar Minoan symbol, the Double Axe. On the south side of the Palace he found remains of a huge specimen of these 'Horns of Consecration' which at one time had evidently surmounted the roof of the Palace, so that all approaching from the southern road from Egypt could see it. Evans reinstated it near the same position. Nevertheless, as his researches continued, he decided that the Bull had not been worshipped as a diety, but that it may have been considered a favourite animal of the earth-god, and was therefore sometimes sacrificed to him. The presence of the Minoan Goddess (as shown in the wall paintings) at the 'bull-leaping' sports, seemed to suggest that this ceremony, too, may have been a sacrifice. Theseus and the Minotaur—the seven Athenian youths and maidens—*was* there some connection?

The bull-leaping frescoes fascinated people far beyond the limited circle of professional archaeologists. Wherever these extraordinary pictures were reproduced, with their slim-figured Minoan acrobats— dark-skinned men and pale-skinned girls both wearing the same scanty costume—they aroused controversy. Was such a fantastic feat possible? In the Villa Ariadne, in his study at Youlbury, Evans pored over the pictures, trying to penetrate the mystery. Here he is describing the fresco.

In the design ... the girl acrobat in front seizes the horns of a coursing bull at full gallop, one of which seems to run under her left armpit. The object of her grip ... clearly seems to be to gain a purchase for a backward somersault over the animal's back, such as is being performed by the boy (identified conventionally by his darker skin. L.C.).

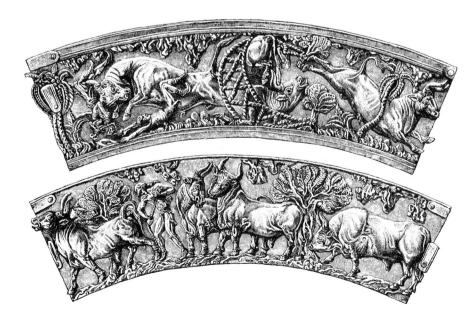

Engraving of the extended design on the two cups found at Vapheio, on the Greek mainland, south of Sparta

164

The second female performer behind stretches out both her hands as if to catch the flying figure or at least to steady him when he comes to earth the right way up. The stationing of this figure handily for such an act raises some curious questions as to the arrangements within the arena.

Some authorities refuse to believe that such a performance was possible. Professor Baldwin Brown, for instance, showed the pictures to a veteran 'steer-wrestler' from the American Far-West, who refused to believe that it could be done. 'You couldn't catch hold of the bull's horns for the start of the somersault,' he said, 'for there's no chance of a human person being able to obtain a balance when the bull is charging full against him.' The bull, he added, is three times as strong as a steer, and when running, 'raises his head sideways and gores anyone in front of him.' So, as no one has so far offered to put the matter to a practical test, the mystery remains a mystery.

It was while studying the Minoan cult of the bull that Evans made a discovery which perfectly illustrates his imaginative interpretation of a tiny detail—one among many such examples. The scenes from the two famous golden cups found at Vapheio and first published more than ten years before Evans dug at Knossos are illustrated here. These richly-wrought vessels were thought at first to be 'Mycenaean'. After Evans's Knossian finds they were recognized to be Minoan in style, probably imported from Crete, or alternatively produced on the mainland by Cretan artists.

The discovery of the bull-frescoes at Knossos aroused new interest in the Vapheio cups, as the subject of their lively reliefs was the trapping of wild bulls.

One side of a cup shows slim-waisted young Minoans trying to catch a bull in a wooded glade. A net was stretched between two trees and the bulls driven towards it. One scene on the cup shows a bull firmly meshed in the net but another scene shows an animal, having evaded the trap, throwing down one hunter who falls helplessly on his back, while the other desperately grasps the animal's horns in an effort to bring him down. And the figure on the horns, said Evans, is a *girl*. 'She has locked her legs and arms around the monster's horns in such a way that it is impossible for him to transfix her.'

The figure on the Vapheio Cup, thus desperately at grips with the horns of the great beast, is certainly that of a girl, in spite of the sinewy limbs it displays. This fact, not apparently noted in any description of the scene, should be clear to any one intimate with Minoan iconography who remembers the parallel wall paintings in which the sex is declared by the white skin colour . . . in the present case the luxuriance of the locks is in striking contrast to those of the fallen youth in front, which have . . . a short appearance in front. . . .

These scenes, Evans thought, paralleled the 'bull-leaping frescoes' which adorned the walls of the Palace of Minos. First the animals were hunted and trapped in the open. Later they were made to perform for more sophisticated audiences in the bull-ring of the Knossian Palace. In each case the young men and women pitted their skill against the animals.

But the most interesting illustration of Evans's observation is in the other scene we have illustrated, which comes from the second Vapheio

165

Cup. The two animals were thought by earlier archaeologists to be two bulls; indeed, apart from their faces they look very similar. Yet, as Evans discovered, the animal on the left is a decoy cow, introduced by the wily hunters to entrap the bull. The Minoan artist, realizing that the body of the cow would be almost entirely hidden by that of the bull had to find some means of indicating its sex. He did this by showing it with raised tail—the normal reaction of a cow when sexually roused. It was this tiny detail which gave Evans the clue. The three scenes on the Cup became perfectly clear. The first now shows the bull nosing the cow's tail. In the second

the bull's treacherous companion, writes Evans, engages him in amorous converse, of which her raised tail shows the sexual reaction. The extraordinary human expressiveness of the two heads as they turn to each other is very characteristic of the Minoan artistic spirit.

In the third scene

the herdsman takes advantage of his dalliance to lasso the mighty beast by the hind leg. The bull is seen with head raised, bellowing with impotent rage.

These reliefs had been known to archaeologists for more than twenty years before Evans pointed out their true meaning.

For season after season he continued his patient excavation, clearing, and, where necessary, reconstituting the Palace of Knossos. Unreflecting visitors to Knossos have sometimes critized Evans for his 'reinforced concrete restoration'. Such criticisms are unintelligent; he had no alternative.

The upper stories (he wrote) of which, in the Domestic Quarter, three successive stages were encountered—had not, as in the parallel case of other ancient buildings, been supported by solid pieces of masonry or brickwork, or by stone columns. They had been held up in a principal degree by a timber framework the huge posts of which, together with the shafts of the columns, were either supplied by the cypress forests, then existing in the neighbouring glens, or by similar material imported from over sea. The reduction, either by chemical powers or by actual burning, of these wooden supports had thus left vast voids in the interspaces. The upper floors had indeed, in a manner that some times seemed almost miraculous, held approximately at their levels by the rubble formation that had insinuated itself below—due largely to the falling of bricks of unburned clay—partly dissolved—from the upper walls.
At the same time, whenever this intrusive material was removed there was nothing to prevent the remains of the upper fabric from crashing down to a lower level.

First Evans tried wooden beams and posts, but they tended to rot rapidly; then pieces of masonry and shafts and capitals cut laboriously from stone, while brickwork arches and girders supported the upper pavements; but this was not satisfactory and cost too much—even for Evans. Finally he decided to use reinforced concrete, which is very strong, looks well, and can be erected rapidly.

The cost of excavation and restoration became greater every year, but Evans was determined that the Palace should be presented to the world in a form that not only the archaeologist could appreciate but so that even the least imaginative lay visitor could feel and respond to its wonder. In this he succeeded beyond measure. But physical restoration of walls, floors, columns, porticoes, satisfied only a part of Evans's nature. It was more difficult, and therefore more attractive, to

Top Vapheio Cup B, side 1, showing a bull being hobbled to a tree by the leg

Centre Vapheio Cup A, side 1, showing 'the bull that got away', leaving a man falling to the ground and a girl clinging to the bull's head so as not to be gored

Bottom Vapheio Cup B, side 2, showing the bull being trapped by the use of a 'decoy' cow (on left)

167

discover the moral and spiritual bases of the Minoan civilization. What had this ancient people believed, hoped, feared? Why this apparent insistence on the propitiation of the Earth? Why the cult of the Snake—emblem of the Earth? Why the mysterious 'lustral areas'—the steps leading down into the Earth?

Further evidence of mysterious religious practices came to light—also linked with Earth-worship. At Knossos, Phaestos and elsewhere in Crete the archaeologists came upon subterranean crypts—dark underground chambers, the central feature of which was always a heavy stone pillar. Sometimes these crypts lay beneath surface buildings, but generally speaking, the central Pillar was far more substantial than was needed to support the superstructure. Sometimes there was no superincumbent building, but the Pillar was still as massive, and often inscribed with the sign of the Double Axe. In some cases there would be a drain near the pillar—presumably to take the blood of sacrifice. Evans called these chambers 'Pillar crypts'.

When Evans was able to date more accurately the successive strata under the mound of Kephala he noticed that although Knossos had been almost continuously occupied since the New Stone Age (*circa* 4000 BC to 3000 BC) until about 1100 BC, there had been breaks in the chain of development—marks of catastrophe in the form of broken walls and charred timbers; three especially severe disasters seemed to have occurred; round about 1700 BC; between the end of the Middle Minoan period and the beginning of Late Minoan; and again in about 1400 BC; and there were signs of others. These could have been caused by foreign attack, by local insurrection or by civil war. Or, thought Arthur Evans, could they have been caused by earthquakes?

He had pondered upon this possibility for some time. He knew that Crete lay in a seismic area, and he consulted the medieval and modern

Right The Throne Room during its restoration: new columns were fitted into the original Minoan sockets and a flat roof was built on top of the structure

Opposite top Evans's excavations of the Servant's House, photographed at the time of work

Opposite bottom Photograph of the Hall of Double Axes taken during its reconstruction. Behind is the tower built so that the excavations could be supervised

history of the island to see if the shocks appeared to follow a definite cycle. He found that six especially destructive earthquakes took place in Crete in six and a half centuries. 'That space of time,' he wrote, 'almost exactly corresponds with the duration of the great Minoan Palace into its successive phases, and we are almost bound to infer that the same natural forces must largely account for the signs of ruin that here mark successive stages of the building.'

Here perhaps, lay the answer to the mystery of those 'Lustral Areas'—flights of steps leading into the earth itself—perhaps they had been used for some ceremony of earth-propitiation?

During his later excavations Evans had a curious and slightly sinister experience, which strengthened his belief in the 'earthquake' theory. He had been digging outside the Palace wall on the south-eastern side, when his workmen 'struck the corner of a small house . . . of the Third Middle Minoan period . . . this little house had been ruined by huge blocks hurled—some of them over twenty feet—by what could have been no less than a violent earthquake shock. . . . The house was never rebuilt but, like another in the adjoining area west, was filled with materials derived from the contemporary ruin.'

The little house appeared to have belonged to an artisan—a lamp maker—and a number of unfinished lamps were found among the ruins. Near this 'House of the Fallen Blocks' was another, which seems to have been damaged at the same time, and here the excavators made a significant discovery. In the north-west and south-east corners of the southern basement had been set the heads of 'two large oxen of the *urus* breed, the horn-cores of one of which were over a foot in girth at the base. . . .' These sacrificial relics which were carefully placed near tripod altars could, said Evans, have only one significance. 'The methodical filling in of the building and its final relinquishment as a scene of human habitation had been preceded by a solemn expiatory offering to the Powers below.'

Bulls had been sacrificed to the Earth-God. As they examined the

View of Knossos from the end of the East staircase showing the main courtyard, the throne room and the West Portico

remains, the excavators found it easy to imagine the solemn warning which may have been issued by the Minoan priest, 4,800 years ago, against all who might attempt to undo his work.

Then, says Evans, just as the workmen completed the task of clearing this 'House of Sacrifice' at 12.15 p.m. on April 20th, 1922, 'a short, sharp shock, sufficient to throw one of my men backwards, accompanied by a deep rumbling sound, was experienced on the site, and throughout the region. . . .'

And he remembered that in the *Iliad*, Book Twenty, Homer had written:

In Bulls does the Earth-shaker delight.

It was two in the morning.

The fire had sunk into a mass of red embers. I felt cold and cramped. Gathering together my pile of books I placed them carefully on the table, hoping I would remember to return them to the library in the morning. Somehow there seemed no point in carrying them back along the shadowy corridor tonight.

I switched off the light, and, as I closed the door before descending the creaking stairs to my basement bedroom, saw, silhouetted against the dying glow of the fire, the profile of the Minoan Bull. . . .

15 PALACE OF THE SEA-KINGS

Early next day, after Manoli had served breakfast in the austere dining-room, I strolled along the winding path past Hadrian and the bougainvillaeas, scrambled down a slope and so reached the narrow lane which leads to the Palace. It was a way which Sir Arthur must have used thousands of times, and I sensed his unseen presence, swinging the formidable Prodger, and acknowledging the respectful salutes of the villagers.

Knossos lies in a hollow, half-hidden by trees, with vine-yards climbing the lower slopes of the gentle hills which enclose it on east, west and south. Only the northern side, the way to the sea, lies open. And though the Palace stands on a mound, it is a mound largely of its own making, the debris of more than 2,000 years' occupation.

Piet de Jong met me at the gatekeeper's lodge. We passed through the screen of cypresses and, as we came out into the sunlight, I saw for the first time the Palace of Minos. Even then it did not reveal itself all at once. A wall of finely-cut masonry hid the view immediately ahead, but to the right, i.e. to the south-west, I saw the spacious north-west courtyard and the north-west entrance to the Palace. Over the threshold, past low walls and carefully-kept pavements, a turn to the left, and I was in the reconstructed fragment of the columned Propylaeum Hall. It was here that Evans had found the Cupbearer Fresco, the first portrait of a Minoan to be discovered. The original pieces now hang in the Herakleion Museum, but here, on the brightly sunlit wall, hung one of Gilliéron's brilliant copies. For a split-second the purist in me protested against all this reproduction but was instantly silenced.

For it is no use comparing a Cretan Palace with the great monuments of Egypt, where the dry air has preserved walls and columns and architraves in their original state for three thousand years. Though hot and dry in summer, Crete has torrential winter rains, and next to human destroyers, damp is probably the greatest enemy of ancient monuments. Its destructiveness is all the greater when, as at Knossos, much timber was used in the construction. The walls, especially in the earlier Palaces, were timber-framed, and the columns which supported roofs, porches, and stairways, were all of timber. When the Palace was sacked (or set on fire by an earthquake— it is not decided) the wooden pillars and framing burned, and such timber as escaped the fire has long since rotted away under the damp earth.

The walls collapsed, the roofs fell, so that the only possible way in

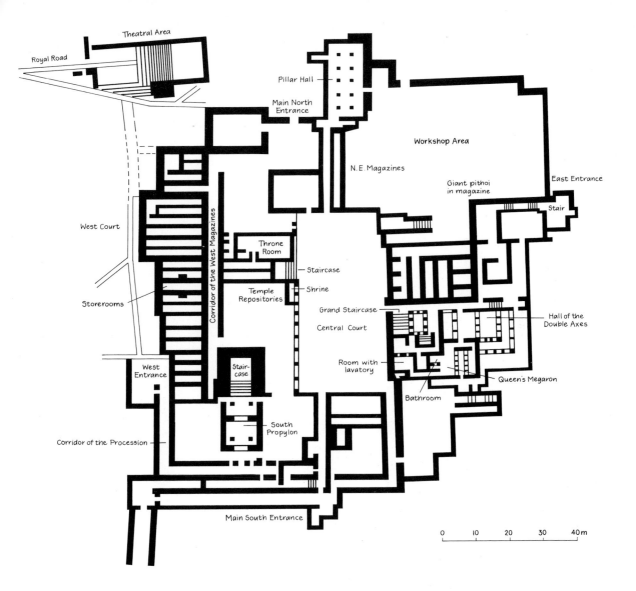

Site map: Knossos

which Evans and his colleagues could show the *original* appearance of
the Palace was by a painstaking reconstruction of typical fragments,
such as the Propylaeum Hall and the North Portico. Perhaps in his
enthusiasm Evans may have gone a little too far—that is a matter of
opinion—but on large parts of the site he had only two alternatives—
to reconstitute, or leave a rubbish heap. None the less, as de Jong
pointed out to me, every fragment of original work which could be
recovered was kept, and an impressive proportion of the Knossian
Palace, especially in the Domestic Quarter, is original Minoan
masonry, untouched for thirty centuries.

Piet showed me the system Evans adopted to denote the original
construction of the Palace in his careful reconstructions.

'In a decayed wall,' he said, 'we would often find evidences of the

173

original stone "chases"' (grooves) 'into which the timber framework was fitted. When we rebuilt the wall we replaced the rotted wood with concrete, and painted it pale buff, to indicate wood. The rest of the wall we rebuilt as far as possible with the original stone blocks.'

Along the wall the two Cup-bearers* marched in slow, stately procession; slim-waisted, broad-shouldered, with proud, aristocratic features and curling black hair. Now at last I began to sense the strangeness of Knossos. We were only a few hundred miles from Egypt, with which the Minoans had been in contact for two thousand

The Royal Road at Knossos, called by Sir Arthur Evans 'the oldest road in Europe'

* Originally there was a long procession of these youths.

The North Portico

years. Yet there was nothing Egyptian in the faces or dress of these people. I thought of the wall paintings I had seen in the tombs of Luxor, those solemn, stiff, hieratic figures in their robes of gauffered linen; these Minoans were quite different. They looked more European than Asiatic—though Evans believed they came originally from Asia. Yet they were not like the classical Greeks. Who were they? *Where* had they come from? How tantalizing of them to have left us no history!

But de Jong, the practical architect, was speaking again.

'People often ask why they made their columns with a downward taper,' he said. 'Do you know?'

'No. Was there any special reason?'

'It's never been properly settled. I think the most feasible theory is that, as the columns were made from tree trunks, they placed them *root upwards*, with the broadest part of the trunk at the top, to prevent the trees sprouting again. Or it may have been just to leave more space at the bottom. These columns here,' he added, slapping the big rust-coloured pillars of the Propylaeum, 'are concrete of course. But we know they stood here, because we found the column-bases, and the capitals lying nearby.'

I asked him how he ascertained the height and proportion of the columns, but this, he assured me, was only a matter of careful surveying and comparison with architectural remains found on other parts of the site. Sometimes impressions of the columns remained in the earth, though the wood had rotted away.

175

'You know,' said Piet, 'one of Sir Arthur's greatest gifts was his capacity for *visualizing*. He could tell, just by looking at a few broken stones, a fallen column, and a few bits of fresco, exactly how the whole room or building originally looked. And he'd get *most* impatient if his architect couldn't see it just as quickly. Yet when the architect had surveyed and measured the site, and studied all the architectural evidence, the fact is that Sir Arthur was nearly always right.'

Among the valuable evidence was that of the painted frescoes, which often depicted buildings with the typical Minoan tapered column. These were a great help when making reconstructions. Some of the most useful information on the shape and appearance of Minoan houses was obtained from representations in the form of small faience plaques only a few inches square.

'But the *colouring*,' I exclaimed. 'The place must have *glowed* with colour. How did you know, for instance, that the columns were a russet, and that their capitals were sometimes blue, sometimes black?'

'From the frescoes,' he replied, as we turned to the left into the great gallery leading to the Magazines. 'You'll see. But first let me show you something.' He led the way into a broad, stone-paved corridor from which opened numerous long, narrow rooms, the walls standing to a height of six feet or more and in some cases roofed over.

Above The tapering columns at the bottom of the Grand Staircase

Opposite The dolphin fresco, Knossos

176

'Now very little of this has been reconstructed,' he said. 'What you see now is practically all Minoan. We just put back the roof.'

We were in the store-rooms of King Minos; the repository of his wealth. The rooms were nearly all full of great earthenware jars, some more than six feet high; originally they had contained oil, grain, dried fish, beans, olives, for in the days of the Minoan thalassocracy wealth was not only in gold and precious things, but in kind. Let into the floor of the rooms were narrow stone-lined cysts or chambers, originally hidden under stone slabs.

'These,' said de Jong, 'were a kind of safe-deposit; at one time in the history of the Palace they were used for storing precious things—the kind of things Schliemann found in the shaft-graves of Mycenae. In fact Evans suggested that the Mycenaean treasures may actually have rested here at one time. But he found hardly anything when he uncovered these cysts in 1900—just a few fragments of gold to show what had been there once. They were all thoroughly plundered when the Palace was sacked and burned. Look at the marks of the fire—see?' And he pointed to the edge of the pit.

There, unmistakably, on the northern edge was the mark of black, unctuous smoke, almost certainly made by burning oil. Elsewhere I saw many other evidences of fire and always the tell-tale stain showed that the smoke had been blown to the north.

So a south wind was blowing when the great Palace fell. . . .

As I followed the Curator up a flight of broad steps to the Central Court, a curious, faint uneasiness began to mingle with my delight and wonder. I am not a superstitious man, I have no belief in the supernatural and my journalistic experience has trained me to observe and report facts. But I have to admit that, in spite of the keen spring air, the sunshine, and my own pleasure in visiting Knossos, the atmosphere of the Palace depressed me. It was—there is no other word for it—sinister.

But now, in the spacious Central Court, I was able to drink in the full splendour of Knossos. Standing in the centre and looking north towards the sea, I could see on my left the official quarters of the Palace, from which Crete was administered in the days of Knossian supremacy. Though only the lower storey of these ruined buildings remained, still they stirred the mind; and above them storey upon storey had once stood; these had been rooms of state approached by flights of broad, shallow steps flanked by columns, and lit by a system of light-wells (as in modern hotels and office blocks) which allowed a soft indirect light to penetrate while avoiding the direct rays of the hot summer sun, or the icy winter winds. Though most of these rooms have vanished, their character is known through the almost miraculous preservation of the Domestic Apartments on the eastern side of the Great Court, to which de Jong now led me.

To reach them we had to descend the famous Grand Staircase, itself the greatest monument of Knossos; a monument not only to the Minoans, but, let it be added, to the extraordinary skill of Christian Doll, the architect who preserved it. We crossed the Court and began the descent. The steps are of gypsum, a smooth white, crystalline

177

stone, much used by the Minoans for the interiors of their buildings. Originally there were five flights, but the two upper storeys have left only slight indications. But as we went lower I walked down three full flights which must have looked exactly the same to the Minoan courtiers and ladies as they followed in the train of the Priest King more than 3,600 years ago. On my left, as I descended, was the Minoan wall, originally covered with gay frescoes in the now familiar tones of pale blue and russet. On the right was a low balustrade overlooking a central wall which gave light to the stairway. Rising from the balustrade were stout Minoan columns of the familiar downward-tapering form, supporting the landings above. The column-bases with their sockets were original, and when Evans, Christian Doll and the rest—aided by Greek miners—tunnelled into these depths nearly fifty years ago, they found the carbonized stumps of the original wooden columns still remaining in their bases. The present columns, of identical shape to the originals, are of stone masked with stucco. I recalled Evans's description of how he and his staff dealt with a huge wall which threatened to topple and destroy all that was left of this masterpiece of the Minoan master-architect (could his name have been Daedalus . . .?)

The Grand Staircase leading down into the domestic quarters

The landing block of the fourth flight of the Grand Staircase being manoeuvered back into position, under the supervision of Christian Doll

The middle staircase wall above the first flight was found to have a dangerous list outwards involving a continual risk to the remains of the whole fabric. . . . Under the superintendence of our trusty overseer Gregorios Antoniou, the wall was first harnessed and secured by planks and ropes; its base was then cut into, along its whole length on either side; wedge-shaped stones and cement were held in readiness for insertion in the outer slit, and sixty men on the terrace above were then set to pull the ropes secured to the casing. The mighty mass was thus set in motion, and righted itself against the solid wooden framework prepared as a stop. This was then removed, and the whole structure refixed in its upright position. By these various means it has been possible to maintain the staircase and balustrade at their original levels, and thus restore to the modern world the structural aspects of this great work which dates back some 3,600 years. . . .

All the expense of this tremendous work was borne by Evans alone; a rich man, admittedly, but it is worth noting *en passant* that not all men of wealth spend it on yachts and racehorses. And, conversely, can anyone—even the most passionate advocate of State control— imagine a modern 'progressive' Government spending *a quarter of a million pounds* on preserving an ancient monument—even if it was vital to the history of our civilization? If Knossos had been discovered in 1952, Evans, presumably, would have had to apply for a grant from the impoverished British Council. . . .

The struggle to preserve the Grand Staircase was truly dramatic. It had all the classical elements of conflict—between the archaeologists on one hand, and Time and Decay on the other. Here is part of Evans's own account from *The Palace of Minos*.

. . . The hewing away of the clay concretions and the extraction of the various rubble and earthy materials of the intervening spaces left a void between the upper and lower spaces that threatened the collapse of the whole. The carbonized posts and beams and shafts, although their form and measurement could be often observed, were splintered up and exposed and, of course, could afford no support. The recourse to mine props and miscellaneous timbering was almost temporary and at times so insufficient that some dangerous falls occurred.

To relax our efforts meant that the remains of the Upper Storeys would have crashed down on those below, and the result would have been an indistinguishable heap of ruins. The only alternative was to endeavour to re-support the upper structures in some permanent manner. In the early days of the excavation the Architect, Mr Christian Doll, who manfully grappled with his Atlantean task, had perforce largely to rely on iron girders, brought from England at great expense, and these were partly masked with cement.... Even then, wood, which it was hard to obtain properly seasoned, was allowed to play a part in these reconstructions....

The cypress trunks and beams that had supported such masses of masonry in the old work were of course no longer obtainable, but we had to learn that even the pinewood of Tyrol, imported through Trieste ... could be reduced to rottenness and powder in a few years by the violent extremes of the Cretan climate....

It was not until reinforced concrete—with its interlacing web of steel wires—was introduced in the twenties, that Evans found an answer to his problem—how to provide enduring support for heavy masses of masonry, and how to roof large spaces cheaply and strongly. So the twentieth century AD came to the aid of the twentieth century BC. Daedalus, one feels, would have approved.

At the foot of the Grand Staircase we entered a short corridor leading to a suite of splendid rooms, and here I knew I was surrounded by genuine Minoan walls. It was the first time I had stood within a King's Palace belonging to a period contemporary with the Seventeenth and Eighteenth Dynasties of the Egyptian Pharaohs (1600–1350 BC) and the effect was overwhelming. In Egypt the royal palaces were usually temporary structures made of sun-dried bricks, of which only foundations remain. There only temples and tombs were built for eternity; how paltry are the remains even of the Palace of the magnificent Amenophis III at Medinet Habou, compared with the tombs of Amenophis and his descendants in the Royal Valley at Luxor. But at Knossos one walks through rooms which once heard the seductive rustle of the Minoan ladies' flounced skirts, and echoed to

Reconstruction of the Hall of Double Axes by Sir Arthur Evans's artist

180

the murmur of gossip and music. There, in his high-backed throne under the wall of shields, sits Minos himself . . . in that far corner a group of elegant young men are gambling—between them lies the inlaid gaming-board which Evans found nearby. And not far away Minoan ladies, jewels glittering on their ivory breasts, are discussing fashion, destroying the reputations of absent friends, and perhaps recalling the amazing performance of that young Athenian in the arena on the previous day. What was the barbarian's name . . . Theseus? 'Did you notice how the Princess looked at him? But it was *obvious*, my dear, he just *had* to win . . .?'

Then Piet broke into my fantasy. 'Sir Arthur called this room the Hall of the Double Axes,' he said. 'Come over here and I'll show you something.'

There was a row of columns dividing the Hall of the Double Axes from the adjoining room. But let into these columns were recesses which proved that at one time folding doors had existed which in winter would be kept closed for warmth. In summer, however, the doors could be neatly folded back into the recesses in the columns, allowing a free flow of cool air.

Then the Curator pointed to a low plinth on the northern wall of the Hall. 'We think there was a Throne here,' he said, 'just like the one in the Room of the Throne on the west side of the Court—I'll show you that later. But that had some religious significance, while these were purely the private apartments of the royal family. You see—Sir Arthur put a wooden replica of the Throne to replace the one that's disappeared.'

On each side of the Throne hung a great figure-eight shield, full-sized, big enough to have covered the body of a Minoan warrior. Behind them on the stucco wall, was a painted spiral band. I had first seen this curious body-shield, so like that described in the *Iliad*, on the Mycenaean daggers which Schliemann found in the shaft-graves, and on the tiny bead-seals which Evans had reproduced in his *Palace of Minos*. Now here it was, hung on the wall of one of the principal rooms of the Palace of Minos itself more than one thousand years older than Homer.

'They're not the original shields, of course,' said de Jong, 'but Evans found that in the rooms which once existed above the Hall of the Colonnades there had been shaped shields painted on the walls, connected by a spiraliform band—like a dado. Well, here, in the Hall of the Double Axes, there was the dado all right—but no shields. Sir Arthur reckoned that instead of painted shields there may have been *real* shields hanging on the wall as a decoration. So he told Gilliéron to make accurate painted copies, and hang them on the wall on each side of the Throne. And there they are.'

Then he led me through a short, twisting corridor into the most private apartments of the Palace, which Evans, sensing a certain femininity in the surviving decoration, named 'The Queen's Mega-ron'*. Here all was lightness and grace. There were low seats around

* Hall or principal room.

the walls, which were bright with gay frescoes of natural scenes. Dark blue dolphins sported on an eggshell-blue ground; there were starfish, and spiky 'sea-urchins' or 'sea-eggs'—realistically drawn, yet all conforming to the overall decorative pattern. One wall opened on to a columned light-well from which a soft illumination filled the interior. On the other side a doorway led to a further suite of smaller rooms, accessible from the main *salon*, but not from outside. Here was a little bathroom, with an earthenware bath shaped almost exactly like its modern descendant. The bath had evidently been filled by hand—presumably by a handmaiden—but nearby was a hole in the pavement through which the waste water could be poured into the main drain.

An adjoining room, smaller than the bathroom, had undoubtedly been a W.C. In Evans's words:

On the face of a gypsum slab to the right is a groove for a seat about 57 cm from the floor. Outside the doorway of the latrine is a flag [stone] sloped towards a semicircular hole, forming a sink, and from this opens a small duct leading to the main drain. The aperture leading to the main drain, partly masked by a curious projection, deviates from the centre of the seat, thus leaving room on the right for some vessel used for flushing the basin. As an anticipation of scientific methods of sanitation, the system of which we have here the record has been attained by few nations even at the present day.

It is typical of our technological age that, for most lay visitors to the Knossian Palace, none of its aesthetic treasures make such a profound appeal as this 3,600-year-old latrine. Indeed, for anyone to whom sanitation and civilization are synonymous, Knossos is irresistible. It is a Plumber's Paradise. Great stone channels led the water from the roof to underground drains, and these shafts, says Evans, were themselves ventilated by air-shafts and made accessible by manholes

so roomy that my Cretan workmen spent whole days in them without inconvenience. The elaborate drainage system of the Palace and the connected sanitary arrangements

Above Reconstruction of how the Queen's megaron might originally have looked, by Sir Arthur Evans's artist

Below The Queen's bath

182

The Queen's megaron as it looks today

excite the wonder of all beholders. The terra-cotta pipes, with their scientifically-shaped sections, nicely interlocked, which date from the earliest days of the building, are quite up to modern standards. . . . The slightly tapering form of the sections of which the terra-cotta pipes were composed . . . were admirably designed to impart a shooting motion to the flow of water so as to prevent the accumulation of sediment. . . .'

But the most remarkable example of Minoan hydraulic engineering is on the North-East Bastion, to which de Jong took me after we had re-climbed the Grand Staircase. Here is a noble flight of steps leading from the north-east angle of the central court to the lower ground near the river. These steps were in the open air, and a channel had been cut at the side of each flight to carry away rainwater. That in itself did not seem very extraordinary, until de Jong showed me the scientific construction of these channels. Each flight of steps (which were quite steep) was at right-angles to the next, and the problem of the Minoan engineers was to get the water round the corners without overflowing on to the landings. If the water-ducts at the sides had been mere flat-bottomed slopes the rainwater would have rushed down them at such velocity that inevitably it would have overflowed at the first corner.

The trick was to slow down its speed; and this was done most

183

cunningly by making the bottom of the water-channels in a series of *parabolic curves*. The curves themselves almost exactly agree with the natural parabolas that the water falling down a slope at such an angle would make. Therefore the water reached the bottom of each flight at about *half* the speed it would have reached had it poured down the slope in a straight line instead of in a series of jumps. 'Nothing,' writes Evans, 'in the whole building gives such an impression of the result of long generations of intelligent experience on the part of the Minoan engineers as the parabolic curves of the channels.'

Nor was this all. A series of catch-pits collected the sediment on its downward course, so that when the water reached the bottom of the steps it was still pure and fit for washing purposes. And Evans adds, with one of those charming Homeric touches of which he was so fond, 'the special fitness of rainwater for washing linen warrants the conjecture that the tank was used for this purpose, and Minoan Nausikaas* may have made their way here from the Palace halls above.'

This north-east quarter of the Palace seems to have contained workshops for the artisans. In one of them Piet showed me a block of purple Spartan basalt half sawn through. There it lay on the floor, just as the workman had left it. Why had he left his work unfinished? Again, I felt that slight sense of unease which I first noticed when I saw the marks of fire in the great Magazines. We walked across the court again to the west side, where in a gallery above the Room of the Throne were hung some of Gilliéron's brilliant copies of the frescoes I had come so far to see. There they were—the fresco of the bull-leapers, the fresco of the grandstand with the chattering ladies, the products of a civilization which, sixteen hundred years before Christ, had already reached and passed its prime; was, in fact, decadent. All the charm, the intelligence, the jaded sophistication of a rich, declining culture were present in those delicate paintings. But there was something else, too, something which had haunted me since I entered the Palace, a sense of doom, a smell of death.

Evans believed that an earthquake brought about the final destruction of Knossos. Pendlebury, a younger scholar, believed that it was sacked, probably by a force from the mainland of Greece. I believe that Pendlebury was right. I feel that the Minoan culture, as represented in the Knossian frescoes, had passed its apogee before 1400, had over-ripened and become rotten, and that when the invaders came, whoever they were—probably Homer's 'bronze-clad Achaeans'—they only hastened an end which was inevitable.

But the end must have been very terrible on that spring day, fourteen hundred years before Christ, when the wind was blowing strongly from the south . . . even now something of the terror lingers in marks of fire, in blackened walls and floors, fragments of charred timber—grim evidence of the fatal day when the raiders came. One draws breath with wonder at the delicate beauty of the wall-paintings, at the slim effeminate dark-skinned youths with their narrow waists

---

* Nausikaa, the daughter of King Alkinous of Phaecia, was surprised by Odysseus when she and her maidens were playing by the seashore after washing the family linen.

184

The Throne Room, restored, with the original gypsum throne and a reproduction of the griffin fresco

and black, curling hair; at the groups of chattering, elegant women with their pale ivory skins, jewelled necklaces and hooped and flounced skirts. And then one thinks of the last day—the women running screaming through the frescoed corridors, the desperate fighting in doorways and staircases, the master-craftsman disturbed at his work, leaving one stone jar half-finished—the warrior lying dead across his great body-shield—the smell of smoke, the sound of crashing timbers, the splash of blood on the white gypsum pavement. . . .

'Come and have a look at the Throne Room,' said Piet.

The Room of the Throne is the most dramatic room in Knossos, and I was glad de Jong had left it to the last. We entered the low-ceilinged outer chamber, opened a wooden gate and were in the Throne Room itself. It was not very large, of rectangular shape, the broadest side being on the right. On this long, right-hand wall crouched two magnificent painted griffins—lion-like creatures with the heads of birds in the now familiar russet on a pale blue ground. Between the guardian griffins rose the Throne of Minos himself still in its original place with its high 'wavy-edged' back and anatomically-shaped seat.

On each side of the Throne, and extending to the flanking walls, were low stone benches. The impression of a 'cathedral chapter house'—as suggested by Evans—was very strong.

In front of the Throne, to the left of the door, broad steps led down to one of those mysterious pits—the 'Lustral Areas' or 'ritual impluvia' which Evans believed had been used in connection with some ceremony of anointing. In the antechamber outside still stood stone and earthenware jars which had been found on the site, and which seem to have been used in this ceremony. Other smaller rooms opened out of the Throne Room. One of them seems to have been a kitchen, and it may well have happened that on certain occasions the Priest King retired to this suite of chambers and isolated himself from the rest of the community for an extended period—perhaps days, perhaps weeks.

It was all so baffling. If only the Minoans had left written records which we could understand!

'Well,' said Piet, 'that's about all in the Palace itself, apart from the North Portico and the Theatral Area, which we can see this afternoon. I'll have to get back to the *Taverna*, but you've no need to hurry if you want to stay. But lock the door after you when you go.'

As the Curator's footsteps died away I sat on the oldest Throne in Europe. It was extremely comfortable. There was no sound outside. In front of me the dim light from the upper storey filtered down into the ritual pit, flanked by its tapering, russet-coloured columns. Then I recalled a passage from a book which, next to *The Palace of Minos*, is probably the most authoritative and scholarly work yet written on the Minoan civilization: John Pendlebury's *The Archaeology of Crete*.

The eastern flight of steps in the theatral area at Knossos

Pendlebury believed that Knossos was finally sacked by an invading force from the mainland, probably men from the colonial empire of Minos, determined at last to throw off the Minoan yoke.

'Now there is a name,' he wrote, 'which is always associated with the sack of Knossos, at least with the liberation of its subjects—*Theseus*. Names have a habit of being remembered when the deeds with which they are associated are forgotten or garbled. . . . It has already been suggested that the seven youths and seven maidens may have been the mainland quota for the bull-ring at Knossos. This is just the type of detail that would be remembered, the more so in that it may well have been the sentimental reason without which no purely commercial war can ever take place. No doubt the rape of Helen was a very good rallying cry when the Mycenaean Empire wished to break through to the Black Sea trade which Troy was keeping to herself.'

'And in the last decade of the fifteenth century on a spring day, when a strong south wind was blowing which carried the flames of the burning beams horizontally northward, Knossos fell. . . .'

'. . . The final scene takes place in the most dramatic room ever excavated—the Throne Room. It was found in a state of complete confusion. A great oil jar lay overturned in one corner, ritual vessels were in the act of being used when the disaster came. It looks as if the King had been hurried there to undergo, too late, some last ceremony in the hopes of saving the people. Theseus and the Minotaur! Dare we believe that he wore the mask of the bull?'

16 THE OLD TRADITIONS WERE TRUE

In the year 1911, at the age of sixty, Evans was knighted; an honour bestowed not only for his work in Crete, but for his overall contribution to learning. Three years earlier he had resigned his Keepership of the Ashmolean, in order to devote all his time to Knossos; but by that time his triumph over the reactionary elements in the University was complete. At the time of Evans's resignation, the new Chancellor, Lord Curzon, had written to him, 'Your real monument is the Ashmolean itself, now organized and equipped on a scale that renders it absolutely unrecognizable to the Oxonian of twenty-five years ago....' At the same time Evans retained the honorary post of Visitor to the Ashmolean, which enabled him to keep an eye on its affairs, as he did to the end of his life, besides making generous gifts to it.

During the 1914–18 war he kept a vigilant eye on those centres of learning which tend in wartime to be brusquely treated by the military authorities. Always in times of national emergency there are jacks-in-office who take advantage of their brief authority to make stupid and arbitrary use of their powers. When such people crossed the path of Sir Arthur Evans they usually got hurt.

For example, in the early years of the war, the Air Board tried to requisition the British Museum, and began roughly moving the collections to make room for Civil Servants. This to Sir Arthur was the 'breaking in of the jungles'. In letter after letter to the great newspapers, in public speeches and in private conversation, he lashed the Philistines.

In a notable speech he described the 'surprise visit' of an Air Board official, followed by a request by the Board to the Cabinet for permission to requisition the Museum as their headquarters. In the teeth of vigorous protest by the Trustees 'the order was actually given by the Cabinet' but 'this monstrous proposal, which both as Trustee of the Museum and President of the Society of Antiquaries, I did something to expose, raised a general storm of indignation, not only among the accredited representatives of Art and the Historic Sciences, but throughout the Press.'

The order was withdrawn—the Air Board suddenly discovering that 'it did not need the building after all....'

But in the meantime much harm had been done. Galleries had been hurriedly cleared to make room for clerks. Evans spoke of 'weeks of labour in the clearing out of three large galleries, to the final undoing of the work of a century and a half ... entailed by the wanton caprice of a Government Department which, after having occasioned all this trouble and expense, came to the conclusion that they did not find the accommodation suitable!' Where was all this to end, he demanded.

'... the treatment of the British Museum, the incalculable destruction there of the results of generations of learned labour and classification, the commandeering—for there is no other word—of the University Press, show that those who control our Administration are inspired by a Philistine spirit for which we shall in vain seek a parallel among civilized Governments. Ruthless proscription, the result of panic action, threatens at every turn the very sanctuaries of learning. Those who represent its interests are doubtless a very inferior race in the eyes of politicians. We are not concerned to dispute their verdict, but it is well to remind them that even the lowest tribes of savages have their reservations. . . .'

Some may smile cynically at this outburst, remembering the far more deadly attacks on the citadels of culture during and since the recent war—the wholesale destruction of museums, galleries and works of art—the persecution and murder of non-conforming artists and scholars in totalitarian countries, the post-war 'witch-hunt' in America. But I think such cynicism is misplaced. Sir Arthur and his generation stood for absolute standards. They could not imagine a lowering of those standards, and when the attempt was made, they fought bitterly. In the end they lost, but they, and not the Philistines, were right. We are the losers.

In 1916, when a move was made to expel certain German Honorary Members from the Society of Antiquarians, Evans, in spite of the wave of hate which was sweeping the country, and in spite of his own revulsion against the barbarities being committed on sea and land, kept his head and spoke for reason and moderation. 'The existence among German Honorary Fellows of savants belonging to that noble class of which the late Dr Helbig stood forth as a conspicuous example—should give us pause before we carry out any too sweeping measures. In spite of the Gospel of Hate, let it be said to their credit, the learned societies and academies of Germany, with inconsiderable exceptions, have refrained from striking their English members from the rolls.'

And he ended his address with the noble words:

'We cannot shirk the fact that tomorrow we shall be once more labourers in the same historic field. It is incumbent on us to do nothing which should shut the door to mutual intercourse in subjects like our own, which lie apart from the domain of human passions, in the silent avenues of the past.'

I put down the account of Evans's address, closed the old, faded pamphlet and replaced it on the shelves of the library in the Villa Ariadne. I felt depressed. These fine exhortations, this splendid, selfless endeavour, had they not all been futile? Another war had come and gone, and the sons of the men with whom Sir Arthur Evans had 'laboured in a common field' of learning, had parachuted from the sky of Crete and themselves occupied the Villa Ariadne as a military headquarters. Admittedly, they had not harmed it seriously, nor the Palace. Only one tomb, at Isopata, has been destroyed by a German N.C.O. who, not realizing what it was, had turned it into a gun emplacement (the punishment which his commanding officer afterwards ordered would have made even Sir Arthur feel sorry for the sergeant). The war had ended, and the Germans had handed back the Villa Ariadne almost intact, with every article of its original furniture, accompanied by an accurate inventory. So perhaps some civilized instincts remained, even during war.... Perhaps Evans and his German confrères had not laboured entirely in vain.

I had been at Knossos for nearly a week, living at the Villa Ariadne and making excursions into the surrounding country. I had seen the Palace many times, in early morning, in the late evening, even by moonlight. I had taken my notes and photographs and tomorrow I was to cross the mountain chain to reach the other great Palace of Phaestos, in the south. And on the following day I had to fly to Athens and so back to cold, misty London.

As I put back Evans's Presidential Address to the British Association I noticed a group of notebooks with faded covers, resting on a lower shelf. I picked out one at random; it was filled with pencilled diagrams of pottery and notes in a small careful handwriting. The signature was 'D. Mackenzie'....

So these were Duncan Mackenzie's own notebooks; Mackenzie, the taciturn, talented Scotsman whom Evans had admired so much, and who had developed a unique system of dating pottery. I fingered the pages ... tried to decipher the abbreviated symbols 'L.M.1b' (Late Minoan, First Period, Second Subdivision) and so on. Poor Mackenzie suffered long under a mental illness to which he eventually succumbed. Long before he had finally to leave Knossos, he had been subject to fits of depression and nervous irritability which Evans, quick-tempered himself, bore with extraordinary patience. When, after long years, news reached Sir Arthur of Mackenzie's death, he wrote, in his *Palace of Minos*, a tribute of extraordinary tenderness.

His Highland loyalty never failed, and the simple surroundings of his earlier years gave him an inner understanding of the native workmen and a fellow feeling with them that was a real asset in the course of our spade-work. To them, though a master, he was ever a true comrade. The lively Cretan dances revived the 'reels' of his youth. No wedding ceremony, no baptism, no wake was complete without the sanction of his presence, and as sponsor, godfather, or 'best man', his services were in continual request. There still fall on my ear the tones of that 'still small voice' as he proposed the toast of a happy pair—with sly jocose allusions, fluently spoken in the Cretan dialect of modern Greek—but not without a trace of the soft Gaelic accent.

After the First World War, Evans had returned to Crete. Costs were higher, but he was a rich man, and after re-engaging his Cretan workmen he continued to excavate and restore the Palace of Knossos. Piet de Jong joined him in 1922—the third of Evans's resident architects. After the First World War de Jong had worked for Professor Wace at Mycenae. Evans had been so impressed by the architect's plans of the Mycenaean fortress that he had invited him to come to Knossos.

In 1921 appeared the first volume of his long-awaited *Palace of Minos*—of which further volumes were to appear at intervals during the next fourteen years. It was a monumental achievement; four great books (Volumes 2 and 4 were so enormous that each had to be issued in two sections) totalling more than 3,000 pages, with more than 2,400 illustrations—many of them in colour. Most of it was written at Youlbury, his Berkshire home. How he worked is described by his half-sister, Dr Joan Evans:

> The library was big enough to take any number of bookcases on the floor, apart from the bookshelves that lined its walls. Here he could work at his great book—classifying the material by the simple process of setting up a fresh trestle table for each fresh section, and moving from one to the other like a chess player engaged in multiple games.... In truth he needed space; his material was overwhelming; and he took advantage of none of the modern methods in dealing with it. He had neither secretary nor typewriter, and still used a quill pen.

Sir John Myres wrote of the work: 'The difficulty of such a composition was exceptional, for new discoveries were being made throughout the forty-two years since Evans landed in Crete. But throughout its 3,000 pages the vast work reads like a saga; there is always the great design, within which each topic and digression takes its place.'

From this work—almost unique among archaeological books in that it combines detailed scholarship with bursts of brilliant descriptive writing—I have already quoted typical passages. I would like to add one more, because it strongly reveals Evans's poetic imagination. Here, in Volume 3, he is describing the re-constituted Grand Staircase:

> The Grand Staircase, as thus reconstituted, stands alone among ancient architectural remains. With its charred columns solidly restored in their pristine hues, surrounding in tiers its central wall, its balustrades rising, practically intact, one above the other, with its imposing fresco of the great Minoan shields on the back wall of its middle gallery, now replaced in replica, and its still well-preserved gypsum steps ascending to four landings, it revives, as no other part of the building, the remote past. It was, indeed, my own lot to experience its strange power of imaginative suggestion, even at a time when the work of reconstitution had not attained its present completeness.
>
> During an attack of fever, having found, for the sake of better air, a temporary lodging in the room below the inspection tower that had been erected on the neighbouring edge of the Central Court, and tempted in the warm moonlight to look down the staircase well, the whole place seemed to awake awhile to life and movement. Such was the force of the illusion that the Priest-King with his plumed crown, great ladies, tightly girdled, flounced and corseted, long-stoled priests, and after them a retinue of elegant and sinewy youths—as if the Cup-bearer and his fellows had stepped down from the walls—passed and repassed on the flights below.'

It was this quality of imagination which helped him to solve one of his baffling archaeological problems—the significance of the mysterious 'Lustral Areas', the subterranean 'Pillar Crypts', and even of the Bull itself. For a long period he had suspected that these pits and crypts were associated with the propitiation of an earth-deity, perhaps represented by the Minoan Goddess herself in her aspect of Lady of the Underworld. That the Bull also entered into this worship he was

191

certain; we have noticed the significance he attached to the two sacrificed oxen found in the House of the Fallen Blocks. But confirmation came in most dramatic form on a warm summer night in June, when Sir Arthur was resting in one of the basement bedrooms of the Villa Ariadne.

My own mind . . . was full of past earthquakes and the foreboding of a new convulsion when on June 26 . . . at 9.45 in the evening of a calm, warm day, the shocks began. They caught me reading on my bed in a basement room of the headquarters house, and trusting to the exceptional strength of the fabric, I chose to see the earthquake through from within. Perhaps I had hardly realized the full awesomeness of the experience, though my confidence in the full strength of the building proved justified, since it did not suffer more than slight cracks. But it creaked and groaned, and rocked from side to side, as if the whole must collapse. Small objects were thrown about, and a pail, full of water, was nearly splashed empty. The movement, which recalled a ship in a storm, though of only a minute and a quarter's duration, already produced the same physical effect on me as a rough sea. A dull sound rose from the ground *like the muffled roar of an angry bull;** our single bell rang, while through the open window came the more distant jangling of the chimes of Candia Cathedral, the belfry as well as the dome and cupolas of which were badly damaged. As the quickly repeated shocks produced their cumulative effect the crashing of the roofs of the two small houses outside the garden gate made themselves audible, mingled with women's shrieks and the cries of some small children, who, however, were happily rescued. . . . Meanwhile a mist of dust, lifted upwards by a sudden draught of air, rose sky high, so as almost entirely to eclipse the full moon, some house lights reflected on this dark bank giving the appearance of a conflagration wrapped round with smoke. . . .

The archaeological *sequitur* of this is very important. When, as in the great Palace of Knossos we find evidence of a series of overthrows, some of them on a scale that could hardly be the work of men, there seems real reason for tracing the cause to the same seismic agencies. . . .

It is something to have heard with one's own ears the bellowing of the bull beneath the earth who, according to a primitive belief, tosses it on his horns. It was doubtless the constant need of protection against these petulant bursts of the infernal powers that explains the Minoan tendency to concentrate their worship on the chthonic aspect of their great goddess, wreathed with serpents as Lady of the Underworld. Certain structural features, moreover, peculiar to the old Cretan cult suggest the same explanation. Such were the 'lustral basins' which were not made for the purpose of holding water, but to which votaries descended, often by double flights of steps, for some ritual function that seems to connect itself with Mother Earth. Such, too, were the 'pillar crypts', windowless, and only lit by artificial light, the massive central piers of which, associated with the sacred double axe, were provided with vats beside them to receive the blood of sacrifice.

He was seventy-five when he had that experience. Some years before he had decided to give the Palace, the Villa Ariadne and its estate to the British School of Archaeology at Athens, negotiations for which took several years.† Meanwhile, from the age of seventy onwards, he had taken enthusiastically to flying, which he found did not make him ill as sea travel usually did. Each year he would fly out to Athens, and if possible, get a seaplane to Crete.

In his eightieth year he still enjoyed travel and delighted in its unexpected accidents. 'When I tried to leave Piraeus for Crete by a Greek boat and was actually on board, a terrific snowstorm occurred, the worst known at Athens for fifty years, and the steamer stayed in

---

* *Our italics.*
† In 1952 it was handed over to the Greek Government, rising costs and post-war stringencies having made it impossible for the British School to maintain it.

port. . . . I decided to spend a few more days in Athens, and to fly to Crete by the seaplane. Incidentally this gave me an opportunity of stirring them up like bees at Athens by sending to the paper that Venizelos reads, a full account of the bad treatment that I and other travellers had experienced both on landing at Piraeus and on attempting to depart from it, at the hands of the "Pirates of Piraeus" the boatmen and porters. . . .'

Age had not brought softening of Sir Arthur's sharp temper and sharper wit. In Crete I was told a story about him which may well be true, though I had no means of checking it. Immediately after one of his arrivals in Crete he was driving through Herakleion when he noticed to his indignation that workmen were demolishing one of the finest Venetian houses in the town. Ordering his chauffeur to stop, Sir Arthur stormed out, waving Prodger, and began belabouring the workmen, commanding them to stop immediately, and demanding to see the Mayor. When that official appeared Evans told him, in the strongest terms, that the building was a national monument of which the Cretans should be proud, and that to demolish it was an act of vandalism unworthy of a civilized people. The demolition ceased.

I cannot vouch for the facts of this anecdote, but it was told me in good faith, and I see no reason to disbelieve it.

In his eightieth year he could still find energy to excavate. 'Here I am with the Pendleburys and de Jong,' he wrote, 'starting some trial excavations which have already led to surprising results including—where I looked for it!—a large built tomb. Probably it has been entirely robbed however.'

In 1932 he returned, after an absence of half a century, to his beloved Croatia and Dalmatia. He saw again the Casa San Lazzaro—the house to which he had taken Margaret after their marriage, and even found, in the neglected garden, flowers which they had planted. Visiting the gaol in which he had been imprisoned, he remarked to the custodian—'I come here every fifty years.'

As the friends and colleagues of a lifetime died, one by one, the old scholar began to feel the loneliness and isolation which is the penalty of all those who long survive their own generation. There is a grave, dignified sadness in the Introduction to the fourth and last volume of his great book, in which he salutes his departed friends and fellow-scholars. After his tribute to Duncan Mackenzie, already quoted, he goes on:

Apart from this sad stroke ... the passage of the years itself has lately taken an untimely toll—even while this present Volume was in hand—of those whom I could most look to for encouragement and advice. . . . Already, when this Volume was well advanced, A. H. Sayce was suddenly taken from us. . . . Much travelled scholar and first hand student of the monuments of Egypt and the East . . . it had been owing to his interpretative genius that the first real light was thrown on the Hittite problem, and the revelations of Minoan Crete nearly concerned him. . . . With him, too, H. R. Hall, most learned and serviceable guide, beyond the Aegean shores to Egypt and the Ancient East, has gone before his time. Gone too, in the fullness of his years, is Friedrich von Duhn, the revered German 'old master'. . . .

Opposite above: The Palace of Phaestos

Opposite below: The Grand Entrance Staircase at the Palace of Phaestos

His warmest tribute was reserved for his old friend Professor Frederico Halbherr, the Italian archaeologist who 'was first in the field, the Patriarch of Cretan excavation', and who, through his seasoned knowledge of local conditions, had helped Evans to make his preliminary exploration of the island in times of difficulty and danger, and paved the way for the excavations at Knossos.

His smile, his kindly manners won all hearts, and his memory still lives among the Cretan villagers. The 'net' under which he slept secure at night, and his coal-black Arab steed that climbed rocks 'like a wild goat' and on which he could gallop—over Turkish roads—from Phaestos to Candia in little over five hours, have become almost legendary. . . .

The Introduction reads like a Roll Call of the dead, and one wonders if Evans realized, as he recorded the deaths of his fellow-scholars, that he was also recording the end of an epoch. Leisurely scholarship supported by private wealth, the disinterested pursuit of knowledge for its own sake, amicable relationships between scholars of varied nationalities—the liberal intellectual atmosphere in which he had been reared as a child, which he accepted like the air he breathed, and had defended in his war-time speeches; did he recognize that these precious things were soon to be swamped by a new fanatic intolerance worse than any he had known in the First World War?

He did not survive the Second World War, though he lived through the first two bitter years—the fall of France, the invasion of Greece and Crete, the occupation of Yugoslavia, all lands which Evans knew and loved. In London in 1941 he visited the British Museum—burned and blasted by enemy attack. He called at the offices of the Hellenic Society to inquire about its members who had been left in Greece and Crete. One member at least, John Pendlebury, Curator of Knossos, the young scholar whom Evans had admired not only for his scholarship but for the touch of knight-errantry in his make-up, had died gallantly fighting alongside the Cretan Resistance.

His health had begun to fail two years before, and now he spent most of his time in his study at Youlbury, though he still came sometimes to the Ashmolean Museum. On his ninetieth birthday, shortly after having undergone a serious operation, he received in his library at Youlbury a deputation of his friends who brought him a beautiful scroll from the President and Council of the Hellenic Society, recalling 'with gratitude and admiration his exceptional contributions to learning' and '. . . his lifelong and strenuous devotion to the cause of freedom in thought and in action.'

'On his knees,' wrote Sir John Myres, 'lay a well-used Ordnance map showing his Roman road' (Evans had traced it on his estate at Youlbury and had become interested in this fragment of local antiquity); 'in reply to a question he showed the fair copy of his account of it, and said brightly "It is finished; it will go to *Oxoniensia*."' It was his last contribution to learning. Three days later he was dead.'

Life, it has often been observed, always falls short of Art. If this had been a novel, Evans would not have lived to hear the hum of bombers over Europe's ancient cities, to know that the Villa Ariadne was a German military headquarters, that his beloved Balkan countries were once again a battleground of the Great Powers, and that civilized standards of conduct which used to be observed even between nations at war, had been abandoned in a brutal struggle for survival. Instead, he would have died in 1939, after his last, triumphal visit to Crete to receive, at Herakleion, the highest honours the Cretans could bestow upon him. It is at that moment that I prefer to think of him, eighty-eight years of age, replying to the address of welcome in words which epitomize the story I have tried to tell, however inadequately and incompletely, in this book:

We know now that the old traditions were true. We have before our eyes a wondrous spectacle—the resurgence, namely, of a civilization twice as old as that of Hellas. It is true that on the old Palace site what we see are only the ruins of ruins, but the whole is still inspired with Minos's spirit of order and organization, and the free and natural art of the great architect Daedalos. The spectacle indeed, that we have here before us is assuredly of world-wide significance. Compared with it how small is any individual contribution! So far indeed, as the explorer may have attained success, it has been as the humble instrument, inspired and guided by a greater Power.

EPILOGUE

Over an hour and a half ago the agonized, ague-shaken old bus had ground its way out of the Cathedral Square in Herakleion, *en route* for the south coast of Crete. At every halt on the long, gear-whining climb into the mountains we had taken on board such a weight of human, animal and vegetable freight, that I calculated—while contemplating the unfenced precipices within a few feet of our wheels—that we must be carrying more than twice the load that our ancient Ford had been built to carry.

Now we were climbing slowly and laboriously over the high mountain chain which is the spine of Crete. Right—left, left—right, swung the bus, and every turn in the road only led to another. At the highest point I estimated that we were at some 5,000 feet above sea level, probably higher, but the mountains still rose above us, some capped with snow like sugar icing. At points the road clung to the edge of the mountain, while enormous boulders seemed poised ready to fall upon us from the upper slopes; the dust rose behind us, and on the rutted, rocky road, our wheels danced on the rough surface.

Suddenly the long agony of the engine was over. It stopped screaming and gratefully accepted top gear; as we began to bowl down the other side of the pass I heard the rumble of the tyres again.

We had broken through the mountain chain and were coming smoothly down into a lovely fertile plain in which were more olive-trees than I had seen in the whole of Crete; from above they seemed almost a forest. The sunlight slanted down over the mountains making the green of the fields glow like emerald, and against this brilliant green of spring grass the old powdery-grey olives stood in ranks, with occasional bands and patches of reddish earth which had been newly ploughed. Away to the right rose a snow-covered peak which seemed unbelievably high and remote—Mount Ida itself. And ahead of us smiled the sea, the southern sea beyond which, only two hundred miles away, lay the north coast of Africa.

It was evening as we moved quietly down into the rich plain of Messara, most fertile region in Crete. Here had been found the tombs of some of the earliest peoples to settle in the island; here also, on its knoll overlooking the plain, near the harbour where once the Minoan galleys had moored, stood the Palace of Phaestos, the southern rival of Knossos. It was at Phaestos that I had arranged to spend the night.

I was relieved when at last the bus stopped near a small Byzantine church. The driver, after courteously carrying out my bag and absurd

Opposite The Palace at Phaestos: view of the corridor leading from the Central Court to the Royal Apartments, with Mount Ida in the background

196

197

typewriter, waved his arm towards a hill on the left of the road. 'Phaestos,' he said with a smile.

'Efcharisto!' I replied, delighted to have remembered enough of my Greek phrase-book to thank these charming people. The dusty old vehicle moved off round the bend, past a dismantled German gun emplacement, and I began to climb the path which wound up the slope through the olive-trees.

Near the top of the hill I was met by Alexandros Venetikos (Alexander the Venetian)—a small, lithe, dark man who, with his sister, is responsible for the Rest House at Phaestos. But I had come so early in the year, he said—long before the students and the tourists usually arrived. However, I was welcome, and though they had only candles and oil-lamps, and could only offer me eggs, a little bacon and a glass of wine—still, I would have a comfortable bed, and the Palace to myself. As I followed Alexandros into the Rest House the first faint stars were beginning to tremble in the night sky.

At supper round the candle-lit table, the light wavered on the dark faces of the caretaker, his sister in her red head-scarf, and a tall mountaineer friend, who, with his broad shoulders and slim waist looked as if he were lineally descended from the Cup-bearer himself. We talked of local beliefs. They told me that in some parts of Crete it is believed that up to the time of its christening a child is surrounded by evil spirits. So, after a birth, all the relatives and friends meet in the house, making merry as noisily as possible so as to drown the child's cries, and thus prevent them being heard by evil ones. This may have its origin in the legend of Zeus, entrusted by his mother to the Corybantes, who drowned his cries by the noise of cymbals and drums to prevent his being devoured by his father Cronos. . . .

It is certain that respect for the old Gods is still strong among some modern Cretans. I was reminded of a true story told me by an English friend living in Crete. One day she asked a Cretan bus-driver, 'Why don't you make the buses run to time?' He replied that it was impossible. 'But in England we do it,' she told him. 'If only you would make a little extra effort the service could be perfect.'

'*Perfect?*' he asked, aghast. 'Perfection is for the Gods. We are but men. . . .'

After supper I left my hosts and walked out into the moonlight, and down the slope to the Palace of Phaestos spread out at my feet. Phaestos is far more magnificently-sited than Knossos. It stands on a high knoll proudly commanding the Messara Plain, with the hills lying well back at a respectful distance on each side. All the familiar Minoan features are there—the maze of rooms, the broad sweeping stairways, the store-rooms or magazines with their great *pithoi*. But in contrast to Knossos the site was in some ways simpler to excavate and preserve, so that Halbherr, unlike Evans, had only to do the minimum of restoration.

The full moon threw a magical light over the noble flights of stone steps, the long, shadowed corridors, the doorways of gleaming white stone. The place seemed compounded of moonlight, like a fairy palace which would disappear when dawn came. The gentle radiance softened the contours of the broken walls, and gave to the majestic

The steps of the theatral area in the west court of the Palace of Phaestos

ruin a strange, dream-like quality, making it possible to imagine the walls at their original height, to replace the great bronze and silver doors, and to people the shadows with Minoans.

I found myself in a room with walls of shining white gypsum, which seems to have been an audience chamber. The original stone benches remained on two sides, and in the centre were bases from which once lofty columns had sprung. To the right and left, doorways rose to their original height. Sitting on one of the stone seats, one could recreate the Palace. Beyond that doorway, if I passed through it, might I not find Phaestos just as it was—with the gay frescoes restored, the walls and ceilings in place; would I hear, perhaps, the hum of voices, gay feminine laughter and gossip, the footsteps of some important court official hurrying along the corridor, the solemn chanting of priests celebrating the sacred rites of the Mother Goddess?

I sat silent, looking at the full moon high in the clear sky, and hearing only the sound of frogs croaking in the valley, and the little

199

night sounds—the flutter of a startled bird, and the fluting of an owl. . . . I looked to my left and there, serene and splendid, high over all, rode the long, snow-covered ridge of Mount Ida, birthplace of Zeus.

Back in the rest-house I sat up in bed, an oil-lamp drawn close to the bed-side, my books and notes scattered on the coverlet, trying to assemble in my mind all that had happened since I had stepped over the threshold of 'La Belle Hélène de Menelaüs' at Mycenae; not very long ago, yet how distant it seemed now! There, too, I had been welcomed by friendly people; there too, I had lain awake, impatient to begin the exploration of Schliemann's Mycenae—the first stage in my long journey into prehistory. Now that journey was nearly over. I had followed Ariadne's thread through the Labyrinth. Where had it led me? Are we now in the full daylight of knowledge concerning the ancient Aegean civilization which began in Crete, then spread to other islands and the mainland, from whence, perhaps, came its destroyers? And where does Homer fit in? And what of old Dr Schliemann and his theories? Are they now quite discredited? I flicked through the pages of my diary. Somehow these questions must be answered, and the results of the journey summarized.

To change the metaphor, having followed the river of Aegean civilization upstream nearly to its source, it was time to turn the boat round and glide rapidly downstream again, noting the chief landmarks. So, in the few remaining pages, I will try to sum up what is currently accepted by Aegean archaeologists, bearing in mind that opinions vary, and that older theories are constantly being modified, or even abandoned altogether, as new knowledge is gained. The following outline of the course of Minoan civilization is based mainly on that of the late John Pendlebury, to whose book *The Archaeology of Crete* I am deeply indebted.

It is believed that the ancestors of the Minoans came to Crete roughly between 4000 and 3000 BC. Their original home seems to have been in south-west Anatolia and Syria—at least, says Pendlebury, their nearest cultural connections were with the people of those areas. They were at the Neolithic stage of development, i.e. they used fairly highly-developed stone implements and weapons, and they were a seafaring people. Their settlements occur in small groups, each one reached from some point on the coast. These people were at first mainly cave-dwellers, though later they built elementary shelters.

But although the Neolithic settlers were probably Asiatic, Sir Arthur Evans believed that 'the determining cause of this brilliant development of early civilization is . . . traceable to the opening out of communications with the Nile Valley across the Libyan Sea.' There is no doubt that there was contact with the Lower Nile and with Libya from extremely early times. The late Professor Percy Newberry, addressing the British Association in 1923, pointed out that at the very beginning of the historic period in Lower Egypt the cult objects of the people of the north-western delta (nearest to Crete) 'included (1) the

Harpoon, (2) *the Figure of Eight Shield* with crossed arrows, (3) the Mountain and probably, (4) the Double Axe and, (5) a Dove or Swallow. With the exception of the Harpoon all these cult objects are also found in Crete.' And even the Harpoon may have been later modified into the familiar Minoan Trident, which appears on the walls of Knossos and Phaestos.

There may even have been a landing by small bands of Lower Egyptian refugees after the conquest of Lower Egypt by Menes, in 3200 BC. It is an interesting fact that the capital of the Western Delta of the Nile, in pre-Dynastic times (before 3200 BC) was Sais, whose goddess, Neith, had as her emblem the figure-eight shield. The people of the Western Delta were known to be closely connected with Libya—in fact the Egyptian language was unknown to the inhabitants.

Now this Libyan connection gives us some most significant clues to the possible cultural origins of the Cretans. For one of the features of Libyan male dress in this remote time—as shown in statuettes, was the 'Libyan Sheath'—which, like the codpiece of medieval times, protected the genitals. The Minoans wore the same sheath. The Libyan men wore their hair with a side-lock falling down from in front of the ear over the breast or through the armpit. So did the Minoan men (see illustrations on pages 127 and 163). There are other curious examples; for instance, in the very early 'Tholos' tombs discovered in the Messara—not far from Phaestos—the excavators found 'idols or human figurines entirely divergent in class from the old Neolithic class but identical with those found in prehistoric tombs at Naquada' (in Egypt).

So we have two main elements in Neolithic Crete; an original stock from western Asia, constantly reinforced by other peoples from the same area; and a quickening influence from the Nile Valley, either through trade, or through the immigration of a small number of refugees from the Western Delta, driven out when the Kings of Upper Egypt conquered the whole country at the beginning of the third millennium BC. They may have taught the original settlers new arts—e.g. fine lapidary work and the manufacture of faience—for which the Delta was famous.*

During the thousand years which archaeologists call for convenience the *Early Minoan Period* (*circa* 2800–1800 BC), the population of the island increased rapidly. Important towns grew up on the coast, at Palaikastro, Pseira, Mokhlos and Gournia. The most prosperous settlements were in the east though in the south the Messara plain became well populated. With the concentration of population in towns and villages arose a class of professional craftsmen; art, especially that of the potter, flourished. Life became easier; communications were improved. Foreign relations—especially with Asia, Egypt and Libya—became closer. But in metal work the Minoans were still backward. Sculpture was in its infancy and the seal-stones were of poor design and quality.

The island was at this time divided into three groups, Central,

---

* Evans suggests that Minoan agriculture may have benefited by contacts with Egypt. 'The beans found in the store-rooms at Knossos were at once recognized by our workmen as identical with those imported from Egypt.'

Southern and Eastern, which appear to have been independent of each other. There were no palaces.

The *Middle Minoan period* (*circa* 1800–1600 BC)* is marked by 'two most important changes; the rise of the Palaces, and, allowing for a local difference due to natural difficulties of communication, unity of culture' (Pendlebury). During these two brilliant centuries the three main divisions of the country began to coalesce. The population began to spread west of Ida. Crete may still have been divided into many states, but Knossos appears to have gained chief political power; Phaestos may have remained independent. Building methods became so similar that it is clear that the Minoan culture is now a unity. Bronze was introduced, making it possible to cut fine ashlar masonry. Gypsum was used as a facing stone; buildings show evidence of detailed planning—to this period belongs the introduction of the marvellous architectural features, the 'light-wells' and the elaborate drainage system. Fresco painting reached a dazzling level of achievement. The potter's wheel came in. A wonderful school of vase painting developed. So did miniature sculpture and the art of making faience (glazed clay). Gem engraving kept pace with progress in the other arts.

In Middle Minoan III, says Pendlebury, the seal-stones reach the highest point of beauty.

Overseas trade had made the Minoans rich. Undisturbed by war, protected from the envy of their neighbours by the sea of which they were masters, they were acquiring a commercial empire. They may not have deliberately planned the conquest of other Aegean islands. Their Empire probably grew like the British Empire. First they would get permission from a local prince to establish a trading-post; perhaps build a port. Then, later, the prince might ask them for help against a neighbour—which would be given, at a price.

So gradually, and probably peacefully, most of the country comes under the control of newcomers. Finally comes the stage when further acquisitions become necessary owing to the need of putting down piracy or rather of ensuring against other seafarers poaching on their preserves.

Such was the origin of the sea-empire of Minos, traditions of which survived until classical times, and were taken seriously even by historians such as Thucydides.

By the beginning of the *Late Minoan Period* (*circa* 1550–1100 BC) Crete was a world power, co-equal with Egypt and the Hittite Empire. These were the days when the proud ambassadors of the Keftiu are shown on the walls of the Egyptian tombs, not offering tribute as members of a subject state, but bearing gifts from one great monarch to another.

By 1550 BC there were fine roads linking the Minoan cities, protected by guard stations. By now Knossos had become the centre of a highly centralized bureaucratic system; from his mighty Palace the King of Crete ruled over many overseas dominions. Hence the size

* The dates for these periods (which in any case are only approximate) differ from those given by Pendlebury in his excellent *The Archaeology of Crete*, as modern scholars tend to place them somewhat later than he did twenty years ago. I am indebted to Dr Frank Stubbings of Cambridge, for the revised dating.

and complexity of the Palace. It was not merely a King's residence; it was a centre of administration.

It was the seat of a government which controlled not merely the neighbouring regions or even the island, but a maritime empire.... We may fairly surmise that there existed a well-developed system of administrative machinery which needed considerable room for its offices. The rich tributes which the Kings derived from their dependencies were stored in the Palaces. (Bury: *History of Greece*).

The other great Palace of Phaestos, in the south, may have belonged to Princes of the Knossian family line.

Round each of these and other smaller Palaces clustered handsome towns with well-built houses of stone for the solid burgher class, and smaller homes for the numerous artisans. The mountains were not bare as they are today, but clothed with magnificent forests, supplying the great cypress beams needed for the columns, architraves and timber-framing of the Palaces.

Then, at the very height of this glory, in about 1400 BC came violent destruction, ruin and death. Knossos, Phaestos, Hagia Triadha, Gournia, Mokhlos, Mallia and Zakros all show traces of violent destruction accompanied by burning. What had brought about this disaster? Pendlebury, as we have seen, believed it was due to an invasion from the mainland, of which the story of Theseus and his companions is the legendary symbol. Evans believed it was due to one of the terrible earthquakes which had brought previous destruction to the Minoan cities, though perhaps in this case followed either by foreign invasion, or local insurrection.

Pendlebury's theory has much to support it. He points out that on each of the sites mentioned above there is evidence of destruction by fire, and that in ancient times earthquakes did not necessarily cause fire, as they do in modern towns with gas and electricity mains. But if foreign invaders destroyed the chief cities of Crete 1,400 years before Christ, who were they, and why are they believed to have come from the mainland?

To find the answer we shall have to go back six hundred or more years and look at the mainland of Greece as it was in 2000 BC—when Crete had already attained a high degree of civilization. In Greece (not then called by that name) as in Crete and some of the Aegean islands, there was a Bronze Age population which had entered the country a thousand years earlier. They belonged to the dark-haired 'Mediterranean' race and may have been akin to the inhabitants of Crete and the Cyclades. Their language, like that of the Cretans, is lost, but they have left us memorials of their presence in certain place-names *which do not belong to the Greek language*. These are mainly names ending in '-os' and 'nth', of which there are many in Greece and—significantly— even more in Crete. For instance *Corinth, Ilissos, Halicarnassos, Tylissos*; these names of Greek towns and rivers are not Greek; they have been left behind by the population which lived there before the ancestors of the modern Greeks entered the country. Other names were of flowers, plants, and birds with which the invading Greeks were not familiar—such names as *hyacinth*, and *narcissus*—which have passed into our own language. In Crete there were scores of such old non-Greek place-names *of which Knossos itself is the most obvious example.*

Most significantly, the very name for 'sea'—thalassa—the sea by which the Greeks lived is not Greek. Scholars suggest this is another indication that the people which invaded what is now Greece round about 2000 BC came from the north—from the interior of Europe where the sea was unknown. Therefore, on arriving on the shores of the Mediterranean they would naturally borrow the name used by the people whom they had conquered. These northern conquerors—for whose presence there is positive archaeological evidence after *circa* 2000 BC—are believed by scholars to have been the ancestors of Homer's bronze-clad 'Achaeans'. And it was these men, a warrior-race from a harder, northern climate, who became overlords of the Mediterranean peoples and set up their mighty citadels at Mycenae, Tiryns, and elsewhere.

Inevitably these people, who may have been organized in a loose federation of states, with Mycenae at the head, came into contact with the great Minoan Empire to the south and so produced the fusion of mainland and Cretan culture which we call Mycenaean. Authorities differ fundamentally in their interpretation of Minoan-Mycenaean relations. Evans believed that the Minoans colonized Mycenae, and Pendlebury agreed with him. 'So Minoanized does the rest of the Aegean become,' he wrote, 'that it is imposible for the present writer at least to avoid the conclusion that it was dominated politically by Crete. . . .'

But Professor Wace, who probably knows more about Mycenae than anyone living, does not accept this view. He believes that the mainland rulers remained politically independent, but were attracted by the higher civilization of Crete. They imitated it in their architecture, dress, and art, and may, in fact, have employed Minoan artists to work for them on the mainland. Those who hold Wace's belief point out that though the style of the objects found in the shaft-graves, e.g. the engraved dagger-sheaths, is unmistakably Minoan, the subject-matter—hunting and fighting—is not. Such subjects would have more appeal to a northern warrior race, and the impression left by 'Mycenaean' art is that of Minoan craftsmen working to the orders of a foreign master. Notice also the decidedly non-Minoan faces on the Mycenaean death-mask (illustration page 71).

Whatever may have been the cause it is certain that, after the fall of Knossos, the mainland cities, and especially Mycenae, rose to the peak of their power and wealth. Pendlebury believed that the Achaeans—or 'Mycenaeans'—attacked and destroyed the Cretan cities as a political move—probably because they wished to smash the Cretan monopoly of trade and obtain a share of the rich traffic with Egypt. They do not seem to have occupied and colonized Crete, since after 1400 BC Minoan culture still continues, though in a minor key, in the smaller Cretan communities. The Palaces, with their ruling class and hive of civil servants, seem to have been destroyed, but at a lower level Cretan civilization continued until it was absorbed into the common culture of the Aegean.

Minoan vase with plants

The scene now shifts to Greece, which from 1400 to 1200 was wealthier and probably more united than it was to be again for five hundred years. Throughout the period Mycenae was dominant; it was then that the Mycenaean princes enlarged their Citadel, built the Lion Gate and hollowed out of the hillsides some of the earlier 'beehive' tombs described in Chapter Five. The shaft-graves were, of course, much earlier (1650–1550 BC). In his lofty Palace, dominating the community, the King entertained his guests with banqueting and minstrelsy, as Homer describes. The Mycenaean nobles loved hunting and chariot-racing. Their women, like the Minoans before them, wore tight-waisted jackets, with open bosoms, huge flounced skirts, elaborate coiffures and lots of jewellery. It was a splendid age, this heroic period to which Homer looked back during the Dark Age which followed the collapse of the Achaean Empire.

But before that happened the Achaeans, having defeated the kings of Crete, broke through to the rich East, founding settlements at Rhodes, Cos, and Cyprus, trading with Egypt, exchanging the products of the Aegean for luxuries such as gold, ivory and textiles. An interesting point is that there has been discovered at Boghaz Keui, the ancient capital of the Hittite kings, in Asia Minor, clay documents referring to the *King of Akhiyava*—which nearly all scholars now accept as the first documentary reference to the Achaeans—the word which Homer used most often to describe the Greeks. He also calls them Danaoi.

Then, in the thirteenth century BC, Egypt adds her testimony. In 1221 BC an invading host moved down on Egypt, led by the King of Libya, but most of the invaders came from the north. Among them the Egyptian inscriptions mention the 'Achaiwasha'—probably another reference to the Achaeans or 'Mycenaeans'. The invasion was unsuccessful, but a generation later a second great wave came down from the north, including a mighty host of the 'sea peoples'. This was the coalition defeated by Ramesses III in a land and sea battle, and among them the Egyptian inscriptions mention 'Danuna'—who may be the Danaoi. It was an age of unrest and vast migrations of people; the last attempt especially seems to have been far more than the advance of professional armies, but of whole tribes, moving down the coast of Syria and Palestine with their women and children and baggage-wagons. 'The Isles,' wrote the Pharaoh's priestly chronicler, 'were in tumult.'

Probably the last desperate venture of the Mycenaean Empire, or coalition of states, was the siege of Troy, which history, legend, and archaeology all agree was fought during the first quarter of the twelfth century. This again seems to have been a political stroke, perhaps to break the Trojan stranglehold on the Black Sea trade. But by this time the Achaens were facing peril at home. The final chapter in this 3,000-year-old drama revealed by the spade—but living more richly on the lips of poets—tells of the destruction of the destroyers. For the Achaeans, who had broken the power of Knossos and inherited the wealth of the old Minoan Empire, were themselves overthrown in the twelfth and eleventh centuries by yet another wave of northern immigrants of the same Greek-speaking stock. These were the Dorians—the ancestors of the 'classical' Greeks and those of today. They broke up the highly organized Mycenaean state into small cantons.

Centuries later, when the old Mycenaean cities lay in ruin and the Minoan Empire forgotten, a Greek poet of genius produced, from a number of much earlier epics, the *Iliad* and the *Odyssey*. These earlier poems, which glorified the deeds of the heroes of the Mycenaean Age, had been transmitted orally from generation to generation, and although they were modified and altered to suit prevailing Dorian fashions, they still preserved the names of the Mycenaean cities, Mycenaean leaders and their deeds, and details of Mycenaean social customs.

They may even contain unconscious memories of Cretan glories, transferred to fairyland by a generation which could not imagine that they had once existed. Consider Homer's description of the mythical 'Isle of Phaeacia' where Odysseus is washed ashore after his shipwreck. Of her country the King's daughter, Nausikaa, says:

... there is no man on earth, nor ever will be, who would dare set hostile feet on Phaeacian soil. The gods are too fond of us for that. Remote in this sea-beaten home of ours, we are the outposts of mankind and come in contact with no other people.

Could there be a better description of Crete in the days of her glory? And in a later passage occur the lines:

For the Phaeacians have no use for the bow and quiver, but spend their energy on masts and oars and on the graceful craft they love to sail across the foam-flecked seas.

Alcinous, King of Phaeacia, tells his guest:

But the things in which we take perennial delight are the feast, the lyre, the dance, clean linen in plenty, a hot bath and our beds. So forward now, my champion dancers, and show us your steps, so that when he gets home our guest may be able to tell his friends how far we leave all other folk behind in seamanship, in speed of foot, in dancing and in song.

May not this be a folk-memory of the luxurious life of the Knossian Palace? For in Homer's own time, at least five hundred years after the fall of the Cretan power, nothing remained in Crete itself to tell the newcomers that the island had once been the centre of a mighty Empire. The curious Dorians found, in the crumbling ruins of Knossos, a few fragments of the bull-frescoes, with youths and maidens, and these may have helped in the development of the legend of Minos and the Athenian captives, and of Theseus and the Minotaur. As for the Labyrinth, this is simply derived from the *labrys*—another non-Greek word meaning the Double Axe, the most familiar symbol on the walls of Knossos. As for the mysterious underground maze in which Minos kept the bull-monster, this story may have been brought back to Greece by venturesome Dorians who found their way into the great sewers of the Palace drainage system—which were big enough to accommodate a man—and were, of course, quite unknown in their own primitive communities.

So thanks to Evans and his fellow-scholars, building on the foundations which Schliemann and Dörpfeld laid, we can survey a vast new territory of prehistoric life in Europe. The old legends and myths have been proved to contain more truth than the dry-as-dust historians would admit. For this knowledge we have to thank first Schliemann, who trusted the ancient traditions, and had the means and the will to justify his faith. But for patient, scientific investigation, analysis and synthesis, we owe our debt to Evans and the line of devoted scholars who have succeeded him.

Homer now appears not only as a weaver of dreams and fairy-tales. He wrote in a period of cultural twilight. He had not seen the walls of Ilium, or watched Agamemnon ride through Mycenae's Lion Gate, or sat in the frescoed hall of King Minos at Knossos; but his antecedents had seen these wonders. So it happens that in the poems there are preserved, like flies in amber, descriptions of noble rooms, works of art, arms and armour, and a way of life which had vanished in Homer's own day, but which the spade of the archaeologist has now proved to have existed.

Ours also is a twilight age, especially for humane studies. The Schliemanns and the Evanses, men who had the leisure and the wealth to preserve knowledge for its own sake, are dead; their successors, working with far more limited resources, are doing fine work; for example, Professor Wace's book *Mycenae* marked another step forward in our understanding of the Mycenaeans. But how much more remains to be learned! The mysterious Minoan writing, which Evans went to Crete in the hope of deciphering, remains still a mystery:* and in Crete, in spite of the work of scholars and archaeologists from Britain, France, America, Italy and elsewhere, more remains beneath the soil than has yet been taken out of it. The valley in which the Palace of Minos stands, could, if excavated, perhaps yield tombs and treasures equal to Egypt's 'Valley of the Tombs of the Kings'. But how is such work to be done today? Where is the man of wealth—who is also a man of genius—who could finance, let alone plan, such work? What Government would dare to ask for a vote of £250,000 for excavating and rebuilding a 3,000-year-old Palace? One is left sadly wondering how many years must pass before the world is settled, and civilized, enough to carry on the great work which Schliemann and Evans began.

The morning sun, shining through uncurtained windows, woke me early. I breakfasted on the terrace, with the Palace spread out a few hundred feet below me in the sun which made the white walls shine like snow, and patterned the courtyards, corridors, and broad-sweeping stairways with ink-black shadows. Mount Ida, with its icy-white crest, rode high and serene in the innocent blue of morning. Ahead, beyond the flat-topped hill, on which the Palace stood, the rich, green plain of the Messara expanded till it met the enclosing hills.

These hurried, fleeting visits, I reflected, stirring my coffee, are also part of the pattern of our time. Fifty years ago, nay, less than that, young men of modest means could spend months in such rewarding places, planning a career, a book, or a university thesis; or perhaps—dare we say it—just enjoying themselves? Today such experiences can be enjoyed only by three 'privileged classes'—the rapidly dwindling minority of tourists who can afford to pay their passage, the even smaller minority who travel on university grants, and very occasionally, fortunate journalists, who 'snatch a fearful joy', conscious all the time of the return airline ticket in their pocket and the impatient editor waiting at home. . . .

Nationalist passions, suspicion, intolerance, the propaganda lie—all the evils which Evans fought—have come near to destroying the world he knew. Yet in our Age of Anxiety we must make the best of what chances we have. For a short time the grip of unreason has relaxed a little—just sufficient to allow a few people to enjoy the stimulus of travel and friendly intercourse between peoples which used to be considered the mark of civilization.

---

* Since the first edition of this book was published the 'Linear B' script has been partly deciphered. See postscript chapter.

I walked down the slope from the Rest House, and slowly mounted the broad, magnificent stairway—as noble as that of Versailles—which leads to the entrance of this 4,000-year-old Palace. I passed through the long corridors, past the innumerable doorways and flights of steps which once led to higher apartments. I crossed the broad Central Courtyard, on, on, up further stairways and along further corridors until I arrived at the furthermost limit of the Palace—the point at which the knoll on which it stands falls away in a sheer cliff to the fertile plain of Messara below.

Suddenly, from far below, piercing the morning air, came a thin, high trumpet-note. A herald announcing the arrival of an Embassy from Egypt? No—just a shepherd's horn.

To right and left rose the low, gentle hills, partly shadowed in the morning sun; the hills in which were found the 'Tholos' tombs of some of the earliest peoples to land and settle in Crete. Ahead lay the Messara itself, a lush green patterned with ranks of powder-grey olives, each throwing a long morning shadow across the damp grass. Among the old grey stones of the Palace pink asphodel sprang, its many-clustered flowers standing quite still in the warm, windless air. There were red and blue wild anemones, and at my feet, painting the green plain with bright gold, sweep upon sweep of the tiny yellow *oxalis*.

Spring . . . Spring had come to Crete from the south, across Homer's wine-dark sea which had been the path of the first Cretan settlers five or six thousand years ago. In a day and a half I would be walking the rainwashed pavements of cold, windy London. But I had seen the arrival of Persephone on

this sea-beaten home of ours,
. . . the outpost of mankind. . . .

—whence came the Spring of Europe.

POSTSCRIPT ON THE DECIPHERING OF LINEAR B: THE EVEREST OF GREEK ARCHAEOLOGY

In Chapter Ten I described Sir Arthur Evans's discovery at Knossos of 'Whole deposits, entire or fragmentary, of clay tablets analogous to the Babylonian but with inscriptions in the prehistoric script of Crete. I must have about seven hundred pieces by now. It is extremely satisfactory,' he wrote, 'as it is what I came to Crete to find. . . .'

It was what he came to find, but although he and other scholars wrestled for more than thirty years with the decipherment of the mysterious writing they were able only to establish that the tablets represented inventories, that there was a numerical system, and that some of the objects listed in the inventories could be identified as chariots, horses, men and women from the 'pictographs' which appeared at the end of certain lines. All attempts to ascertain the grammatical basis of the language—if it had one—failed.

But while this book was being written the script—or rather one form of it—was at last yielding its secrets, and now, more than fifty years after Evans discovered the 'Linear B' tablets, they can be partially read. Moreover it seems fairly certain that the language in which they were written was an early form of *Greek*.

In the first volume of his *Scripta Minoa* Evans showed that there were three stages of writing in Crete. First hieroglyphs represented on the early engraved seal stones. Then came a more cursive form of writing which he called 'Linear A'. Finally came a third script, a modified form of the 'Linear A' which Evans called 'Linear B'. This was the commonest form, and it was in use at the time of the destruction of Knossos. The same form of writing has been found at places on the mainland, such as Mycenae and Pylos. It is this 'Linear B' script which has been partially deciphered, largely through the efforts of a young Englishman named Michael Ventris, unhappily killed in a motor accident in 1957. Ventris was not an archaeologist, nor even a professional philologist. He was, in fact, an architect.

Nineteen years ago the British School at Athens was celebrating its fiftieth anniversary with an exhibition at Burlington House, London. Among the speakers was Sir Arthur Evans, then in his eighty-fourth year. And among the audience was a thirteen-year-old schoolboy studying classics at Stowe. The boy—Michael Ventris—heard Sir Arthur say that the tablets he had discovered thirty-six years before still challenged decipherment. Ventris was intrigued, and decided to make the subject his hobby. From that day he began to struggle with the problem, but it was to take him seventeen years to solve.

Why did the writing take so long to decipher? Largely because there was no bilingual clue such as that provided by the Rosetta Stone which set Egyptologists on the road to understanding the hieroglyphs. Champollion and other philologists were able to decipher the writing of the Ancient Egyptians because (*a*) there existed, on the Rosetta Stone, the same inscription written in both Ancient Egyptian and Greek, and (*b*) because elements of the ancient language still survived in the Coptic tongue. The Behistun Rock supplied the same kind of bilingual clue for the *cuneiform* writing of Babylonia. No such help was provided for those who tried to wrest the secret of the Minoan script from the baked-clay tablets found in the Palace of King Minos. The symbols bore no relation to any known form of writing. In vain archaeologists sought for a bilingual clue—perhaps a bill of lading written in Minoan and Greek. Nor has any such aid appeared, even today. How then, has the feat been accomplished?

If no bilingual clue exists there are other ways in which one can attempt to decipher an unknown language. As Ventris himself says:

Since 1802, when Grotefend first correctly read part of the Old Persian syllabary, the basic techniques necessary to a successful decipherment have been tested and developed on many other initially unreadable scripts. Each operation needs to be planned in three phases; an exhaustive analysis of the signs, words and contexts in all the available inscriptions, designed to extract every possible clue as to the spelling system, meaning and language structure; an experimental substitution of phonetic values to give possible words and inflections in a known or postulated language; and a decisive *check*, preferably with the aid of virgin material, to ensure that the apparent results are not due to fantasy, coincidence or circular reasoning.

(*Antiquity*, Vol, XXVII, December 1953.)

Let us consider the first phase of the operation: 'the exhaustive analysis of the signs, words and contexts'. If sufficient material exists one can begin to sort out and classify the words and signs, to notice how many times the same group of signs occurs, and how often and in what way a word beginning with the same group of signs has varying endings. For instance, if the reader was confronted with a book written in English, without knowing the language or any related tongue, he might notice that the words 'AND' and 'THE' occurred more often than any others, and that sometimes one found a word beginning with the signs G-R-O-W which ended in different ways, e.g. GROW ... GROW*ING* ... GROW*N*. Looking further he might find another word containing some, but not all, of the same signs but which also used the same endings as in the other group of words, e.g. THROW ... THROW*ING* ... THROW*N*. Then he might have a setback on finding that whereas ROW and ROW*ING* semed to be governed by the same grammatical rules, the third form of the word was not ROW*N* but ROW*ED*. In this way, if he had enough material and sufficient patience, skill and application, he might be able to hazard a guess at the grammar, and then, by comparing it with that of known languages, see if there was any possible link. Did the thing *work*, or not?

This is only one example of the ways in which the script might be attacked. Another would be to find out the total number of symbols used. If, for example, there were only twenty-four signs, as in Greek, the language would probably be alphabetical, each sign representing a

211

consonant or a vowel (though some ancient languages such as Egyptian had no signs for vowel sounds). On the other hand, if there were, say, seventy or eighty signs the language is probably syllabic, each symbol having the value of a consonant plus a vowel, e.g. one sign for TA, another for TO, a third for TE, and so on. A number of syllabic writing systems, e.g. Hittite and Cypriote, have managed to make do with between sixty and eighty signs.

At the outset Ventris was handicapped by lack of material. 'When I started,' he told me, 'only 142 out of the 2,846 tablets (and fragments of tablets) found by Evans had been published. The most useful work on the material was by Sundwall, a Finnish scholar, who had access to more tablets than other people. But we made slow progress.'

Then in 1939 Professor Blegen, of the University of Cincinnati, began to excavate at Pylos, in the Western Peloponnese, the traditional home of Nestor, the aged counsellor of the Greeks before Troy. He found a palatial Mycenaean building in which lay some six hundred tablets in the 'Linear B' script. These tablets, published in 1951, showed that though the script ceased in use at Knossos after the sack of 1400 BC, it was still in use two hundred years later on the mainland. Then in 1952 Sir John Myres, Evans's lifelong friend, published *Scripta Minoa*, Volume Two, which Evans had left unfinished at his death. This volume contained all the 'Linear B' tablets found at Knossos, and, with the Pylos tablets, provided Ventris with valuable new material.

Already by 1940 it was generally recognized that the script contained some seventy common signs for sound values, apart from the 'ideograms'—the small pictorial signs which indicated such objects as chariots, swords, horses, men and women. The script was therefore clearly a 'syllabary' like modern Japanese and the Hittite hieroglyphs.

The Pylos tablets discovered by Blegen had been deposited in the Bank of Athens, but Blegen had had them photographed, and one of his students, Emmett L. Bennett Jr, studied the tablets and helped to prepare them for publication. In 1947, after his return from cryptographer service in the U.S. Forces he submitted a thesis on the tablets. He examined the shapes of the signs in a more methodical way than Evans. In 1940 Ventris wrote an article in *The American Journal of Archaeology* suggesting that the language might be like Etruscan, and that the Etruscans may have spoken an Aegean language. Working on this hypothesis he tried to decipher the script but his theory was based on too small a part of the material, and came to nothing. Meanwhile, between 1944 and 1950 the late Dr Alice Kober of Brooklyn wrote suggesting that by looking at the Knossian tablets which had been published one could see that the script had a certain grammatical pattern. She suggested also that by studying the order of the words and how they changed, e.g. by noting inflexions and word-endings, one might get at the grammar even without knowing the pronunciation.

Ventris, in the meantime, had joined the Royal Air Force and become a navigator in Bomber Command. It is typical of him that he chose to be a navigator rather than a pilot because the mathematical problems involved in navigating an aircraft seemed to offer more interest than 'being a driver'. Then the war ended and he was able to take up his hobby again, devoting to it all the time he could spare from his profession of architect.

Up to 1950 it was generally assumed that the 'Linear B' script contained a non-Greek language, like 'Linear A'. (1700–1450 BC). Evans thought that 'Linear B' was developed from 'Linear A' when the Knossos ruler centralized the government of the island in his palace, and overhauled its administration methods. It remained the same language, Evans believed, but better written. But the young American scholar, Emmett L. Bennett, thought differently. He made a close study of the two scripts and in 1950 published an article pointing out certain vital differences. *The signs looked the same, but the words were different.* To make this clearer, at the risk of over-simplification, imagine a Martian studying two manuscripts, one in English, the other in German, but both using the Latin alphabet. Not knowing the languages, and seeing that the same signs were used to write it, he might at first think that both manuscripts were written in the same language. Only after careful study would he discover that they were two different languages using the same signs.

This vital discovery led to a new approach to the 'Linear B' script. 'Linear A', the earlier form, was used in Crete over many centuries. Then suddenly one finds an entirely new system, though using the same signs, and this is used not only in Crete at the end of the Late Minoan Period but also continues on the mainland for centuries afterwards. Wace and other archaeologists believed that at this period mainland influence in Knossos was strong, that, in fact, the Mycenaeans, who were of Greek stock, may have conquered Knossos. *Could the 'Linear B' script have been an archaic form of Greek, using the Minoan syllabary?* This possibility had already occurred to Ventris, and he corresponded with Bennett in order to test his theory. He was on the brink of an important discovery.

Blegen's six hundred Pylos tablets, which had been published in 1951, furnished him with new material, and there was also Myres's *Scripta Minoa* Volume Two which came out later. The latter volume, based on Evans's fifty-year-old material, might possibly contain errors, so Emmett L. Bennett went out to Herakleion in Crete to check up on the originals in the Museum. The two young scholars kept in touch, and between the spring of 1951 and 1952 Ventris worked away at the script, testing and discarding theories, and every month taking a particular line of inquiry. At regular intervals he would send out Roneod copies of his investigations and conclusions, so that other scholars could study and comment on them.

In May 1952 Professor Blegen was back at Pylos, excavating the Palace of Nestor. He explored the other end of the Archive Room in which he had found the six hundred tablets in 1939. To his delight *another* four hundred came to light, including the broken halves of some already dug up in 1939. They were entrusted to Bennett to prepare them for publication and the contents of a few of them were made known to Ventris and other scholars in early 1954.

A complete explanation of Ventris's methods is outside the scope of this book, and readers who wish to study the subject in greater detail should read the presentation of his theory in the 'Documents in Mycenean Greek' which he and John Chadwick, a Cambridge philologist, published in 1957. But, briefly, he built up a huge dossier which showed, for example, how many times a certain sign occurred, how many times it occurred at the end of a word, how many times in the middle, how many times at the beginning, etc. Then he and other scholars began a long process of analysis and gradually began to recognize the apparent grammatical structure of the ancient language, and the relative frequence and interrelationships of the phonetic signs with which it was written. Ventris wrote:

Once the values of a syllabary are known, its signs can be most conveniently set out in the form of a chequerboard 'grid' on which the vertical columns each contain a single vowel, and the horizontal lines a single consonant. A vital part of the analysis consisted in arranging the signs as far as possible in their correct pattern *before* any phonetic values were tried out; this was made possible by clear evidence that certain groups of sign shared the same vowel, (e.g. *no ro to*), others the same consonant (e.g. *wa we wi wo*).

There were also several pairs of spellings which alternated in such a way as to suggest masculine and feminine forms of the same word, and Dr Kober had detected the presence of inflexional endings.

CONSONANT	VOWEL 1	VOWEL 2	VOWEL 3	VOWEL 4	VOWEL 5
(H-)	A / AI	E	I	O	U
D-	DA	DE	DI	DO	DU
J-	JA	JE		JO	
K- G- CH-	KA	KE / KWE?	KI	KO	KU
M-	MA	ME	MI	MO	
N-	NA / NWA?	NE / NEKO?	NI	NO	NU
P- B- PH-	PA	PE / PTE	PI	PO	PU
QU- GU-		QE	QI?	QO	
R- L-	RA / RJA	RE	RI	RO / RJO	RU
S-	SA	SE	SI	SO	SU
T- TH-	TA / TJA?	TE	TI	TO	TU
W-	WA	WE	WI	WO	
Z-		ZE		ZO	ZU?

Syllabic grid showing suggested phonetic values for 68 of the 88 signs of the Linear B system

During the fifteen months following Bennett's publication of the Pylos tablets, Ventris had been able to form some idea of the grammatical structure of the 'Linear B' language, and to fix the relative positions of many of the signs on his 'grid' (see illustration).

'There now seemed to be', he wrote in his cautious scholar's way, 'sufficient material for a reasonably controlled experiment in allotting phonetic values.'

Thus, after years of preliminary research, classification and analysis, he had reached the second phase of the operation: 'an experimental substitution of phonetic values to give possible words and inflections in a known or postulated language.'

'Previous attempts at decipherment,' wrote Ventris, 'had all relied, for fixing of key phonetic values, on supposed resemblances between "Linear B" signs and those of the classical Cypriot Syllabary, whose values are known.'

What was this 'Cypriot Syllabary'? Mr R. D. Barnett, Keeper of Western Asiatic Antiquities of the British Museum, writes:

It has been thought for some time that the actual language of Homeric times was probably nearest to the archaic dialects which still survived in Classical times, isolated by later Dorian and Ionic invasions and restricted to Cyprus and, on the mainland, to the mountain district of Arcadia. This view is now likely to receive unhoped-for confirmation. When the Dorian and Ionian invasions came at the beginning of the Iron Age, the Mycenaean civilization collapsed and with it all recollection of the arts of writing, except for the memory of the tablet inscribed with 'baleful signs' which Proitus gave to Bellerophon to carry to the King of Lycia, which was really a request to have him killed.

This theory—that the 'Linear B' script might be related to the Cypriot Syllabary, though attractive, cannot yet be proved. The Syllabary shows few superficial resemblances to either 'Linear A' or 'B', except in the shapes of some of the elementary signs. 'The differences,' wrote Ventris, 'might be due to a reduction in size and a more "cuneiform" writing technique, but they make parallels between "Linear B" and the classical Cypriot Syllabary almost impossible to trace. It is clear that the values of the "Linear B" signs must be fixed on internal evidence, and to satisfy the "grid" and inflexions already found, *without taking into account any other doubtfully related writing systems.*' (Our italics.)

Ventris decided to 'go it alone' and turned to the work of Alice Kober, who had worked on the 'Linear B' script during the War, and who had recognized certain inflexions. Among the words which she had studied there was a consistent series which recur in different contexts in three different forms. Dr Kober called these words 'paradigms' and Ventris, 'triplets'. These, Ventris thought, were possibly the names of the chief Cretan cities, together with their corresponding adjectives.

Now it is characteristic of most languages (he wrote) when syllabically written, that the signs for the plain vowels A-E-I-O-U- are exceptionally common in an initial position; and the first sign of the first 'triplet' suggested the value A to Kober and Ktistopoulos. The decisive step was to identify the first words with Amnissos, and to substitute values which would turn the others into Knossos, Tylissos, Phaestos, and Lyktos:

A-mi-ni-so	*Ko-no-so*	*Tu-ri-so*	*Pa-i-to*	*Ru-ki-to*
A-mi-ni-si-jo	*Ko-no-si-jo*	*Tu-ri-si-jo*	*Pa-i-ti-jo*	*Ru-ki-ti-jo*
A-mi-ni-si-ja	*Ko-no-si-ja*	*Tu-ri-si-ja*	*Pa-i-ti-ja*	*Ru-ki-ti-ja*

Since about 50 signs had already been assigned to their places on the 'grid' the substitutions in these five words automatically fixed most of them as well, by a kind of chain reaction. If these names were an illusion, then the resulting system of values must inevitably be a completely dislocated jumble, with which no further sense could be extracted from the texts by any sort of jugglery.*

But they did *not* become a 'dislocated jumble'. When Ventris began to apply the experimental phonetic values to the pattern of declensions which he had already analysed he found to his surprise that 'these fell into line, not merely with the known Greek system of declensions, but specifically with its most archaic forms as deduced from Homeric and other dialects.'

Ventris was now at the third stage of the operation a 'decisive *check*, preferably with the aid of virgin material, to ensure that the apparent results are not due to fantasy, coincidence or circular reasoning'. At first, like Evans and other scholars, he had assumed that the unknown language was Minoan, and that it had no connection with Greek or any other known language. But now, by attributing, experimentally, Greek values to the signs, he began to realize that the language could be read as an archaic form of Greek, and the similarities occurred too often to be mere coincidences.

For example, here is one tablet from Pylos.

Linear B tablet 140 (Eb 35). For a more precise discussion of this tablet see Ventris and Chadwick's *Documents* (1973), page 256

If one attributes to the signs the values given them by Ventris this could read, in Greek:

Hiereia echei-que, euchetoi-que etonion echeen theon, ktoinoochons-de ktionaon kekeimenaon onata echeen. (Tossonde spermo;) WHEAT 3–9–3.

which in English would read:

This the priestess holds, and solemnly declares that the god has the true ownership, but the plot-holders the enjoyment, of the plots in which it is laid out. (So much seed) $3^{57}/_{60}$ units.

Another tablet, from the armoury of Knossos, could read:

Hiquia, phoinikia harrarmostemena, araruia haniaphi; wirinios 'o-po-qo' keraiaphi opii(sta?) iaphi, ou-que 'pte-no'; CHARIOT 1.

which in English would read: . . .

Horse-vehicle, painted red, with bodywork fitted, supplied with reins; the rail(?) of wild-fig-wood with jointing of horn; and the *pte-no* is missing; 1 CHARIOT.

In decipherment the real test is simple; does it make sense? It appears to. For instance there is an inventory of swords, recognizable from a 'pictogram' which clearly illustrates this weapon. It ends with a number and the 'total' *to-sa pa-ka-na* (so many swords). The classical Greek equivalent for this would be *tossa phasgana*, which is good

---

* Ventris: 'Greek Records in the Minoan Script', *Antiquity*, Vol. XXVII, December 1953.

Greek and makes sense. There is another tablet with a pictogram representing chariot wheels. The accompanying description, read with the values Ventris ascribes to it, describes the wheels as *kakodeta* or *kakia*—'bound with bronze' or 'brazen'. The thing appears to work.

Most remarkable of all, two tablets from Knossos and one from Pylos, deciphered by the Ventris system, carry the names of Greek gods 'Lady Athena', Enyalios (an old name for Ares), Pan, Poseidon, Zeus, Hera, and 'The Lady'.

John Chadwick, another British scholar who worked with Ventris, points out that 'it is certainly surprising to find names which can be read as Hector and Achilles (but not Nestor or Minos). . . .'

However, all the above examples were taken from the earlier Evans and Blegen 'digs'. They did not fall into that category of 'virgin material' previously unknown, which Ventris needed for his 'decisive check'. But in 1952 this was forthcoming. A tablet was found at Pylos in that year which has almost the effect of a bilingual. On it are drawings of tripods and vases. Ventris, reading the signs which accompany the picture, gives them the values *ti-ri-po-de*—unmistakably the Greek word for 'tripdos'. And the rest of the tablet is in the same strain, proving the decipherment on the right lines. Other tablets yielded similarly interesting results.

Ventris himself was very modest about his achievement. At the end of his article in *Antiquity* he wrote cautiously:

There is some doubt whether the present 'Linear B' material is large enough for the decisive proof of a solution, but a substantial check is promised by the still unpublished Pylos tablets found by Blegen in 1952 and 1953. At all events, I do not anticipate serious competition from any rival decipherment—not out of conceit, but because of this unfair advantage; if the tablets are written in Greek, they can hardly be explained otherwise than we have proposed; but if they are not, their language is probably in the existing circumstances unknowable.

R. D. Barnett, Keeper of Western Asiatic Antiquities at the British Museum, writing about Ventris's achievement in the *Manchester Guardian Weekly*, hit on the happy phrase 'The Everest of Greek Archaeology'; for such truly it is. The death of this brilliant young man, at the age of 34 was a tragic loss to archaeology. To the layman, the disappointing fact is that now, when the mysterious script seems to have been deciphered, all that is revealed are, as Evans and others suspected, mere inventories. It is as if some future excavator, searching for the clue to the unknown English language, and having heard of a great poet named Shakespeare, had found somebody's laundry bill.

But the important fact is that, (assuming that Ventris is right in his conclusions) scholars now have the key to the Minoan-Mycenaean writing should any more interesting inscriptions turn up. It is amazing that a brilliant and a gifted people, whose achievements are immortalized in the epic poems of Homer—which may indeed be based on oral poetry handed down from that remote age—have left no written documents apart from these inventories. Their contemporaries, the Egyptians, have left us tomb inscriptions, historical annals, stories, poems and letters. So have the people of the Euphrates Valley. The

Mycenaeans must have been in touch with these contemporary civilizations; objects found in their cities proved that. But they have left us no written record of their history save what survives in the poems of Homer, which was first set down in writing many centuries after the last Achaean King ruled from Mycenae.

Homer mentions writing only once. There is a passage in the *Iliad* Book VI in which Glaucus, the son of Hippolochus, challenges Diomedes 'of the loud war-cry' to single combat. In one of these long, discursive orations with which the Homeric heroes address each other before proceeding to battle, Diomedes asks if Glaucus is a man or a god in disguise, since, he says, 'I am not a man to fight against the gods of Heaven. . . . But if you are one of us mortals who plough the earth for food, come on, and you will meet your doom the sooner.'

Glaucus, to reassure him, gives him a long piece of family history. He is descended, he says, from the redoubtable Bellerophon, son of Glaucus and grandson of Sisyphus—'as cunning a rogue as ever there was.' Bellerophon was subject to King Proetus, a far more powerful nobleman than himself. Queen Anteia, the wife of Proetus, fell in love with the handsome youth 'who was endowed with every manly grace, and begged him to satisfy her passion in secret. But Bellerophon was a man of sound principles, and refused.'

Whereupon, like Potiphar's wife, the Queen told her husband that Bellerophon had tried to ravish her, and urged Proetus to kill him, or be killed himself. Proetus dared not put Bellerophon to death, so he sent him to Lycia, and it is here that Homer mentions writing for the first and only time:

. . . he packed him off to Lycia with sinister credentials from himself. He gave him a folded tablet on which he had traced a number of devices with a deadly meaning, and told him to hand them to his father-in-law, the Lycian King, and thus ensure his own death.

The Lycian King gives Bellerophon a number of arduous and dangerous tasks, hoping he will be killed, but each time the young man triumphs, even when the King sets an ambush for him.

He picked the best men in all Lycia and stationed them in ambush. Not one of them came home. The incomparable Bellerophon killed them all. In the end the King realized that he was a true son of the Gods.

Now until recently this passage in the *Iliad* was regarded as a later interpolation, but, says Stubbings:

There is no reason why it should not refer to Minoan or Mycenaean script, and I think myself that it does. The writing materials are not identifiable from what little is said. Little is yet known of Mycenaean contacts with Lycia in Asia Minor, though I hope one day will be, even though we can hardly expect to find the actual death-warrant for Bellerophon which Homer alludes to.

It is interesting to note, moreover, that Bellerophon belongs to an earlier generation of heroes, to be dated definitely earlier than the known examples of 'Linear B'.

So the torch is handed on; from Schliemann to Evans; from Evans to Ventris and Papadimitrou; from Ventris and Papadimitriou to whom? For though a corner has been turned and fresh vistas spring to view, the end is far from being in sight. Much more work on the tablets will be needed, in fact the work has only begun. And there still remains the 'Linear A' script which may be truly Minoan and may baffle all attempts at decipherment for years to come.

To conclude, let us take a forward look and consider the problems and possibilities arising from these new discoveries. It now appears very possible that people of Greek stock were dominant at Knossos at the close of the Late Minoan Period. Professor Wace has long believed that in Late Minoan II (1500–1400 BC) Knossos was under mainland influence. His case grows stronger with the evidence that Greek was written there at that time. In a letter to *Antiquity* he wrote:

For some time past several of us have been pointing out that in L.M. II at Knossos (but not in the rest of Crete) there are features which are mainland; beehive tombs, throne-rooms, the Palace Style, alabastra, imitations of Ephyraean pots, and so on. Also the Knossian frescoes, as Luisa Banti points out, agree with the mainland more than with the rest of Crete. Now Knossos alone in Crete has the 'Linear B' script, and it is known on tablets at Pylos and Mycenae and on pots from Thebes, Mycenae, Orchomenos, Tiryns and Eleusis. 'Linear B' is more spread on the mainland than in Crete. 'Linear B' is Greek. So at Knossos in L.M. II there were Greeks. The Mycenaeans were Greeks; they were the Middle Helladic people developed after contact with the Minoan civilization and the Near East in Late Helladic I, or rather from just before the end of Middle Helladic through Late Helladic I. Thus the decipherment of the tablets confirms the result already arrived at archaeologically.

There is another aspect. The earliest known date for the Phoenician alphabet as adapted by the Greeks is the eighth century BC. Historians used to believe that after the Dorian invasion there was a Dark Age during which the Greeks were illiterate. Now we know that the 'Linear B' Mycenaean script was in use down to the fall of Pylos, which presumably came towards the end of the Bronze Age. Wace poses the question 'is it likely that such an inventive, intelligent and wide-awake people as the Greeks would ever have stopped reading and writing once they had learned to do so?'

Perhaps—who knows—the end of the 'Linear B' script and the beginning of the Phoenician Alphabet may have overlapped?

If only, writes Wace, we could find an inhabited site of the Late Bronze to Early Bronze Age to Early Iron Age period we might find tablets in it. All our knowledge at this period is from tombs. . . .

The crying need now is for more documents from Pylos, Mycenae and other sites, and an Early Iron Age inhabited site, in order to find out what the script and language situation was at that time. The so-called Dark Age, thinks Wace, is dark only to us.

We are on the eve of great developments. We can no longer speak of pre-Hellenic Greece, because from 2,000 BC onwards the Greeks were in Greece, and Mycenaean art is the first manifestation of Greek art. . . . One would like to see applied to the Dorian invasion the same methods of study and the same archaeological technique as have thrown so much light upon the arrival in Britain of the Anglo-Saxons and upon our own origins: the two problems have much in common.

ILLUSTRATION ACKNOWLEDGEMENTS

The Ashmolean Museum, Oxford, pages 7, 66 (above), 69, 70, 100, 108, 113, 114, 115, 124 (both), 125, 131 (both), 140, 146, 151, 155, 161 (both), 163, 168, 179, the colour plates opposite pages 97 and 128 (and back jacket). *British Library*, page 51. The two colour photographs opposite page 96 were reproduced by Courtesy of the Trustees of the *British Museum*. *B. J. Brooke-Smith*, colour plates opposite pages 33, 81 and 193. *Colour Library International*, front jacket photograph. *Sonia Halliday*, pages 45, 66 (below), 67 (margin), 80, 81, 132, 162 (above), 175, and the colour plates opposite pages 32, 80 and 176. *David Herbert*, pages 24 (above) and the colour plate opposite page 177 (above). *Hirmer Fotoarchiv, München*, pages 58, 67 (above), 83, 117, 133 (margin), 144, 157, 170, 183 and 205 and the endpapers. *Wyn Jones*, colour plates opposite pages 145, 177 (below) and 192. *Mansell Collection*, pages 24 (below), 31, 39, 46–7, 49 (both), 53, 59, 61, 63 (above), 64, 65, 75, 77, 79 (both), 86, 92, 129, 130, 135, 143, 145, 162 (below), 163, 164, 167, 169 (both), 176, 178, 180, 182 (both), 185, 186, 197, 199 and the colour plate opposite page 17. *National Tourist Organisation of Greece*, pages 25, 63 (below), 73, 74, 88, 90, and 134. *Photoresources*, pages 127, 137, 174 and the colour plate opposite page 16. *Sunmed Holidays*, the colour plates opposite pages 129 and 144.

The illustrations and maps on pages 19, 57, 68, 123, 142, 173, 214 and 216 were drawn by Hilary Evans.

INDEX